MW00436634

*The Price of Achievement*

*The Cassell Lesbian and Gay Studies list offers a broad-based platform to lesbian, gay and bisexual writers for the discussion of contemporary issues and for the promotion of new ideas and research.*

# *The Price of Achievement*

## *Coming Out in Reagan Days*

*W. Scott Thompson*

CASSELL

Cassell
Wellington House
125 Strand
London WC2R 0BB

215 Park Avenue South
New York, NY 10003



First published 1995

**British Library Cataloguing-in-Publication Data**
A catalogue record for this book is available from the British Library.

ISBN 0-304-33301-8 (hardback)
0-304-33303-4 (paperback)

Typeset by York House Typographic Ltd, London
Printed and bound in Great Britain by Mackays of Chatham plc

# *Contents*

# *Acknowledgements*

SOON after Calvin Trillin published his widely reviewed and well-received *Remembering Denny*, he and I appeared on a Public Broadcasting Service book program. I assured Christopher Lydon, the anchor, that I would be forthcoming, as is my style, but wished not to be introduced as 'gay' as such – since I still had yet to discuss my homosexuality with Heidi, my thirteen-year-old youngest child. The very next day, however, I was driving her to Andover for dinner with son and brother Nick. Could we chat, she asked, and started commenting very shrewdly on the program. What *was* all this, asked her innocent father? How much *do* you know? 'Oh, Dad, if it's about your being gay, I've known *that* for at least three years.'

Once my little circle saw how I planned to handle this bundle of sensitive topics, and given the current profound salience of such issues, they were skeptically encouraging. For this is a book for today's world, where the issues of coming out, gay parenting, and the treatment of gay people in transition in the workplace, in the suburbs, indeed at church, is more and more before the general decent citizenry of America.

A book like this, observes the formidable Edward Luttwak, is not like a scholarly essay which one can revise in later editions, or explore developments on the same subject in further learned volumes in later years. A book like the present one, rather, is here to speak to human emotions at its own irreproduceable time, in the lives of the writer and those in whose lives he has partaken, to inflame as well as to inform, to transform as well as to analyze. It sets out to *affect* as well as to reflect upon. This, after all, is where I have taken my stand; I could do no other.

Let me first thank Mr Timothy Dickinson for not having encouraged me on this project earlier, secondly for an extraordinary amount of disciplined attention to draft after draft. Few people are kind enough and smart enough to get to the heart of a long manuscript so as to be able to see better than the author what he is trying to do. Tim

Dickinson is one of them. Young friends bring a critical perspective, and in Kenneth Weisbrode's case a brilliant one too. He has been more my teacher than student. Dr John Luce as always gave me the best kind of encouragement and thoughtful suggestions, as did my very special friend Richard Lewis. Marie Aruña Ward, on faith, led me to my publisher. I also received incisive comments from Jacqueline Almassian, Robert Bagnall, Siddarth Dube, Warren Coats, Mark Falcoff, Nathan Hasson, Robert Heglar, Amie Hoeber, John Milstein, Constantine Pleshakov, Mitchell Reiss, Tony Smith, Ronald Steel, Edward Wilson and also Janne Nolan, who in addition hoped for my safety in seeking publication of these thoughts. Rictor Norton, for Cassell, did the most perceptive editing I have encountered, but even he could not surmount all the problems my text presented, for which – along with all its errors – I accept full responsibility. And thanks to Steve Cook for seeing the book's possibilities in the first place.

Homer's Jove has casks of good and evil, to determine our fates. From the cask of good I was blessed for four decades. This book concentrates on the ensuing decade, where the gods seemed to be free with the cask of evil, at least toward my worldly concerns. But how far did my own mistakes, perversities and idiosyncracies bring misfortune upon me – not to mention my children or their mother? And where do societal perversities – most obviously homophobia – bulk as large as the failings of any one weak heart? I have tried to deal essentially with homophobia; my own mistakes are simply private material for me to learn from, which is the reason why no lasting pain or grief comes from such, since no one could have had so much opportunity to grow from what time has put him through.

The writing of this book psychologically and empirically overlapped the working out of its subject matter – it was done in 'real time', as the soldiers say. No people could know this better than my three equally gifted and loving, and thus endlessly enquiring, hostages to fortune, Phyllis, Nick and Heidi Thompson. They were the ones who bore the costs society imposed on my drawn-out emergence from what I believed was a launching pad but in the end proved a prison; and their forbearance now – I claim no more – as I try to make some communicable sense of it is part of the most important thing in my life: for which reason I dedicate it to them, and to the new generation of decent young folk which they represent.

*For Phyllis Elizabeth Pratt Thompson,*
*Nicholas Edwin Scott Thompson,*
*Heidi Alexandra Nitze Thompson*
*and their generation*

*. . . we are, as it were, posted at a window, badly placed but looking out over an expanse of sea, and only during a storm, when our thoughts are agitated by perpetually changing movements, do they elevate to a level at which we can see it the whole law-governed immensity which normally, when the calm weather of happiness leaves it smooth, lies beneath our line of vision . . .*

● Marcel Proust, *Time Regained*

# *Introduction*

WHEN news of the Soviet shoot-down of Korean flight 007 came to the senior executive branch on 1 September 1983, I was, improbably, in an EST (Erhard Seminar Training) seminar across the Potomac in Roslyn. There were three hundred of us, bewildered and confused enough by life to endure four days of belligerence, intrusion, pressure and indignity in hopes of throwing off a few of life's shackles; even willing to give up two long weekends for our souls' enrichment.

My buzzer went off with a White House code, telling me to go straight to that splendid center of the Western world, where I knew we would be squeezed into the Situation Room – probably the least grand operational hub of power in history – to devise a retaliatory strategy, and where I would predictably, as the government's chief external information officer, urge us to press a case based on truth, not force.

I am not a patient sort. Thus the whole EST exercise – sitting on hard chairs and floors with none of the deference to which I had grown accustomed as a sub-cabinet member – had been building steam against my safety valve; but three-fourths through, I was finally able to run heat to work. Only an hour earlier a beautiful young man, to whom all the women and, seemingly, many of the men appeared to be looking, in 'sharing', had stated at the outset that he was unloved, unlovable, unloving – and gay. 'Is it all right to be gay?' the trainer asked.

'Yes, it is, I guess,' the young man said, staring at his feet.

'Look up', snapped the trainer. 'How many people here are gay?'

I was still married to a socially prominent daughter of the type Max Beerbohm spoke of as, 'Oh, isn't he just of an eminence,

Sir?' I even had a girlfriend, but seeing most of the good-looking young men stand up – this being Washington in all but zip code – and seeing that this was an EST seminar, a reasonably secure environment in which to take my first stand, I got up on shaking legs. I didn't know how much longer it would take to stand up Outside, but I now knew along what bearings my life must head.

For the meantime, however, I was still in the Reagan administration, which apart from the small share of glory offered was also my livelihood and my security blanket as I was whiplashed through a bitter million-dollar divorce. At EST, the whole psychology was to keep everyone under mounting pressure, against the enormous temptation to quit the distressing exercise of hypnosis, self-revelation, tears, and interminable ramblings of the trainer. 'Don't go, Scott, Don't go, Scott', the whole crowd chanted, on cue from the front, as I got up to leave, until someone whispered in his ear that a very important-looking car was awaiting me out front.

And to the White House I went, trying to devise a strategy for the United States against the predatory Soviets, whose unprompted strike in the dark provided an apt personal analogy for what I was being subjected to. I, of course, was the Korean airliner and only hoped in the real world that I could do better for my country than I was doing for myself.

Only a year earlier I had been living with my three children and wife in a mansion in Boston with outlying compounds in the country, at the seashore, and first-class tickets for family jaunts to Aspen, and chateaux and music festivals in Europe, along with shuttle tickets for New York. Then I was preparing for an at least modest ascendancy in national affairs that had been predicted ever since a national magazine in my junior year at Stanford said I would surely be president.

Now I was fighting week by week for access to the children and trying to find the money to pay a lawyer to defend me against the onslaughts that my wife and Paul Nitze, her distinguished father, were mounting on me. In ten days, I was to return from a conference in Canada to find my house, in enough of a mess from the rehab going on throughout, being robbed of all my divorce papers, but that was just the warmup. In due course I was threatened with extinction if I didn't agree to divide up family assets 94 per cent in favor of my wife.

I was soon to be hollowed out by hepatitis B, which I shook off only to walk for several years under the diagnosis of AIDS. And the one unequivocal fulfillment of learning at life's mid-point what others learn at sixteen – how to mate among one's deepest kindred spirits – brought with it the highest, because most intimate, costs at the heart of the reward.

What, asked some whippersnapper, had the great Abbé Sieyes done in the French Revolution? 'I survived,' said he, with depths of felt achievement that only come when it has long been apparent that one probably will not; and if one does it will be by one's own efforts above all. This, in short, is the setting of one man's coming out amid chaos. It is the story of a new consciousness emerging of the forces at work in his own life as a specimen case of the battle overall for gay rights in the larger world, and of his own small triumph in that struggle, as he became the first openly gay man to receive an appointment from the President of the United States with the advice and consent of the Senate, a public accomplishment dwarfed by finding the spirit to transcend private chaos, misery and bitterness. It is a manifesto, applying such dearly bought lessons to the movement, hoping above all to bring with him gay men from the closet, and allies from the straight world, in the great American model so often repeated of an oppressed community finding the strength to withstand the awful tyranny, the mass of decent people feeling no alternative but to join in the cause of justice.

Gayness is now the frontier and cutting edge of civil liberties. No less than Harvard's swift and well-spoken president Neil Rudenstine said so, at Harvard's 1993 gay and lesbian annual dinner during commencement week, while General Colin Powell was visiting as the commencement speaker. For at the heart, it is not the same as seemingly open-and-shut external, group-defined issues like race or gender, but in some ways the more essential and interior issue of how we all psychologically imagine, judge, and understand ourselves. A man can't be a woman – without horrific surgery; and a shadow line still cleaves crucial parts of the white and black experience for virtually all participants. But we all, argues Freud, have evolved through a stage of bisexuality, some staying there, some of us coming back to it as gay men and women, and for the rest posing the question of how they accept themselves in dealing with a minority that has throughout history been victimized, laughed at, and done historic, unimaginable violence to, beneath the foot of pride. The soil which homosexuals have trodden has been one where we were psychological beasts of burden, kept in place by the ultimate whip – that of the old libel phrase, hatred, ridicule and contempt. What is happening on a wide scale right now is that homosexuals are beginning finally to stand up like African-Americans before, and say 'No more.'

Progress in civil rights has hitherto benefitted those from whom the mainstream can plainly differentiate itself. Now America is being asked to open its hearts to a segment that emerges among rich and poor, black and white, Jew, Methodist, Muslim. America has been the country that dissolved the notion that one had his 'place' or station, fixed, unalterable; in Stanford's first president's phrase, the country where hatreds died. But that makes it both easier and harder to open itself to a minority that wanted no 'place' to begin with – indeed one to which too much 'place' had been assigned already – the place of sissy, child-molester, irresponsible (because without progeny) – and wanted just fairness and privacy, as three-dimensional real people. In other words, it isn't good enough, in fact it isn't good at all, to take your sex, have it in the bedroom, but for God's sake don't talk about it. That's two-dimensional. Gay people want full lives, including sexual, but not limited to sexual, ones. For gayness, we will see, is about sexuality, and only starts with sex. And sexuality is about culture. That has been the specter haunting middle America in recent years, which has evoked its own witch doctor, the religious right.

We cannot confine our sexual activities to the bedroom and go on living like the majority. This book tells why; it simply doesn't work that way. Until the bedroom act itself is *accepted* as non-threatening, then even it is constrained, as in fact by this Supreme Court. But beyond that, whom do I take to dinner parties – a tame 'cover-girl'? And who protects the publication of the novels and papers I like to read some of the time? Where can I safely look for partners without being slapped in jail for prurience? Great victories of justice entail the defeat of false imaginings before real imagination of the oppressed's plight is possible.

The fact is, homosexuality is not and cannot be an erotic isolate hanging suspended in a vacuum; it is a body of individual ways of living and an aggregate lifestyle, a culture, for most of us, never just a matter of 'sex'. The closeted gay who proclaims himself happy to live silently among the majority and keep his sex out of the way is no different from any other brand of appeaser – an appropriate term because the appeaser's reward is further aggression. Sadly but truly, gayness has the worst brand of all – it has always been deemed undignified – a far more disabling stigma than 'menacing' or 'evil'. Oscar Wilde said that war would never be ended by calling it wicked, but only by persuading people that it was vulgar. Why else was it impossible until 1994 for even one gay person to become a federal judge, upon the inspired appointment of an African-American lesbian (but when a more 'conventional' candidate for the bench was rumored to be gay he was promptly scuttled). This isn't something to be fought by bragging about living 'like' straight people; Anarchists, Zoroastrians, Vegetarians, Circus Exhibits do not spend their time stressing what they do 'like' the Tory, Moslem, Carnivore, single-jointed sea of fellow human beings they live among: they know that overwhelming mass of common nature and experience which unites all islands to the human continent: they also know – and if they are to prosper in themselves and be profitable neighbors to those around them – they know where differences set in, and are civilisedly committed to them, as well as to the greater union of the human family. Bruce Bawer, in his widely-reviewed *A Place at the Table*, does so brag; he argues for a very banal suburban brand of gayness, as if we could already be there, in as tedious a life as he describes his and his lover's – and as if any minority ever got a place at the table by aping the manners of those already dining in state.

But the problem remains: the distinctiveness of the gay minority revolves around the delicate issue of sex, something that is in practice private for almost everybody. But not *everybody*, since the reader may recall that even the Supreme Court has as recently as 1986 backed the right of states to snoop literally and intrusively in gay bedrooms and has sustained the conviction of a gay man for consensual sex on his own turf.[1] But the question for society is not the private sex act; the question is sexuality.

Let us assume, heroically, that all gay Americans are suddenly free to commit sodomy in their own homes, as most straight men and women, according to many polls, do regularly and equally illegally; only as I write was sodomy decriminalized in my home city of Washington – for gays and straights. That still leaves unanswered how society is going to treat homosex*uality*. The emphasis is on the culture, not the sex. That is because there are some five to ten per cent of the population who deserve the right to develop themselves according to their own lights, but who know that if they do so they will be systematically discriminated against: outright in the military, but with varying degrees of crudity or subtlety in virtually every field except hairdressing, modeling, and ballet. Let us not put too fine a point on it: in 1993, in the Big Apple, where sophistication is supposed to reign, a multimillion-dollar-a-year lawyer got killed in a cheap motel, presumably by a young hustler: according to the *New Yorker* he and his gay partners and associates weren't free to be open about their gayness at his powerful law firm, and so he had to seek sex on the dark side of town.[2] True, many gay men seem to like it this way – in the manner of Tom Driberg, the gay British parliamentarian, who once said that ideal sex was conducted with someone whom you had never met before and would never meet again, and this hardly helps our image.

There is of course a paradox here. We have seen evidence – and we will see more later – of the disproportionate influence the gay world has borne on the development of modern culture. But it is the contribution of a marginal culture, one that has an incentive to 'overproduce', like the Korean grocer turned large-scale merchandiser, or the Jewish money-lender turned merchant-banker. One friend commented that the *TLS* was alternately Jewish one week and gay the next. Of course if we were accepted even with our identity intact, the incentive might dry up in the sand. But then so what? we would be successful. Others would set cultural and artistic standards the way we have been doing at least since Leonardo, without ever having had a chance for secure private lives as we wish to live them. But it is not morally self-evident that even that cost is an obligation of the civic life rather than a pathology of it.

But clearly there's a long way to go: and even if, where my children go to school, there is a new atmosphere of openness, we only have to listen to the teenager from a public school in a lower-middle class Boston suburb, who shared a TV screen with me recently, and who talked of suicide attempts and despair because of the attitude of his peers toward his homosexuality – at least at his far more populous station of society. Mr Bruce Bawer should visit redneck suburbs before concluding that passing is possible much beyond the shadow of the corner Episcopal church.

The argument about gays in the military is less symbolic than representative for the country as a whole, an existential compression justified by references to war, intimacy, and so on, and therefore more revealing than vaguer manifestations of the topic. And the issue is seldom put in terms of what soldiers in real time can put up with among their gay colleagues. It is rather how they think of themselves. Over and over my students from the military reiterated – or, rather, protested – their own lack of personal prejudice during the great military debate of 1993. 'It is, rather, that we just can't put up with men dancing with each other at our officers' club', I was told. In other words, it is their own image of their masculinity that gays threaten, not something real and substantive. And that is the problem in America as a whole, where security of one's masculinity is so low – and with which homophobia is inversely correlated.

That we are now going to be drenched by the discovery of more and more injustice is also evident. Randy Shilts's book *Conduct Unbecoming* is seven hundred sometimes tedious pages of the history of the (mis)conduct of straight society to gays in the US military: even in the past few years the vilest illegal coercion has been used to get out of gays the identity of their gay comrades, and then they are drummed out of uniform for crimes they didn't commit. Such a record acts as a call to arms.

What is holding back the gay movement right now is less the intractability of 'straight' opinion toward gay people, than the unwillingness of mainstream gay[3] people to come out – though one does not wish to understate the problem of persuading straight friends and families of gays to talk openly about sexuality. I had no inkling how high the price for honesty would be – positions denied, old roommates turning against you, and outright extortion and blackmail in legal processes: but my story also shows that it's a price worth paying with the right spirit. For me, the correct option was so overpoweringly right that the possibility of doing otherwise had ceased to exist. In the previous incarnation I had the worst of both worlds: I didn't have the comfort of the world to which I knew I belonged, and my own confused self torn between head and heart could hardly do its best when it was, ever more inescapably, living a lie externally and starving on insufficient truth within.

What do I mean by 'mainstream' gay people? I do not mean to set up categories of worthiness. But I do mean in the first instance those who have managed a career, have tried relationships, have achieved something in the eyes of the world, but most importantly of all, are a moral force in America, in living lives as exemplary as any others. And here I mean gay people, not merely people who have same-sex bedroom games: again we speak of sexuality, not sex, a culture, not something that can, on the grounds of that decency which is the reciprocal of privacy, be swept back into the bedroom – whether by straight society or individual gays.

In the eyes of God I believe that everyone's story is equally important. But the fact is that civil rights for gays will come when there are more than two acknowledged gay congressmen in public life (there certainly are reserve armies aplenty), and a smattering of minor officials elsewhere; when major movie stars don't wait until they are dying of AIDS to come out;[4] when role models of excellence stand out throughout society not just for struggling gay youth, but for mainline America. Mainstream America has to realize we are everywhere; and then relax. It is doubt, suspicion, fantasy, not truth that jar and keep a society off balance.

We *are* everywhere. There are at least two gay senators, one effectively outed recently, the other a known quantity, and I would guess there are a third and a fourth; perhaps more, to conform to our putative tenth of the human world in all its manifestations. A major figure in official Washington, with vast influence on current events, is widely thought to be gay. In the arts, of course everyone knows that certain fields seem virtually dominated by gays. Frank Rich, *New York Times* drama critic, wrote perceptively in 1987 that the 'story of American life over the past two decades is often, for better and for worse, the story of the homosexualization of America'.[5]

That may be an overstatement, of what was in fact the incorporation by mainstream America of gay themes; but whether it was the fashion that gay men brought to men's clothing, bisexual (and gay) imagery in pop culture, gay characters in *Dynasty*, the body culture of the 1980s which the gay community now found straights grabbing, it all radically changed American life and made gay culture far more available.

But until a senior military officer, a governor, a leading partner in a great law firm, a big-city mayor and some major executives – perhaps, most tellingly, a few labor leaders – come out, and until thousands more at each level of leadership follow suit, mainstream America is simply not going to realize that we are worthy, and that their contumely, bad jokes, and bad attitude reflect only on themselves. Until there is an openly gay university president, until boards choose gay people for any kind of leadership position without needing to weigh such a factor, until *gayness*, as such, is no longer a factor in life's competitions, any more than left-handedness or eye-color, we will remain America's oppressed minority: indeed the most oppressed, given the dearth of legislation prohibiting discrimination against or oppression of gays and the energy with which we are pursued. And to the argument that gays have the option, unlike most African-Americans, of 'passing' as straights, and thus avoiding discrimination, one merely notes that discrimination against oneself and his true self, in order to avoid it from society, is a still higher cost. For that involves the obliteration of the self, more accurately its unconscious whittling away, a sort of anesthetizing death.

This then is a manifesto, drawing on private experience where this is apt. Once I came to terms with myself, I was making choices at the key turning point of the gay movement autonomously, sometimes ignorantly, but increasingly with full awareness of consequence, I hope enlightening our understanding of the gay struggle a small bit. In essence I write as a existentialist, believing that the unique and particular of each given human experience cannot but be the starting point of our endeavor to picture the world as a whole; while each of the great common factors that unite the two currents bring a deeper vision than either alone can give. But these are the years in which gay people are striving to make their first priority that understanding and that determination which make possible full moral choice, to act justly on which is the necessary condition of a full life for those who come hereafter.

## Notes

1. See *Bowers, Attorney General of Georgia* v. *Hardwick, et al.* No. 85–140, Supreme Court of the United States. 478 US 186, argued 31 March 1986, decided 30 June 1986.
2. See Stewart, J. B., 'Death of a partner', *New Yorker*, vol. 69, pp. 54–62, 21 June 1993. As this particular partner was married, his constraints were surely the greater.
3. I use the term 'gay' to denote men and women, but my reference is in general to men; lesbian women are more in the forefront of gay civil rights efforts than men, one suspects in relation to their numbers. But my knowledge of lesbian issues and lesbians is limited.
4. *Newsweek* makes the point that however many powerful gays there are in Hollywood, 'few are "out" publicly, and those who are tend to be, as one young dancer puts it, "discreetly out . . . the truth of the matter is that the gay community doesn't support itself in Hollywood",' 'Hollywood and vice', 23 August 1993, p. 49. Whether Tom Hanks's emotional 1994 Oscar speech, for his role in *Philadelphia*, changes this remains to be seen. Coming from a 'safe' heterosexual actor, his courage may have less effect than had it been from a gay, or coming out, actor.
5. Frank Rich, 'The gay decades', *Esquire*, November 1987, p. 88.

# *Part One*
# *Contradictions*

Chapter one

# *'He whom the gods wish to destroy . . .'*

*. . . a reprobate part of the human whole, but an important part, suspected where it does not exist, flaunting itself, insolent and unpunished, where its existence is never guessed; numbering its adherents everywhere, among the people, in the army, in the prison, on the throne; living, in short, at least to a great extent, in a playful and perilous intimacy with the men of the other race, provoking them, playing with them by speaking of its vices as of something alien to it; a game that is rendered easy by the blindness or duplicity of the others, a game that may be kept up until the day of the scandal, on which these lion-tamers are devoured . . .*

● Cities of the Plain[1]

LATE that Friday afternoon, the eighth of February 1991, I was gazing out at the noble west slope of Rock Creek Park, Louis Hallé's wonderful *Spring in Washington* beside me. It had been a mild winter and just the faintest touch of green was opening among the woods framed by my windows. I was hopeful. 'James',[2] a friend of mine with AIDS, that new cross and powerful stigma, swiftly growing in the dark to replace the slowly-dying old one, wished to borrow my house at Rehoboth Beach, but I couldn't find a spare key. The previous week, another friend, Roger Hansen, a distinguished scholar at SAIS, as we academics call Johns Hopkins University's Paul H. Nitze School of Advanced International Studies, had asked to borrow the house, telling me that the deep depression of a month before had lifted and that he needed to lock in the good feeling with some time at the beach where we had spent many happy weekends – frolicking by the sea or reading, by what grim coincidence, galley-proofs of Frank Fukuyama's celebrated essay *The End of History*. I had been delighted to be helpful, but he hadn't returned the key and was answering the phone at neither end.

The phone rang – a Rehoboth neighbor who had been asked to lend James his key. Was I calm and stable? 'Because your friend Dr Hansen is dead. He committed suicide . . . his body is in your garage.' It took time even to acknowledge the news, much less to accept and absorb it, unsurprising though it finally had to be. And the subsequent publication of Calvin Trillin's elegiac best-seller about Roger and his ineluctable steps from extraordinary fame as a 1950s Yale undergrad to a lonely death would only intensify the pain.[3]

For Roger and I were in a sense twins, or *Döppelganger*. At New Haven Roger was an intellectual star as well as captain of the swimming team; Alfred Eisenstadt trailed him around for a *Life* magazine feature, following up on it once Roger was at Oxford. The *Saturday Evening Post* did one in smaller vein about me in my junior year,[4] after I had been elected, to my astonishment, president of the Political Union at the end of freshman year – and of dozens of other organizations before I was through. This was toward the end of the era when one's college record stood on its own, as a part of one's life not just a preparation for it; the sort of attention Roger got, and I to a lesser extent, was equally distracting and profoundly centering. An adult celebrity lives off by himself and buys privacy according to his means as he wishes; a student celebrity physically lives among his peers twenty-four hours a day; in my case I slept for three years on a sleeping porch with the rest of my fraternity, including a recent head of the CIA.

We were Rhodes Scholars seven years apart; teachers at the two leading – at least two of the oldest – American graduate schools of foreign affairs, equally preoccupied by third world issues and US foreign policy.

There may have been a slight degree of competitiveness between us. Roger was my elder and I considered him my intellectual better – and a most attractive man, indeed much more so in those fine-drawn last years than when Eisenstadt photographed him at Yale. But I did not realize that he was slipping rapidly in his colleagues' professional esteem and even more in his own by the time we met, as depression flooded more and more of his time and energies. I tried to get him invited to professional conferences and meetings where his first-rate mind could contribute so much more than most. And, by the time we met in 1986, we were both consciously gay – I openly, Roger only among a small circle of friends and to fellow-customers at a few bars on the edge of town. Finally, we were both disposed to depression, which I am convinced in many gay men is a function of, or compounded by, guilt and an inability to accept the whole self – something hardly surprising given the large number of us who were rejected by family, and sometimes by many of our peers. With Vincent Foster's suicide in 1993, society has finally and above all happily interested itself in this scourge and the costs thereof, for not only does society act as a central cause but it must serve as the essential way out.[5]

But this book's main purpose is to show the other side of the coin. I believe that many of the same forces that drove and then consumed Roger have lived in me from birth, but for me the ones that determined his choices could not be the roads taken. Many differences stood between us – for instance my fifteen years of marriage, indeed to the daughter of the man, Paul Nitze, after whom Roger's school had recently been named. With her I shared what was always most important for me, two daughters and a son, each loving, bright and talented, and around mere access to whom my own life was to revolve for almost a decade as it continues to do in joyful contemplation.

The principal parting of our roads was that unlike Roger, I came to terms with my homosexuality, despite having walked the difficult turf of a marriage in so many ways successful over so many years. Roger, in contrast, as Christopher Lydon has tellingly observed, spent years fitfully courting a woman in the manner of John Marcher with May Bartram in James's 'The Beast in the Jungle', turning to her not so much as a cover as a way to work through the agonizing uncertainties of his sexuality; he was covering one Roger from another Roger, not from the rest of the world. Just as irresolutely, he involved himself with a man of real character who loved him, but whom he forsook (he claimed on his psychiatrist's advice) and because the young carpenter showed HIV status – an additionally painful cross for this young man to bear. Roger never fully acknowledged his gayness, especially to himself.

In the last year of his life, I noticed a growing distance between us in the affections we had always expressed toward and felt for each other and the occasional intimacy we managed, despite the ties we had from shared experiences with our overlapping circle of friends and our times at the beach and Storybook Farm, my children's and my Virginia retreat. There had always been a tentativeness to Roger in the years I knew him, but now I felt a veritable chill creeping across his body, something he could do nothing to warm or stop. He couldn't even discuss homosexuality in the last few months of his life. He was wholly within the logic of his depression.

For my coming out I paid an enormous price, but not that which Roger paid, for forty years of throttling the voice that sought to speak out. And that is also part of our story, not so much about me as about our society and its insecurities. Living a life as a gay man in a straight society is a perpetual run up a down escalator: but with training and a bit of skill, one learns how to do it. Trillin's book, for example, I described as 'Hamlet without the Prince' on a television broadcast, because of Trillin's inability, like the society of the 1950s which he describes, to deal with homosexuality, Roger's especially. Rather did it seem that Trillin was trying to write a morality play, a Gatsbyesque story, the more he refused to grapple with Roger's essence. I am equally convinced that my ability ultimately to deal with depression was a function of the healthy attitude I developed toward my homosexuality.

Let me note that I refer to myself consistently as gay or homosexual, though the record would make obvious, given fifteen years of marriage, a certain bisexuality. Society does not make choice easy here; proclaim yourself bisexual and you are suspect in both camps, without support. A useful test is to rank-order a room of attractive people with respect to their sexual desirability; invariably there are some women I place ahead of some men. So to call oneself gay is in part a political choice, not a scientifically accurate description.

## 17: *'He whom the gods wish to destroy . . . '*

Cyril Connolly, the British man of letters, is the most recent writer to observe that 'he whom the gods wish to destroy, they first make promising'. It was a phrase one was to hear frequently in the past year. Ved Mehta wrote in the *New Yorker* of one friend of his at Balliol, the Oxford college he attended just five years before my time, that 'we imagined that few people at Balliol . . . could have fulfilled the Oxford dream of a Renaissance man' better than did his friend Roger Ogilvie, who committed suicide in 1981.[6] And those dreams of Oxford remind us that we are dealing with the imagination of times as well as of persons. Thus of Roger Hansen again, Calvin Trillin wrote of everyone's expectation, back in the 1950s, that he must surely some day be president:

> What an enormous burden for a young person who may not have had the emotional or social strength to absorb such a claim and not entangle his soul. A fear of failure and disappointing others can be paralyzing, and we can suffocate our young by creating unrealistic expectations.[7]

There was a Stanford junior back in the 1960s, of whom an article in the *Saturday Evening Post* reported a coed as saying:

> 'I'm sick and tired of listening to the bull sessions on "Is there a God?" and "What makes Scotty Thompson tick?" ' said Senator John F. Kennedy after speaking at Stanford in 1960, at Scotty's invitation, 'I'll see you in the White House in a few years, Scotty – if you haven't beaten me there.'[8]

This created a set of expectations which took at least a decade, if not to the present day, for me to live down – or recast. For that is not what I had grown up thinking about. Who wouldn't have been affected? The trouble was, everyone but me seemed to know what made me tick. Children dream about many things – but political power is rarely among these – and then when at any stage they get it they wonder why it isn't satisfying. Is it therefore surprising that George Stephanopolous, also a Balliol Rhodes Scholar, replied 'No' to the question of whether he had read *Remembering Denny*? 'I'm too scared,' he said, as well he might.[9]

Add homosexuality to achievement and the mixture can be lethal. It is hard enough to match early expectations; success coming early or out of season is always difficult to deal with, if only because it sets up conflicts with one's peer group ahead of schedule and enhances them. 'One never knows self-contempt until he's praised', one hears, especially when one gets so much of it so early. But homosexuality, if it is there, has almost necessarily been suppressed or repressed, and repressed more than in a less conspicuous youngster.

Repression causes conflict. Moreover, it causes overt adjustment problems – one cannot have had so much 'evidence' of his inability to adapt to the dominant lifestyle without appalling consequences to his self-esteem. Though Roger and I had continuing reminders of our achievements we were alike in finding them suspect, precisely because of the artificiality of our reaction to the world of sexuality as we acculturated as adolescents; there was just no point at which our homosexuality was to be tolerated or even understood. I know that for my part I continually had to remind myself of – rather than naturally accept – my achievement so that I would appear as natural as possible about the recognition about which I was exceedingly nervous. But when fourteen Rhodes Scholarship regional finalists were summoned into the inner sanctum of the Cal Tech faculty club for the announcement of the four winners from the western United States after a weekend of grueling interviews, I automatically assumed that the other Thompson – Robert Thompson – was the winner when that family name was announced last of the four. It was a minute before the confusion was straightened out, a minute of course that changed my life.[10]

Though does this beg the question; how much gay achievement is a flight from the intolerable? Roger's case and mine raise that question in spades; I had to achieve because my father expected me to and so prepared me, and had bequeathed me his drive – though alas like so many gay men I was unable fully to come to terms with him during his lifetime, no doubt because of that scary issue of masculinity. But my marriage, and the surrounding factors, precluded some avenues of happiness and fulfillment while reinforcing some very tempting substitutes; so then I was in real trouble. Any serious commitment precludes other choices; 'Renunciation marks the master', we remember, but the incipiently gay man may well use his homosexuality to avoid choice by making multiple superfluous commitments. I knew only that the world which yielded to me was largely built on illusion – and the hollow echoes of this knowledge rang through my sense of power, beauty, understanding, from very early on. The harder I strove the more I felt I was grasping a snowflake in the desert.

There are many in the same boat. In June 1993, when the Rhodes Trust held a reunion of all North American Rhodes Scholars in Washington, the widely-known Cambridge gay activist Jack Wofford and I arranged for all nine hundred attending (including President Clinton) to have in their packets an invitation bidding gay, lesbian, and bisexual members to a get-acquainted party at my Washington house. Rhodes Scholars, achievement-oriented and smart, are not always the most creative and courageous of people, though Jack and I had high hopes. Unsurprisingly, none of the truly famous Rhodes Scholars whom one or the other of us knew or assumed to be gay accepted the invitation – though some thirty came in all.

One just slightly less famous, like Roger and me highly visible in college days, much written up in magazines, did accept: then failed to attend. But it struck me as slightly more than coincidental that the three perhaps most famous 'student leader' types of that era each turned out to be gay: if homosexuality was a stigma, a closet gay might be driven forward to deflect or displace these devouring phantasmagoric anxieties about his self-worth.

So I was certified and commanded to be promising at Stanford, in that I got things done, something earlier teachers had proclaimed of me from the second grade. Now I was in the big world and the real one, or so it seemed: and the promise must therefore be taken seriously from within – as it was, oh so wonderfully and excruciatingly, from without. I have no doubt that the anxieties I had about sexuality were an underlying motive for my political career there, through which I sublimated and diffused my pain until I had fairly well papered over the interior cracks, soared, in other people's eyes, over the exterior chasms.

I had girlfriends, a few of whom counted briefly as lovers, and it seems that some very attractive and now very eminent coeds fell in love with me. Political power, even in the small goldfish bowl of a campus, is as much an aphrodisiac as John Dean said it was at the White House.

And make no mistake, my political ambition was very intense and, to some, overpowering or obnoxious. 'Yes, that's another picture of Scotty Thompson; this is something of a Thompson issue', said the Stanford Alumni Review of its 'once in a generation student'.[11] And of course by then I was quite immodestly revelling in it.

But my ambitions were a little different from that of the more conventional political activist, perhaps growing out of my incipient homosexuality – my cultural and artistic sensibilities, nurtured by my musician-mother and, to a lesser extent, my poetry-loving (but predominantly athletic) father. As early as Andover, these took the form of frequent visits to the Gardner Museum and the Museum of Fine Arts, or today by incessant collecting, with the walls of my home covered by everything from a sketch of a male torso by a student of Michelangelo, to a serious collection of paintings by contemporary Filipinos. My first words, quite late in my third year (my sister always teased that I never ceased thereafter to try to make up for lost time) were to ask my mother to 'Put on the Eine Kleine Nachtmusik.' Surely this is part of my gay side – or at least as those sensibilities have always been seen in this culture – and it always both tempered and filtered my ambition.

A Stanford Classics professor told me that he had, not unreasonably, thought me the most consummate Philistine on campus until he learned that I was studying Greek and reading, appropriately enough, Euripides' *Bacchae*. I wanted power, but was never willing to devote myself fully to it. I would only go to a political event on campus that I wasn't running if there weren't an opera in San Francisco or a poetry reading by Kenneth Rexroth or literary discussion by Frank O'Connor. I had in effect bumped into power, which was magic; I was power's favorite ally. I loved it, but was never fully comfortable with it, then or later.

Anxieties about my sexuality unnerved my hopes of getting into one of the powerful fraternities. Here, as so often, sexual anxieties were also a cover for mundane fears, in this case related to America's dirty little secret of class, which I had discovered at Andover, and was still haunted by. Just before rush season I was invited and went to a 'dirty rush' party, a canvas outside the times and places stipulated, given at Newport Beach by men from the fraternity house I would most have liked to join and at which the most glorious men at Stanford would be present. The important fraternities celebrated the great masculine virtues, chief among which were lady-killing, studliness, and athletic prowess, precisely those areas where my self-confidence was lowest.

I fantasized setting up my own fraternity to preempt rejection. As with so much social engineering, I expressed the fantasy in idealistic terms, as if to set a higher intellectual standard for the Stanford fraternities (not exactly a steep hill to climb in those days). In fact I wanted to build a Magic Mountain, as in Thomas Mann's novel I was then deeply into – though I skidded over the original mountain's being a resort for the well-bred dying.

One day I happened to bring up my private vision to Professor James T. Watkins IV, a very popular and senior political scientist, who rushed me to his house and broke out champagne to celebrate the meeting of dreams. More saliently, he had discerned a weak cell for us to implant our DNA – the Sigma Nu house, which had fallen into such disrepute and disrepair that its survival was in question, threatening the stability of the whole Stanford fraternity system. A drunk member had accidentally run over a fraternity brother, killing him, a very predictable catastrophe given behavior in the house at that point. And it was at the top of a hill. He had only lacked a surrogate – and now had found one. Our relationship was to be extraordinary in the annals of teacher and student, with Jim for my last three college years driving over in his well-marked Chevy convertible virtually every day to enquire after my well-being, and to offer solace or any of the prizes in a professor's gift.

Though married, Watkins was assuredly gay, preferring the company of apparently straight, but unusually good-looking, male undergrads, through whom he seemed to project a rerun of his own Stanford undergrad career, whence his fascination with the fraternities' survival. Of course he had never belonged to one. His motives thus paralleled mine, and he assured me he could deliver the Dean's backing, and probably that of the Sigma Nu rump.

I went first to Maynard Toll, now a successful Wall Street merchant banker, because he had been a heavy hitter at Andover and conveyed the right kind of intellectual-athletic image. The two of us then went to an intellectual star who got things done, Jim Woolsey, recently the Director of the Central Intelligence Agency. We three went to a fourth, and so on, picking up Tom Grey, who now has a chair at Stanford Law School, John Luce, now a prominent physician in San Francisco, John Steinbrenner, for the past decade head of foreign policy studies at the Brookings Institute. We carefully negotiated with the Sigma Nu old guard to give them plenty of dignity, without affording them any illusion that they would still run the house. We even permitted them to run an admittedly tame initiation – in which I was made to sit, rather conspicuously, on the mantel all evening, not just surveying the scene but chanting 'Tick Tock, I'm a clock . . . Tock Tick, I'm a ____.' It turned out that we all found many more friends among their number than we expected – I my close friend Jim Wood, an entrepreneur in Caracas.

Before rushing was supposedly complete, we had, for disinformation purposes, made numerous appearances at the other open houses; and then, having pledged as a group of thirty-five freshmen to Sigma Nu on the first night of parties, we let news of the coup spill across an astonished campus.

A fraternity is a band of brothers, a potentially readymade team, tightly bound then and in many ways more so as the years roll on. John Luce and Jim Woolsey testified, at dinner at my Washington house, to the great import Beta Chi – so we were known after we withdrew Sigma Nu, owing to its exclusionary racial policies, from its national organization – has had on their lives. In our senior year, we matched Harvard College in Rhodes Scholarships, and we unleashed considerable energies in almost every area of campus life.

But Stanford, and Beta Chi, showed me how powerfully denial could work – denial at so many levels, personally and as a team. Along the way I maintained the job of rush chairman every year, because I instinctively knew that was where quality control would be maintained: as any anthropologist will confirm, replacement of the species is where it's at. And the homoerotic aspect of fraternity life brought my suppressed gay side near (and then briefly to) the surface. In my sophomore year one most attractive freshman whom we had just pledged started sticking close to me. One night soon after rush week he showed up in my private room, at the far end of the ground floor below the dining room, bringing cheese, beer and wine, which we proceeded to drink steadily.

Soon his leg was on mine; then things mingled more and more. Finally, he locked the door and to my astonishment asked me to remove my jeans. I quickly realized that, unlike me, he knew what to do next. And indeed what followed was the most erotic hour of my life before or since. But the next morning we put exactly the *Boys in the Band* spin on it, demanding in theatrical overtones just what had happened, letting the record show that we had been too drunk to remember. We were to reenact this scene so often that in the end even we had to drop pretense that it wasn't happening. My fraternity brother, though far more sophisticated in things gay than I, has settled in, by all reports, for a lifetime of married denial.

For me, denial endured and intensified. Thus despite – or, grimly, because of – the extraordinary amount of time spent with Jim Watkins, extending to a whole summer sharing his house to 'take care of it' while his wife was away, I never put two and two together, even despite my occasional advice to him to keep his hands off his young friends – and me.

Not only Watkins. The famous Al Lowenstein, whose troubled memory has been reinvoked by a new biography that lays out *his* homosexuality very clearly indeed,[12] invited me to his Stern Hall flat when he turned up at Stanford at the start of my sophomore year, and over several highly-charged months made clear that I held the secret to every plan and dream he had for Stanford. He insisted that I take keys to his flat and car, tried to press money on me, and took me to expensive dinners until, up against the wall with my own plans and dreams for Stanford, I ceased to take his calls. Then, a spurned queen, he got literally vicious and incipiently violent. Again I failed to see what underlay his obsession, both when he was, as it now seems, briefly, if only slightly, in love, and when he had turned on me (only after, as he would naturally see it, I had turned on him).

Nor did the fact that Al like Watkins focused almost exclusively on muscular, blond and gorgeous undergraduates as the instruments of his crusades (I being the manifest exception) help me to discern the forces driving him. Dennis Sweeney, an object of both Al's and my erotic admiration, once tried to convince me that Al was gay – to my unfeigned astonishment: but that conversation was wrapped in double denial, since the two of us were sharing a motel bed while watching the famous 1962 California election returns and awaiting Nixon's great adieu, which we celebrated affectionately. Eighteen years later a deeply disturbed Dennis was to walk into Al's New York office and shoot him down, with plainly preposterous accusations. It is the unacknowledged demons that drive their victims to the furthest bounds of darkness. But as for me at the time, I can only find it astonishing that for a quarter-century I failed to notice, let alone draw conclusions from, the fact that for a few months the two best-known adult male political figures of the Stanford family were in some sense infatuated with me.

Denial manifested itself in other ways. Every psychiatrist or counselor to whom I would retell the story of that first encounter in my fraternity house, would respond immediately, and with overwhelming dismissal, 'Do you think you're gay because of that *one* episode?' I *had*, after all, been declared promising; I had delivered on enough of the promise to keep myself in play, even though what these therapists might better have considered was how my 'promise' had come to be a way of smothering my needs. I paid my psychiatric bills. So the therapists I sporadically saw over two decades conspired in the denial.

Anyway, their profession only got round to declaring that homosexuality was *not* an illness in 1973, *fifteen years* after Dr Evelyn Hooker made her famous examination of Rorschach and Thematic Apperception tests showing that they could detect no correlation of homosexuality to neuroses or psychoses. Perhaps that will surprise even some gay men accustomed to our antics in the stressed circumstances within which we live, but her finding of slightly higher intelligence among us gays will not surprise.[13] The first openly gay graduates emerged from the famous psychiatric institutes only in the 1990s, so my therapists, trained in the 1950s and 1960s, were only a little lagged behind – but enough.

The problem of my 'promise' was apparent to me before I left for Oxford. It was other people's projection, but I would have to live it out until I had a clear hold on it, had found something better – or had fulfilled it. Promise, after all, is less a lens society holds up to itself for its own purposes than a lens to make the future look more familiar. One can, alas, remain 'promising' for the rest of one's life, as with Zbigniew Brzezinski or Robert McNamara – aging distinguished figures with unfulfilled potential giving them the air of elderly brilliant youths. My 'promise' was hardly connected to my needs and provided an obsessive means of avoiding them, but I was trapped by it for the greater part of my adult life; society quickly alchemized its aspirations into mine. That same promise is a poison. Orwell said that 'seen from within life is a series of defeats', and how much more so when such high external goals were set by the unobservant for the unawakened.

## *Notes*

1. Hereafter epigraphs of each chapter are from Marcel Proust, *Remembrance of Things Past*, translated by C. K. Scott Moncrieff and Terrance Kilmartin (New York: Random House, 1982). Tellingly, throughout his 3000-plus pages, Proust changes Albert of his own life into the fictional Marcel's Albertine.
2. Hereafter wherever a name has been changed to protect privacy, only in the first instance are inverted commas used.
3. Calvin Trillin, *Remembering Denny* (New York: Farrar, Straus & Finoux, 1993). Roger Dennis Hansen was known as 'Denny' to his Yale classmates but evolved into Roger well before I knew him.
4. Roger never mentioned the *Life* article, a revealing indicator of the decline in his self-esteem, since he was clearly aware of the *Post* article about me, the picture from which was displayed in the 'trophy room' at my Virginia farm where he often visited. See 'Farewell to bright college years', *Life*, 42 (24 June 1957), 130–6, and see also 'Men of Eli at Oxford', *Life*, 43 (2 December 1957), 81–2.
5. See Dr Elizabeth Hersh and Dr Susan Lazar, 'Politics didn't kill Foster', *New York Times*, 12 August 1993.
6. Ved Mehta, 'Casualties of Oxford', *New Yorker*, 2 August 1993.
7. Trillin, *Remembering Denny*, p. 14.
8. 'People on the way up: "Campus dynamo",' *Saturday Evening Post*, 7 April 1962, p. 28.
9. Marjorie Williams, 'George in the jungle', *New York Times Sunday Magazine*, 20 February, 1994.
10. But happily changed Robert Thompson's life too: by sheer chance I ran into him on a train in Spain (and in rain) a year later with his

new wife, he in sheer bliss. He had met her in grad school in America – and of course would not have done so had he gone to Oxford. For once both sides were winners – or, in social sciencese, a non-zero sum game.

11. *Stanford Alumni Review*, April 1961, p. 16.
12. William Chafe, *Never Stop Running: Allard Lowenstein and the Struggle to Save American Liberalism* (New York: Basic Books, 1993).
13. Evelyn Hooker, 'Male homosexuality in the Rorschach', *Journal of Projective Techniques*, vol. 22, no. 1, 1957.

Chapter two

# *Nurture or Nature?*

*. . . shunning one another, seeking out those who are most directly their opposite, who do not desire their company, pardoning their rebuffs, moved to ecstasy by their condescension; but also brought into the company of their own kind by the ostracism that strikes them, the opprobrium under which they have fallen, having finally been invested, by a persecution similar to that of Israel, with the physical and moral characteristics of a race, sometimes beautiful, often hideous . . .*

● Cities of the Plain

WHAT is the gay world? In Whitaker Chambers' Washington it was furtive glances among people deemed cripples and criminals by their peers and themselves, around the fountain-statue of Admiral Dupont looking over its circle. But even before that not only were there celebrities and little people who harbored a secret, but some who acted it out, as early as our first native-born naval hero, Stephen Decatur, if Randy Shilts's diligent research is to be believed.[1] Walt Whitman's poetry leaves little doubt that he certainly did. And we know that in all cultures at all times there has been a homosexual, if not always a gay, world: open and jubilant in Hellas, all but invisible – though omnipresent – in tropical Africa. A European student of mine claiming homosexuality was an American vice – which he would commit suicide over were he to find it within – was astonished to find thirty bars, listed in my edition of *Spartacus*, in his modest-sized home city. Europeans who scoffed at the Ottomans for alleged pedophilia can ponder the Porte's emissary in Paris under Napoleon, who was shocked to discover male brothels in the Palais Royal, the house of freedom and revolution, containing '1500 boys exclusively occupied in sodomy'.[2]

The gay world is hardly at a mid-point in its own evolution, from obscurity and persecution, then to a self-hating and closeted stage, never better caricatured than by Tony Kushner's version of Roy Cohn in *Angels in America*, denying to his physician that he is gay.

> Like all labels they tell you one thing and one thing only: where does an individual so identified fit in the . . . pecking order? Not ideology, or sexual taste, but something much simpler: clout: Not who I fuck or who fucks me, but who will pick up the phone when I call, who owes me favors . . . Homosexuals are not men who sleep with other men. Homosexuals are men who in fifteen years of trying cannot get a pissant antidiscrimination bill through City Council. Homosexuals are men who know nobody and who nobody knows. Who have zero clout.[3]

And then one reaches the present, the beginnings of open defiance and pride in gayness, twenty-five years after Stonewall; and possibly to a later stage where, with society's easy and familiar acceptance of gay people – as in parts of California today – the defiance ends, the insistence on a separate gay culture is muted, and the differences between gays and straights become less marked than the similarities. But that is a good time off – and it is worth nothing that the separate gay culture will not go out of existence; indeed it will deepen in its meaning for its members but will be less a wall of protection than a set of opportunities and a stage for self-exploration.

Within today's gay world there is something of a backfire by those resentful that societal images of gaydom are forced by outers, Queens, transvestites, and every other form of the gay world *except* the 'silent majority' that quietly lives and/or works in the suburbs, attending church, drawing no attention to itself, otherwise indistinguishable from all the other couples that make up that bedrock of America. Bruce Bawer has written what he calls a 'meditation' on, but more a 250-page lament over, the absence of celebration of those suburban virtues.[4] The problem is, that kind of life may buy gays a certain mutually nervous acquiescence: but it develops within them no substance, no imaginative presence in their surroundings. As the late Darrell Yates Rist quotes a poor San Franciscan gay who doesn't live in the 'white, male, educated, and affluent' Castro: ' "They think if they buy a house and a couple of cars and mimic a heterosexual marriage, *then* they'll be accepted like straight men. But none of that changes the fact that to straights they're still queers. After all, that's what *queer* means." '[5] Congressman Barney Frank, at the New York march on the United Nations in June 1994, articulated the anxieties of the politically sensitive, in fearing that transvestites and their kind would marginalize the gay movement just when it was gaining mainstream attention – yet in doing so he raised the question of what the gay movement was doing to itself if it disallowed all but the safest-looking marchers.

More mercilessly, I recall my own uncharitable thoughts, sitting with my wife in a pew of our of course Episcopal church, looking at an obviously gay couple in front of us. They were devoted to each other, they were effeminate, and I was contemptuous. 'I won't have any of *that*', thought I, self-servingly reinforcing my own 'choice'. I was trying my best to sympathize, yet knew that for them to earn the respect I could give them as a Pillar of Society, they'd have to make me see them in their own terms, not as mimicking striped-suited fellow-worshipers and ending up a caricature of them.

The problem is also that, although most gay people live quietly (if not in the suburbs), they are not the ones advancing the political agenda. Every group has its quiet majority – but blacks didn't get to where they are now because some quiet dudes hung around the mall. So the gay world, like every world of political activism but more so, is colorful, vocal, and of desperate necessity, verbal.

Gayness also is an emerging sensibility, a set of almost coded reactions, attitudes, mental constructs – and it is the same everywhere. It must come from something deep within. It is an appreciation of the feminine, embodied artistically in centuries of pictures of Ganymede or, a different slant of the sensibility, of the eroticized extremity of St Sebastian, so strangely different from the Crucifixion. It is an urge for order, and a search for completion; it is male and female together, something we know we are all born with, says

Freud, but among men we gays alone are able to keep the strengths of both within us. The traits of gayness seems so basic that they cannot emerge trivially.

Indeed, as I write, a celebrated article has emerged from a study of the National Institutes of Health showing the propensity of gay brothers to share certain chromosomes. The DNA was analyzed in forty such pairs. Dr Dean Hamer, a gay Washington scientist, examined the reference points on the X chromosome where there are genetic markers that vary from person to person. 'According to the scientists' analysis, 33 out of the 40 pairs of brothers had in common a particular region of the X chromosome, containing a few hundred genes, where the gene favoring homosexuality is believed to be.'[6] This was the first study to demonstrate *any* connection between disposition to behavior and genetic markers on chromosomes. It may well be, as Dr Charles Krauthammer keeps bitterly arguing, that such biological correlation only accounts for half of those who become gay (the NIH study was careful not to claim what it didn't prove), making vigilance for those of his persuasion necessary to protect the other half who travel that road without genetic predisposition – or at least of any of which we are currently aware;[7] but two psychologists, Michael Bailey of Northwestern and Richard Pillard of Boston University, put the figure at up to 70 per cent,[8] which is more intuitively satisfactory. In any event, 'Predisposition is not predestination'; the mysterious gene was evidently not a sufficient condition of homosexuality though it may have been a necessary one.[9] But the scientific method is a ruthless and rigorous sieve of truth, of which evidently a little was precipitated here.

It is increasingly clear not just that there are biological differences between very substantial populations of gays and straights, but that the differences between gay and straight people are for the most part and start with the biological. It is also clear that many factors intervene and combine to affect the timing, nature, and smoothness of a child's acculturation,[10] but most gay men among themselves know they are biologically different, however persuasively psychiatrists or psychologists may have made the opposite case.

Long before the compelling contrary data began emerging, my counselors had helped guide me to conclude that my own homosexuality arose from an immediate and intense family context rather than genetics: and they could offer a strong prima-facie case. When I was thirteen, my strong-willed father was locked in battle against my only sibling, a stunningly beautiful sister eighteen months my senior, who died tragically in 1992. Many young men wanted her and Father was determined to screen them, indeed to exclude whole categories; of course those screened out were precisely the ones my sister preferred. With one she fell hopelessly in love: tall, blond, gorgeous and immensely self-confident at only sixteen, Larry Cutter was bent on having her whenever he wished, and did so.

My own anxieties were not just derivative; Larry came over to me at one point in the school's gym shower, towering over me and looking for all the world like a Roman centurion in David's *Rape of the Sabine Women*, to make it clear that I'd regret it if I got in his way. He made castrating jabs and piercing gestures, terrifyingly erotic, which I shouldn't have taken seriously but which of course transfixed me, dominating my dreams and nightmares for years to come. I felt like a small state next to a great power, hoping the interests of the big fellows didn't trample me under in the process. As always, I saw potential adversaries as ten feet tall while seeing myself smaller than the reality. Incredibly I couldn't believe my sister was actually having sex with Larry – sex was a verboten, murderous, mysterious, sacred rite to me – but it soon became evident that they were doing it every day and night, in cars, boats, trees, under my nose in the attic at one end of which was my room – and sheltering womb. My systems were, so to speak, overloaded.

Life was ugly for a while around the household, and I too was left with many psychological scars, enough to be greatly relieved in due course to get a scholarship to round out my high school days at Phillips Academy, Andover; my sister went off to live with a favorite aunt in New York.

Our family spirit was wounded from the crisis, and from that point I probably blamed my sister – plus women in general – and so started my search for appropriate female mates with an underlying but mostly unconscious grudge. And surely I had a great sense of inadequacy as a young male, three years Larry's junior, seeing him as having used his magnificent naked body and head to shatter and despoil the sacred family jewel chest. But still, at this stage I didn't blame Larry, I blamed my sister – and women. 'They' had destroyed my happy family life. In therapy thereafter one psychiatrist after another thought this a probable, possibly a sufficient, explanation of my emerging bisexuality; which, by denying the intrinsic force in my nature of the power at the gay end of the spectrum, was another way for the profession to reinforce my 'heterosexuality' at the other end.

I was from then on always to have an unconsciously fearful attitude to women, but was a magnetic attraction for at least a few of them. Attending a conference at Sarah Lawrence as a Stanford freshman, I was approached by a good-looking woman several years older than I who had seen such an article about me as to make her, she said, fall in love. I went scarlet, and fell back in disorder. Finally she demanded to know whether I was scared. Didn't I want to go back to her motel and get laid? As so often I had been cornered by success. Fifteen years later when I was starting a round of psychotherapy, this incident came up. Dr McMahon was struck by my lack of feeling about it. He finally got out of me that Jody was simply acting the way I assumed all women behaved. I assumed that she had been trying to use me, not that she was simply attracted to me. It wasn't even a Freudian slip. He, however, was incredulous, and tried to show me the connections to the series of older, powerful and successful women to whom I had, in various ways, attached myself and from whom I had benefitted.

So was it all nurture? As I recall the themes and patterns in my boyhood dreams, which are plainly susceptible to homoerotic interpretation, and reread my childhood diaries, and examine the configuration of my friendships back then, there were strong propensities and tendencies, even if I wasn't 'effeminate' or didn't exhibit other outwardly gay characteristics, long before the family crisis. And why did I blame my sister for our family troubles? Had I been dispositionally straight I might well have identified with her.

My belief came to be that the family crisis made a full and life-long acculturation into straight life much more difficult but not impossible, especially had I had, as more than one psychiatrist (and even more importantly, my mother-in-law) was convinced, a more sympathetic spouse. And yet, and yet . . . the more I think back without intervening ideologies supplied by therapists and society more generally, I see my genetic predisposition as conclusive; the only question was to what late point in life would I wait to flow with it. One of my earliest memories, when I was about five, is of a teenaged baby-sitter telling me he was going to 'pull my pants down' and spank me on his lap if I repeated a particular misbehavior, which of course I promptly did. Forty-five years later I discovered that this same baby-sitter is a fellow professor – a married gay man. The games I played in the pastures and woods with friends, when I was eight or nine, were explicitly homoerotic, however much clothed (or, more pertinently, unclothed) in 'medical' or 'cowboys and Indians' form; and several studies reveal that persistence in such childhood games surely presages homosexual behavior in adulthood.

The bottom line in this debate is an intuitive one, however. No man who has spent some of his life in both straight and gay worlds needs scientific data to establish the biological differences between the two groups; it is overwhelmingly obvious. True, they overlap: but the weight of propensity in the two groups is compellingly opposite, not just in the sexual partners but in the patterns of daily life.

It may be that cultural sources can be found for many apparently universal gay and lesbian traits. My therapist suggested, for example, that the gay male mania for neatness, for instance forever ironing one's clothes or rearranging rooms, is essentially to prove one no longer needs his mother; at a deeper level it is manifestation of a sense that the world is not in order. But all such observations need empirical testing, and science will find, in one year or ten, the ultimate sources of biological diversity among men, on the central issue of sexuality, in their genetic and cultural proportions.

In any event, it is extraordinary how opposite are the foci of the two groups: fantasizing about sex and life among gay men is literally a world apart from heterosexuals fantasizing about sex – and life, and love – with women; they are the two opposite ends of the earth, their separated poles identifying the opposite signs of straight and gay men in every tribe and every culture.

The straight world, like any majority on its own turf looking at minorities, fails to see the variety of type that it sees so well among itself. A much older friend of mine who knows I am gay will deny it to others, since I am 'masculine' and 'have children', the daughters feminine, the son a masculine and athletic type, in the popular notions thereof. But effeminate men are sometimes straight, and leather bars are full of hunky gay men, many of whom despite appearances are passive in bed.

Kinsey's extraordinary data, never really contradicted except by noisy assertions of disbelief, show that thirty-seven per cent of American men have had sex, through orgasm, with another man *after* puberty; in light of that we have to see gayness across a vast range of our puritan nation, let alone our species. True, there are persistent attempts to discredit those numbers – like the Pentagon-influenced Battelle study purporting that barely over one per cent was gay; but the old percentages always reassert themselves – because they are right.[11] A pastoral-counseling husband and wife interpret Kinsey as saying that 'less than 50 per cent of the men could claim no homosexual experience.'[12] Kinsey further showed that about a tenth end up as exclusively homosexual, which makes sense to me: in my Rhodes group of thirty-two men there were two eventually openly gay, one closeted, and possibly others; my fraternity house showed a similar percentage, and in groups of thirty I can usually spy out at least two gay men besides myself. Whether it is the Kinsey '1', mostly heterosexual, probably married, like the many married men I have had flings with, or the Kinsey '6', who may prefer not to be alone in a room with a woman, and who usually does have a range of effeminate behaviors, we see too many types of gays for easy characterization.[13] Of course among ourselves gay men tend to be able to recognize each other, through subtle or unsubtle behaviors and codes, but many of us easily 'pass' in heterosexual society. Thus in the trial between my wife and me in 1984, her legal team laid out my 'transformation' in terms of my beginning to wear 'fashionable' clothes!

Given the enormous pressures to marry – from employers like the Air Force, from parents, and from the structural incentives embedded in the tax code and elsewhere – a substantial percentage of Kinsey 1–4 types do marry, but one is bound to wonder whether these would consider marrying in the absence of societal pressures.

There are empirical data on this matter. An Australian study rings true in every respect for American practice. The motive for gay men to marry turns out, not surprisingly, 'to be a highly anti-homosexual expected peer and societal reaction' to the alternative; but conformity 'to social norms [on the part of the married homosexual] appears to be highly situation-specific: there is no evidence that such conformity is a general characteristic of the married homosexual respondent in other areas'; indeed he turns out to be rather less conservative than his heterosexual counterpart, except in matters of sex-role fulfillment.[14]

There are two ways of looking at sexuality, which amplifies both the confusion and choice a homosexually inclined man faces. Masters and Johnson say your sexuality is whatever you say it is, that that's the only fair basis for evaluation.[15] Others argue that behavior isn't the salient thing, since society *induces* too much behavior that might otherwise not be our choice. And what is behavior, once we transcend crudest definition? Ask Al Lowenstein. What one fantasizes about, especially while making love,[16] might thus be a better indicator of sexual preference and long-term choice. Richard Isay, a psychiatrist with many gays in his practice, adopts this point of view.[17]

What are the choices faced by a young man with contrary tendencies shaking in his soul? One thing for certain is that his self-respect will suffer symmetrically with society's pressure to conform to something with which he is constitutionally uncomfortable. The straight adolescent has the reinforcement, as he acculturates to manhood, of society's qualified approval of his love-making and his own pleasure from it. The young gay adolescent, if he tries to conform, finds himself assenting to rituals of his own unworthiness, trying to feign feelings, trying to make his sexuality work at cross-purposes with his psychic and physical endowment, exacting from himself a price that he will be repaying all his life.[18]

True, one may feel forced to find in this a great moral quandary and challenge. My colleague and friend Richard Neuhaus, our century's answer to John, Cardinal Newman, has done so in a blistering review of Bruce Bower's civilized (but wrong-headed) defense of gay conservatism, *A Place at the Table*,[19] which we have already encountered. Pastor Neuhaus's response to every gay argument about the innateness of homosexuality is that life is moral choice, and all sex is fraught with difficulties, of whatever variety:

'... sexual desire is a realm of ambiguity, confusion, gradation, temptation, and decision. It is also a place of moral possibility.' And so, guys, play it tough, because however you fashion the argument it comes back to the same thing: there isn't any 'choice' if the 'right' and 'moral' choice is preordained. No, he can't even accede to Bruce Bawer's plea that his union with his lover be blessed:

> But there is an awful sadness. Those who understand homosexuality as an objective disorder and homogenital sex as intrinsically wrong cannot in good conscience offer their moral approval of the way of life chosen by Mr Bawer and [his lover] Mr Davenport.

Indeed Pastor Neuhaus notes they have made their 'choice', and hopes that these apparently enviably happy men will 'reconsider'!

But in the real world, how would Dick Neuhaus respond if, whatever *his* sexuality, he was told that the 'moral choice' was to have sex with giraffes or trees? The fact is that 'moral possibility' exists on both sides of the street, and there are differences only of degree in the extent to which gay and straight people conventionally must work out their choices along moral lines, but on their separate sides of the street. What Neuhaus has forgotten is what Burke and Grover Cleveland both said so pointedly in other contexts, it is a 'condition that confronts us, not a theory'.

In fact the tables can be turned. How meaningful – and moral – is it to ask a woman to accept an intrinsically gay man as her husband? In most circumstances she will do so only in the context of a lie; exceptions are mostly of convenience. What sort of marriage is this? The problem for Neuhaus is that there is no magic, no magician, by which or through whom his moral gay man can so transform himself. I know – I tried; precisely in the latter part of my marriage as I became more conscious of my homosexuality, it became more and more painful to accept my duties as a heterosexual man. Indeed I became less and less of a man as I denied my increasingly obvious identity, with terrifying consequences not just for my self-esteem but for my wife. It is the same thing that psychiatrists were asking so many of us to do in suggesting that we adapt to the socially dominant model – causing much family hardship and many wretched marriages. You can't morally live a lie – yet that is precisely what Neuhaus would have of us.

And one must finally ask Pastor Neuhaus, what of *God's* will? I exulted when a priest at my university urged *all* of us at a Lenten service to delight and give God thanks for our sexuality. As he is a member of Integrity, an episcopal association for gay men, which has Sunday services like its Catholic counterpart, Dignity, I knew that his blessing included my tribe.

The Classical tradition supports my argument as well. In the most eloquent articulation of the nature of love, Plato's *Symposium*, Socrates, speaking through Diotima, thus defines true love, which ascends upwards in its contemplation of the truly beautiful.

> . . . life above all others which man should live, is the contemplation of beauty absolute; a beauty which if you once beheld, you would see not to be after the measure of gold, and garments, and fair boys and youths . . . But what if man had eyes to see the true beauty . . . ?

Surely the 'true beauty' could not come in its ultimate form through the pursuit of a sexual union from which gay men can have only contrived pleasure, for the sake of satisfying external demons and false gods, rather than the fulfillment of their true selves.

The 'moral' question for me is better stated as a matter of humanity and of how we treat people, ultimately, who are 'different', but whose differentness lies atop a world of similarities. No one ever said it more universally than the Bard, who treats the issue several times but never more bluntly than through Shylock and through Jewishness.

> Hath not a Jew eyes? hath not a Jew hands, organs, dimensions, senses, affections, passions? fed with the same food, hurt with the same weapons, subject to the same diseases, healed by the same means . . . and if you wrong us, shall we not revenge? If we are like you in the rest, we will resemble you in that.

One thing, however, about which there is no debate as between nurture and nature, is that the prejudice against gays is developed. It is nurtured in society. Or against any group, for that matter, its first step being hyper-awareness. When I was seven years old my parents had to leave the house briefly though my father was expecting a friend in a cause allied to his own, that of the American Indian. When my parents returned they asked if anyone had turned up. I told them a man had, and he would come back shortly. I could not remember his name. Asked for a description, I said he was tall and had bushy eyebrows like my father's. That is all I could recall.

The man was the state executive of the National Association for the Advancement of Colored People, and he was pitch black.

Stage by stage, I can recall how I came to acquire prejudice against gay people. In junior high school, the only other boy who shared my cultural and intellectual sensibilities was the son of the high school football coach, just as my father was a former champion athlete and looked it, still indeed coaching his college boxing team. Young Paul and I shared a problem, though we never discussed it: a mutual dislike of the competitive sports at which our fathers had always excelled – and in which they continually pestered and encouraged us to participate. Ask most gay men and they will come up with similar stories of fathers giving them endless baseball bats and footballs for Christmas while starving them of affection; indeed if anything was the cause of my wanderings in quest of self-esteem between my youth and midlife crisis, it was the perception that my father, while loving his son, insufficiently appreciated me with my bookish pursuits and avoidance of athletics. My particularities were too superficially different for him to feel these lesser emotions than love – identity and pride – in which nevertheless love stands upright.

In any case, I recall sitting in the back seat of Paul's mother's Cadillac during lunch hour (she taught at our junior high school) and talking about Mozart, as he tried unsuccessfully to get me off; we were twelve, and this is one area in which I was not precocious, if only because of the mounting tension between father and sister which I intuitively translated into sexual terms, and which inhibited my conscious sexual activity for several years. We were happy in the big car, insulated from all the Western equivalent of the flanneled fools at the wicket, the muddied oafs at the goal. But when he came out to visit me on the college campus over which my father presided, Dad warned me about him – 'he looks homosexual' (not an unfair description); and of course I knew Father, who by and large was a pretty reasonable fellow, was right. *I* picked up that associating with such people carried dangers, both internal and external. So I converted my father's warning into a denial of my own nature, especially since, for all my father's anxiety about my lack of interest in athletics and his constant erosion of my self-esteem, I wasn't considered effeminate. Looking back on it, it is obvious that an unconscious self-selection governed the bonding between my closest friends and me during the ensuing decades, given the high proportion who turned out to be gay, bisexual, or closeted.

Several close friends who attended Eton told me that while at Eton they and everyone like themselves – good-looking and athletic – had slept with everyone else of like mind and body while there, and then generally outgrown such behavior, or been embarrassed by it, and, with few exceptions, slept only with women ever after. But at Andover, I found that the New England private school shared none of the well-known predilection of the English 'public school' for teenage homosexuality. Two inseparable roommates who looked effeminate were whispered about as if they carried the mark of Cain; one died in recent years of AIDS. But status in those years at Andover consisted of standing on the steps of the Commons after dinner, vaunting one's conquests on the athletic fields that day or, were it soon after vacation, one's conquests under young ladies' skirts at home. Paul Monette's lengthy and painful description of life at Andover as an effeminate day-student, marked as a queer at least in his own mind, and only a few years apart from my time there, is extraordinarily painful.[20] But my problems there were of my own making and had nothing to do with homosexuality.

To visit Andover today, with its gay club and open attitude toward all minorities, so many of whom predominate in the school's life, is to go from the unwitting darkness of my day into bright light. My son, his class's 'athlete of the year', also played a horny nurse in a student drama there, and seemed wholly unthreatened by the gay roles acted by peers in the production.

In the perspective of half a lifetime, the Stanford of 1959 – one is tempted to say the Leland Stanford Junior University – was so dominated by the fraternities and traditional social life of football and booze that it was possible to go four years, thirty miles from San Francisco, and have no awareness whatsoever of a gay minority or gay issues. Stanford's Institute of International Relations, of which I was vice president as a junior and president as a senior, had as an advisor one Bill Vatcher of the Hoover Institution, who was to be killed in the gay tenderloin area of San Francisco under circumstances never elucidated, but such thoughts never occurred to any of us. Another mentor to the Institute (and to me among many other Stanford men) Professor James T. Watkins IV, whom we have already met, was very effeminate, in a sexless marriage by his own account, and dangerously given to putting his hands all over the shoulders and necks of attractive undergraduates in a way that would bring instant punishment today. Indeed I warned him even then of the consequences, at least to his reputation among his chosen targets, and squirming away one summer told him at all costs to keep his hands off undergraduates. This did deter him for a short time. He was never to know of my underlying bisexuality, dying in 1982 just before I came out. But that he was 'gay' in a sense that this provided a separate option in life did not occur to us any more than it had to him. What he was to me was a wonderful supporter, with channels of patronage; he was a man of moral principle and intellectual stimulation. I put my gay instincts in the same category of every apathic instinct or temptation which my superego had routinely to overcome. It was just something that you got over, though I feared that I had more to get over than most.

Although my own consciousness of a gay stratum inside me came closer to the surface in these years, I recall only three discussions of homosexuality – like Denzel Washington's comment about homosexuality in *Philadelphia*, when he said, in the role of the homophobic attorney-turned-hero, that when he grew up it just wasn't really thought of or mentioned – it was just those faggots out there. The first was when a highly devious fraternity mate saw into my soul and decided to frighten me, developing fears of a homosexual outing, with allusions to the then current novel *Advise and Consent* (by Stanford alumnus Allen Drury), in which a blackmailed senator commits suicide. The situation was bad enough for me to discuss it with the Dean of Students Donald Winbigler and Professor

Watkins. The latter, however, cautioned me never to allude to the novel when discussing what had happened, because in it the protagonist actually had a homosexual affair. Think of my career! And my mentor knew of what he spoke, while assuming my complete innocence.

The second time was in our senior year, and several of us were discussing our careers, including my political ambitions. One person mentioned experimenting sexually, including with another male. A close friend, later a successful merchant banker, held me eye-to-eye. 'Don't even think about it. If you had even one short encounter in bed with another man, it would come out, and you'd be dead politically.' And public office was my highest ambition.

The third was a thirty-something faculty member who found me desirable, made passes at me, and was astonished when I confessed to (slight) homoerotic thoughts around Stanford's best-looking men. He wanted me to set up blind homosexual encounters for him in one of my fraternity's johns, which of course I laughed out of court. But for the first time I had met a consciously gay – though married – man, one with four children, one who talked of bisexuality as the ultimate sophistication, one with whom Europeans, and 'more advanced' Easterners, were perfectly comfortable – though, ironically, within twenty years California, the land beyond categories, would have the most tolerant atmosphere in the world toward homosexuality. I was to find my professor's words largely true – all the way across the spectrum to the phenomenon of bisexuality among upper-class (and sometimes decadent) young Europeans.

I went up to Oxford in 1963, just after the great civil rights march on Washington, in which I participated, plainly threatened by the rising tide of ambivalent sexuality in me, enough so that in four years at Oxford I never explored this side even though it would have been surely 'safe' and easy so far from home and within so tolerant a culture. But I also slacked off on my search for a suitable woman precisely because I was so confused. While doing doctoral research in West Africa I had a long but not very successful affair with a European diplomat; she wanted more of me than I could psychologically spare at that point of my life. I was living through *coups d'état*; at one point the Ghanaian Chief of Criminal Investigation,

Tony Deku, jailed me. It turned out that he was trying to send a message to the high-powered diplomatic community with which I spent my social life, had a less than fully adequate understanding of the ancient concept of diplomatic immunity, and had been informed he couldn't directly jail the British diplomat who was gossiping about his undeniably interesting sexual activities. A stunning South African 'colored' woman, who had been a close friend of deposed President Nkrumah, had become a prize catch as between army and police sharing the powers of the transitional government. Reportedly, when the army froze her assets – the police having seized her favors – she responded, with anatomical substantiation, that *her* assets were 'unfreezable', a comment diplomats thought very funny; the CID was officially unamused. Among those in Accra's lively diplomatic corps at that time were Jack Matlock, later US ambassador to the Soviet Union, Wim van Eekelen, later Dutch Defense Minister and then head of the Western European Union, and William Depree, later American ambassador to Mozambique.

I got my fun horsing around with my handsome wiry Fra-fra steward and cook from Burkina Faso, in what were plainly pre-gay relations; but my excitement came from elsewhere. I had the good fortune at Stanford to have been assigned by President Wallace Sterling to introduce new student William Windsor around the Bay area, and we became friends; while studying at Oxford, I often stayed at his rather special London digs in St James's. About the time I went down to Africa, William was assigned to the British High Commission in Lagos, Nigeria, as third secretary, but since (as HRH Prince William of Gloucester) he was *inter alia* quite a bit higher than that in Nigerian estimation as seventh in line to the throne of his cousin Elizabeth, he got too much attention to dare misbehave.

So he needed to get out of town. My first escapade with William was up the estuary a hundred miles or so out of Lagos in a rubber dinghy that he had elaborately outfitted, and since it was our Christmas celebration for ourselves, he brought along cases of champagne and other wonderments from his mother, Princess Alice, sent by way of Fortnum and Mason's and other purveyors to royalty on Piccadilly. Our scheme, so he put it, was to enjoy ourselves by picking up village girls with whom to splash in the ocean; previous voyagers had told him these would be wonderfully available. But in the event, his first sip of Christmas champagne on the flawless sand of the beach was so unpleasant – he spat it out – that I thought the bottle must be bad. I tasted it and it was perfect: it took other symptoms to demonstrate that William had jaundice, and his medical travel kit gave only one remedy – stay put and rest for a week. I would have Princess Alice's champagne to myself.

It was an extraordinary experience. I knew William well but had never spent any serious time alone with him. There was almost nothing to do beyond talking, but after we had discussed British history for several days – that is from the usual point of view, of his ancestors – he went on to tell me in great detail about his sexual exploits with classmates at Eton, as well as about some of the rest of the British swells, royal and otherwise. Subsequently I proposed to give him a medicinal massage out in the sun with the tanning oils and skin lotions he had brought in abundance. One thing led to another, and it turned out that, although jaundice slowed him down considerably, his old talents, put aside for London's best women in recent years, were still available. And I didn't know what to make of it, since denial would have been a little absurd, though I managed with myself, saying that I was helping a friend. 'Denial', Paul Monette wrote in his gay autobiography, 'is compulsion's middle name'. It certainly was for me on that occasion up the estuary from Lagos as on so many others.

When he recovered, he would fly himself to Accra, where we could be mischievous in more traditional ways. Not to put too fine a point on it, I threw parties, but rather restricted ones. They were organized by two gloriously and stunningly good-looking men, Colonel (as he then was) Amankwaa Afrifa, the tall lean thirty-year-old co-head of state who had organized the *coup d'etat* earlier that year,[21] and Colonel Robert Kotei, his associate, both of them ruthlessly executed on the beach by the gauntly Puritan Flight Lieutenant Rawlings, in one more instance of the increasingly weary violence some years later.

Few people could take their eyes off Afrifa. At twenty-nine he had seized power from by far the best known African potentate while leaving its exercise for the next months to his six elder colleagues on the 'National Liberation Council'. He had the habit of command and was so stunningly handsome with his exquisite features and build that he needed a security guard to protect his life not above the waist but below, where people in crowds were always grabbing. Kotei would round up a number of large and demanding women, who at first frightened me. My stewards would feed them, and, I suspected, give them their first round of the evening. By the time we were all thrashing around on the mattresses spread around on the living-room late at night, after a great deal of beer, I would be blissfully unclear as to what was happening or who was with whom, which made it far easier. For in the melée there was plainly considerable homoerotic activity, not just by me, over and beyond the systematic penetration we were all expected to make of the women. Afrifa unclothed looked like a Greek statue (though far better endowed than they), but so did all the other men to a lesser extent, and it was pretty sensuous and satisfying – a combination of black power and 'Black Mischief'. I got a political and erotic education in Ghana.

Perhaps with a few more such rumbles I could have skipped some steps and come out far earlier. For now in my subconscious I was dwelling on all that erotic play, by ostensibly, and absolutely gorgeous, straight men – like William and the plainly polymorphous Afrifa. But by his nuance and hints, William made clear once again, after we departed Africa, that our 'horseplay' was Eton-era stuff, put aside when we returned to reality, and also something to be, on the whole, embarrassed about. I don't doubt that that's how he really felt about it. And when he gave a party for my wife and me a few years later in Tokyo, he gave us a Japanese sex instruction booklet as an additional, humorous wedding present (deeply resented by Nina) – and another nuanced reminder that our horseplay on the beach was a childish thing which I was well to have put away, even though at the dinner he gave in our honor feet and hands were moving rather freely under the restaurant table among a very fay Englishman, William and myself. I never saw William again, since he was killed the next year in a flying accident. But he had educated me both in sexual technique and in the place of homosexuality for a man of the world: amusingly unadult. I sought to digest both, which since the two didn't mix, caused me lots of stomachache.

I had another example in the same period, also in Africa. In Dar-es-Salaam I met an anguishingly beautiful tall and thin local, about my age, who drove me to distraction. I followed him around, taking him to lunch, dinner, and films. Always previously able to contain my enthusiasm for dancing, when I learned that it was within the local mores for men to dance together I suggested that, and thus had my first body contact with Joshua. He picked up his unlearned suspicion at some point, however, and without delay suggested we go to the house of 'woman business'. So indignity piled on indignity: not only had I to sleep with a woman I loathed, but to pay for his manifest pleasure in the next cubicle. When we reemerged on the beach, he told me that now he felt like a 'man' again.

I got the message: so much so that, when I had a perfectly good opportunity to be seduced by an attractive man the next day – an American professor in town to advise President Nyerere – I deflected his every move, lecturing myself on the sickness of homosexuality on the presidential beach to which my suitor had brought me in hopes that my attitude would evolve. I felt nauseous at this New Yorker's moves, when I should have felt a redeeming touch of deliverance.

So, like every other child of this country at that time I *learned* prejudice against gays over the years and reinforced my shame at these attitudes within. And, I have further had to learn, the unlearning of such attitudes invariably will be slower the older the community.

Gay African-Americans would supply the confirmation that it is harder to be gay than to be in any other minority; since those I have known always agree that their gayness is the harsher stigma to bear. As one psychologist notes:

> The ostracism incurred for being a gay man runs deeper than it does for being black or Indian . . . Like witches, we [*sic*] called them heretics. The very word *faggot* means a bundle of sticks that were burned in the fire. When homosexuals were burned at the stake, they were called *faggots*.[22]

But attitudes *can* change fast. When I was involved in civil rights (for African-Americans) in the 1960s, it was a verity that wherever else progress was made, Mississippi would be at the tail end, and whites from that state reinforced the attitude with their frequently expressed statement that 'there'd never be a nigger in Ole Miss'. Federalizing the National Guard changed that rather quickly, and attitudes changed, *pari passu*, far more quickly than any of us had thought possible. Charlie Colson, Nixon's adviser, was right: When you've got'em by the balls, the hearts and minds will follow.

After I came out, the average age of my friendships shifted downward – my new friends were much younger, the old ones that remained were on the younger side of my circle. Even my gay friends, but of course much more the straight ones, who had graduated from college before 1968, with its first sea-change of attitudes, found it difficult to 'get it', and the gay men who had come out were encrusted with guilt. Today, the youngsters brought up in the steadily-widening circles of enlightenment are about as much concerned with one another's sexuality as with their hairstyles or comparative advantage on the athletic field. And telling them about attempts by parents in recent years, indeed today, to force their gay children into a procrustean straight bed is like telling them about those who, fifty years earlier, tormented their left-handed children into favoring their right. For they have grown up knowing, instinctively, that gays are gays for the same reason that Hispanics are Hispanics – they are born that way. When there isn't any societal prejudice supplying 'reasons' why 'gays don't have to be gay', or when the young have been happily spared such nonsense until their views are well-formed, then it is plainly obvious.

And surely in an enlightened society, those people not clearly genetically destined for one camp or the other – whom we perhaps in a different sense label as bisexuals today – would feel the freedom to range more freely across the societal spectrum in the search for intimacy. Distilled, all experience shows that John Boswell, in his masterpiece of history of the gay experience (and bigotry thereto), is right: society at its cost and loss throws all people into only two bins for purposes of romantic attachment, namely male and female:

> It can well be argued that the homosexual/heterosexual dichotomy is not a real one, and this would have been the response of most ancient authorities. At best these categories group together according to one arbitrarily chosen aspect of

> sexual actions – the genders of the parties involved – varieties of sexual behavior which may be more dissimilar than similar . . . Moreover, it is not clear that in most humans it is the gender of the other party which makes the sexual act desirable or not: many people are apparently more aroused by the acts themselves (penetration, oral stimulation, etc.) than by the persons involved, and some people respond only to blonds or to people with blue eyes.[23]

Discussing the issue with straight people expressing prejudice toward gays, I routinely ask the characteristics of the people to whom they are attracted. If thinness, youth, and charm are highly prized qualities, a straight man is likely to admit he would prefer to sleep with a young man exhibiting those qualities than with a middle-aged, overweight and cranky woman. But one can narrow the spectrum of choice and still encounter startling responses – if the respondent commits to honesty. For here is the overlap for those of us who have walked in both gardens, as well as those who behave solely heterosexually and know there can be longings in the soul for both sexes.

Alexis, Marguerite Yourcenar's young narrator, writer of the longest letter of love and regret ever, articulates one traditional set of alternatives.

> I therefore had to choose between my penchants, which I judged to be criminal, and complete renunciation, which is perhaps not human. I chose. I condemned myself, at the age of twenty, to an absolute isolation of the senses and the heart.[24]

But in time Alexis of course does marry, a third path so many like him eventually choose, only to realize that that too would isolate the senses from the heart. Certainly the most powerful impulse I was ever to feel was that to bring the senses and the heart together.

## Notes

1. Randy Shilts, *Conduct Unbecoming: Gays and Lesbians in the US Military* (New York: St Martin's Press, 1993) pp. 12–14.

2. Cited in Noel Malcolm, 'Types of the Turk', reviewing Andrew Wheatcroft, *The Ottomans*, *TLS*, 5 November, 1993, p. 21.
3. Tony Kushner, *Angels in America, Part One: Millennium Approaches* (New York: Theatre Communications Group, 1993), p. 45.
4. Bruce Bawer, *A Place at the Table: The Gay Individual in American Society* (New York: Poseidon Press, 1993).
5. Darrell Yates Rist, *Heartlands* (Penguin Books, 1992), p. 14.
6. 'A gay gene?,' *Economist*, 17 July 1993, p. 80; David Wheeler, 'Study suggests X chromosome is linked to homosexuality', *Chronicle of Higher Education*, 21 July 1993, p. A7.
7. See 'Media hype about the "gay gene" ', *Washington Post*, 23 July 1993.
8. See Chandler Burr, 'Homosexuality and biology', *Atlantic Monthly*, March 1993, p. 64.
9. 'A gay gene', *Economist*, 17 July 1993, p. 80.
10. See Chandler Burr's excellent synthesis on the evidence accumulating on this issue, 'Homosexuality and biology', cited above.
11. The Battelle study reported that 1.1% of adult men between 20 and 39 were exclusively homosexual. The study brought hoots and protests from across the gay world. In fact the methodology of the study was wholly dubious, relying on interviews (and that largely from suburbs in 'households'), where reporting is always suspect on homosexuality, and financed by the Pentagon, which had an interest in a low percentage during this period of debate over gays in the military. See 'Honest answers?', *Seattle Times*, 23 April 1993.
12. Morton and Barbara Kelsey, *Sacrament of Sexuality: The Spirituality and Psychology of Sex* (Warwick, New York: Amity House, 1986), p. 183.
13. The Kinsey scale is as follows:
    0. Exclusively heterosexual;
    1. Predominantly heterosexual, and only incidentally homosexual;
    2. Predominantly heterosexual, but more than incidentally homosexual;
    3. Equally heterosexual and homosexual;
    4. Predominantly homosexual, but more than incidentally heterosexual;
    5. Predominantly homosexual, but only incidentally heterosexual;
    6. Exclusively homosexual.

    See Kenneth Lewes, *The Psychoanalytic Theory of Male Homosexuality* (New York: Simon and Schuster, 1988), p. 127.
14. Michael W. Ross, *The Married Homosexual Man* (London: Routledge, 1983), p. 146.

15. William H. Masters and Virginia E. Johnson, *Human Sexual Response* (Boston: Little, Brown, 1966), and subsequent publications.
16. Married gay men almost invariably talk of summoning from their arsenal of images a gloriously attractive man to help them ejaculate in love-making with their wives.
17. Richard Isay, *Being Homosexual: Gay Men and their Development* (New York: Avon Books, 1989).
18. See Isay also, p. 52, for a clinical example.
19. 'Table for One', *National Review*, 13 December 1993.
20. Paul Monette, *Becoming a Man: Half a Life Story* (New York: HarperCollins, 1992).
21. See Colonel A. A. Afrifa, *The Ghana Coup* (London: Frank Cass, 1966).
22. Warren Farrel, *The Myth of Male Power* (New York: Simon and Schuster, 1993), p. 207.
23. John Boswell, *Christianity, Social Tolerance, and Homosexuality* (University of Chicago Press, 1980), p. 42.
24. Marguerite Yourcenar, trans. Walter Kaiser, *Alexis* (New York: Farrar, Straus & Firoux, 1986), p. 49.

Chapter three

# *Marriage amid Ambiguity*

*For a desire seems to us more attractive, we repose on it with more confidence, when we know that outside ourselves there is a reality which conforms to it, even if, for us, it is not to be realised.*

● Within a Budding Grove

PETER Magowan and I had known one another slightly at Stanford: at Oxford we became close friends. Subsequently he became the owner of the San Francisco Giants and long served as the head of Safeway, which he revitalized and saved from a formidable take-over threat. Thirty years ago and more he introduced me to Bill Nitze, his complicated but endearing Groton classmate, son of Paul Nitze, Secretary of the Navy, who had first made his name as financier, had married a Standard Oil heiress and who since 1940 had thrived and been humiliated in executive-branch politics. Peter and Bill and I became a trio traveling Europe together in my little Morris, renting an apartment in Chelsea on the Thames as our London *pied-à-terre*, and plotting to take over the world, or at least California, some day. Peter, a handsome man who was then coming into his own, was by far the most confident of us, but I played senior partner for the moment. I simply hadn't a clue as to the silent and effortless networks to which the two of them were connected, and which opened doors to them everywhere they went, from Britain to my own home ground of California. For the moment my networks were better.

## 51: *Marriage amid Ambiguity*

Oxford for an American Rhodes Scholar could be heady stuff in those years. Ministers of the Crown popped into Oxford Union debates as if it were an extension of Downing Street. History lurked in bell-towers, echoed down cross-streets, and shone from High Table silver. In fantasy, from *Zuleika Dobson* onwards, Rhodies hobnobbed with peers and peeresses of the realm; in fact I found that to be true. For English nabobs Yankee blood was easy to assimilate (over the short term); they wouldn't have known how to befriend a middle-class English graduate student, but a bright and saucy middle-class American could, in a funny way, fit right in. And so I did, though it came about by a real sidewind.

The summer before Oxford, two young English ladies armed with my name from a fraternity brother in St Louis awakened me in my San Francisco flat at five a.m., in need of beds. I put them up for two weeks and had no end of return bounty for four years and half a further lifetime. One was a Mayfair Baring and the other a stepdaughter of the under-secretary of state for the colonies, Sir Nigel Fisher, who more or less adopted me for the duration. At his and Patsie's houses I met a stream of interesting politicians and foreign statesmen. They were even able to take me to Winston Churchill's funeral to stand on the cold flats of St Paul's Cathedral. And through them I met beloved Harriet Berry, the loveliest woman I have ever known.

Probably just because I really didn't even remotely appreciate who they were when she brought me to Oving, her parents' Adam country house, I wasn't intimidated or overwhelmed – and thus stood up and answered back in full measure. It turned out that Lady Pamela Berry (as she then was) happened to be Churchill's goddaughter and daughter of F. E. Smith, Churchill's best friend and Lord Chancellor, as well as friend to the powerful everywhere: *The Times*' lengthy 1981 obituary observed that she had carried on the 'last salon of Europe'. Her husband, later Lord Hartwell, owned the *Daily* and *Sunday Telegraph*, which afforded Pamela additional channels of influence. My chutzpa somehow become charisma worked: I came down for innumerable weekends at Oving, meeting more distinguished Americans (through the Berrys) than I ever saw again – from my boyhood hero Adlai Stevenson to Katherine Graham and Arthur Schlesinger, Jr.

I usually pushed things right to the edge of appropriateness, especially with British guests. One lunch, prior to our going in the evening to a great dance ('small dance' to them) at Mrs Peter Fleming's, I held forth with my opinions on *perfide Albion* at Suez with respect to the then foreign minister Selwyn Lloyd. Later in the afternoon while I was swimming, Pamela came over to the pool with a gentleman on her arm and asked me to get out and go over my argument once again about British guilt. I jumped right out of the pool and into the abyss. In six words – 'Do you agree with that, Selwyn?' – Pamela got deep revenge for every jab I had ever taken at (very) Great Britain.

Congressman John Brademas, then a boy wonder of Democratic politics, gave me numerous letters of introduction to British politicians, most interestingly Jeremy Thorpe, whose later public gay outing was no surprise given the care with which he looked me over (obviously finding me wanting in key aspects). John also told me I would read more at Oxford than ever again, so I was to enjoy it. It was the 'wall absorption theory'. In rooms that had housed such distinction in times past (my own had sheltered Asquith) surely we could pick up something, *faute de mieux*, by osmosis; I read more novels, philosophy and plays than ever before or later.

It at least occurred to me that I should experiment sexually. Surely it would be compelling to investigate something so central to one's life, especially given my powerful libido, and particularly since I had no motivation for the moment to seek out feminine company. But I didn't. How slowly life's processes work. I was determined to get married on return to the States. Real tectonic change may be inexorable, but it moves like a snail. Shorter cycle changes – like my marriage – may overtake it even for a decade or so.

Alas, Washington politics, vintage 1967, the year that I completed my Oxford doctorate, was not an option for me. The Vietnam war defined it, I was against it, and I realized that I wasn't ready to return to California to enter the elective political fray. I hadn't a cent with which to do so anyway and still assumed that only the rich went into politics. Great dreams were hurtling down the chute. The alternatives the world presented to me, in that glorious Oxford spring, much of it fitly spent drinking tea on the almost polished lawn, were a year teaching at Princeton, a research fellowship at Berkeley, and a three-year faculty research position at Tufts' Fletcher School of Law and Diplomacy, which provided for writing and travel in Asia as well as opening up prospects of tenure. No doubt I should have gone to law school to widen my options – but I had no fellowship for that and did have paying jobs waiting.

Anyway, my priority now was to get married, and given my competitive approach to life, I had promised friends I would be at the altar within a year of return. I had missed catching the garter at Jim and Sue Woolsey's wedding in 1965, but caught it at the first wedding I attended on my return to America in 1967. The omens were good. Boston seemed the best marriage mart, which is the main reason I chose Fletcher, about which I was otherwise ambivalent. Despite its vaunted connection with Harvard, its reputation was only a hint of what it has come to be today. I arrived in Boston, aged 25, notionally wrapped in the Oxford D.Phil. gown from my defense literally the day before, and set out immediately on that search. But it was what my friend Timothy Dickinson described as a 'chaos of impulses', and that search would be accompanied by the still unresolved problems of sexuality that had always hovered over me. I was just more determined this time to ignore them completely.

I had changed in four years. No sooner did I approach Customs with my British cape and at least a few European manners than some stonefaced functionary held me up for several hours while my friend Bob Legvold waited. They stripped and searched me in most ignominious ways, and when they didn't find the suspected drugs, one of the few sins that has never interested me, they said, simply, that I looked European, as if somehow that excused their barbarity. My enthusiasm about returning home flew out of the window of Logan Airport security.

Of course there were men I found attractive, but the notion of a gay option still did not exist. It is remarkable to me that I had attended Stanford and never even noticed a gay bar in Babylon-by-the-Bay; now I was seeing no more clearly in Boston. But to an achievement type, the necessity to marry was all the greater. It wasn't something you worked out and thought about in those days; it was dictated. I suppose it also has something to do with where you are on the Kinsey scale: a Kinsey 'six' will simply go find the gay bar, in Boise or Boston; a Kinsey 'one', as I would describe myself in 1968, would automatically look to marriage.

In my case, as an ambitious mobile young professional, I had affair after affair with attractive women, none very satisfactory; and by winter of 1968 I was getting nowhere, of which I was bemusedly reminded by my friends as my one-year deadline for marrying approached.

Looking back on it, I wonder how conscious I (or anyone in this position) could have been of the forces impinging. There is literally no question that new friends, approaching intimate levels of conversation, wish more to ask than 'How did it feel to go into a marriage as a, well, gay man.' My students, usually in their mid-twenties, invariably want to ask it too as the barriers between us break down, and this is natural given their marriageable age.

I wish I had as convincing an answer as Stephen Spender contrived when he was forty-seven, long into his second marriage in which he would stay for the duration, but as gay as I ever was.

> Love for a friend [man] expressed a need for self-identification. Love for a woman, the need for a relationship with someone different, indeed opposite, to myself. I realized that self-identification leads to frustration if it be not realized . . . a certain sterility if it be realized. [With women it] is a relationship of opposite poles. They complete, yet never become one another . . . I could not develop beyond a certain point unless I were able to enter a stream of nature through . . . experience of women.[1]

But he is not completely convincing – especially when he goes on to say he needed to share his creative and intellectual adventures with a man. Not to put too fine a point on it, he continued to have gay affairs. He separates the two worlds as two opposite poles:

> The two needs . . . seemed . . . to be mutually exclusive, so that whilst I was with a friend it might seem that I had renounced a whole world, of marriage, of responsibilities, and I had been received into another where everything was understood, where work, ideas, play and physical beauty corres-

> ponded in the friend's life with my own. On the other hand, when I was with a woman, it was as though I had shed my other personality . . . and that instead of reflecting and being reflected by my physical-spiritual comrade, I had entered into the wholeness of a life outside me, giving to the woman that in myself which was not contained in her, and taking from her what was not in me.[2]

This is unconvincing because the most successful gay relationships in any event are usually built on differences of race, age, class, something Richard Isay virtually prescribes for gay men as heightening erotic tension and interest; and because what Spender does write, always so cautiously, of his erotic life, is so overwhelmingly gay in its sensibility. Spender's erotic imagination from early adolescence, as he reveals between the lines, was gay, not bisexual; the sexual experiences he had before his second marriage, and the failure of his first marriage, all bear the stamp of homosexuality. But despite the experience of living with a man – one which had I done I would never have turned back from, I am confident – he lacked the courage to go forward. Jimmy Younger, Spender's working-class lover, went off to his death in Spain, like David Leavitt's likeness of him in *While England Sleeps*, because neither he nor Spender had really tried to confront their differences, and in addition had the hostility of all but the immediate world around them. But Spender reveals just a bit too much of his own narcissism in his relation to Younger to make the completeness of his life with his two wives wholly credible. And recent rumblings, by one account that the lawsuits about alleged plagiarism were largely initiated by Lady Spender, against David Leavitt, reinforce my perception.[3] What caused Spender to pursue David Leavitt, so mercilessly, fifty years later, so far beyond the actual offense, was, in addition to his wife's act of denial and possession, his terrible sense of guilt because Leavitt got it so appallingly right: not just the details of the flight to Spain, but the triviality of the soul in that phase of Spender's life which caused the lover's deathly flight in the first place – after which his creativity dulled, he set 'his sights lower [and] has achieved a decent competence' as Ian Hamilton devastatingly notes of Spender's later *vita*.

I wanted a wife (in the abstract sense) for the same reasons everyone else did. It was the only game in town, the only way to have a family and a career, the only admissible and legitimate sex-life, the only way to have someone to come home to, the only way to have someone to travel with, and dammit, it was the easiest way to have a complementary soulmate, just as Spender says, a yin for one's yang, and because one simply didn't know there was any alternative around. People had cheered me all along my life's path thus far, and I did not contemplate a choice between going off with a fellow because that held some erotic interest and that alone, and coming out of Washington's Cathedral with my new wife on my arms and to the cheers of my classmates, as was soon to happen. I wasn't going to 'give up [my] dick' (to use a phrase only Paul Monette could have contrived),[4] and didn't, in marrying. The minute I feared I had, fourteen years later, I let fate take over and I promptly fell in love with a man for the first time. A gay man who destroys his creative impulse for the duration of his life in a soulless marriage might be a better candidate for Monette's cruel phrase.

One night I dined with Bill Nitze, by now at Harvard Law School, who was late because he had been out to Wellesley College to see his younger sister. In all our trips together – to Africa, to California, and around Europe – he had only mentioned his older one. But that is the habit of older brothers. I accused him of holding out on me and demanded he bring her to dinner, which the next week he did.

Neither of us – Nina and I – knew what hit us that evening, but while it was subtle it was strong. She had (and has) the most marvelous voice, modulated and elegant, and the finest sensibilities of any young woman I had ever met. She had a comeliness and dignity that I found attractive, and a tentativeness about life that obviously hid some insecurities and made me feel safe about mine: her mother had abused her psychologically far more than my father had me, and her father was always quick to concede that he had no role whatsoever in her upbringing, busy as he had been in great affairs of state. She was a Wellesley junior, I a faculty member almost six years older than she was. She ate my spaghetti appreciatively and then was soon off on a Caribbean jaunt with girlfriends.

But her postcards revealed feeling. It soon got hotter though not yet, at least for me, exclusive.

Then a quirk – though a Washingtonian, she took a summer post at Boston's Museum of Fine Arts, while I had one at the Brookings Institution in Washington, though Boston now was my only home. Knowing that I wanted to marry her, I commuted as often as possible, and one scorching night proposed to her in her little Beacon Hill apartment. I told her that I couldn't provide generously, but surely in the longer term I could do better than my modest apartment near Fletcher. She replied that, after all, she wasn't entirely without resources to fall back on . . . for example, her unmarried sister Heidi, who had no obvious source of income, owned a farm in Maine in addition to her apartment in the Dakota. I didn't understand, in fact I hadn't a clue (I hadn't even heard of the Dakota), but was reassured.

She didn't give an answer then; but after I left she dialled all night trying to reach me in the dorm where I was staying and in the morning when she finally reached me she made me the happiest man in the world. We were at Tanglewood for a concert that weekend, to celebrate and to start planning our life together, when she dropped a bombshell – or rather, appropriately enough, took it out of her purse: a listing of securities that would pass to her name when she turned twenty-one in a very few months from then. It would provide an income, she said most unpossessively, of what I silently figured would amount to seven times my salary at Fletcher. Her mother had told her that we needed to 'choose' an income level or allowance, a concept which was as wholly new to me as to all but a tiny few of the other five billion people on earth, who find it difficult to live on everything they earn.

I couldn't handle it. My father was quite possibly dying of peritonitis in California and here I was in the position to marry not just a wonderful woman but the kind of fortune that changes lives – how much I could not know. I couldn't even afford the ticket to the coast, and had to ask Peter Magowan for a loan, the blank checks for which I was happily able to return to him the next week when Father suddenly recovered.

I rushed to the university health center to talk to a counselor, who asked what on earth was the problem; I seemed as much in love as anybody he had ever talked about it with, and shouldn't penalize *her* by breaking up just because she was rich. Sartre says we pick our advice when we pick our adviser, and no doubt that was what I wanted to hear. In retrospect I am bemused by my inability to comprehend that a *woman* could have a trust fund; I knew that Bill Nitze had inherited income, though what one might usefully spend as a graduate student seldom seemed to exceed what the Rhodes Trust generously provided its charges. No doubt I self-servingly underestimated his resources by at least one order of magnitude. My male-chauvinist father, so representative of his generation, had up to then provided me with an unconscious point of view that women were dependencies of men, though my mother was a professional musician for over fifty years, and always able to supplement family income at least somewhat while I grew up. My daughters in time were to watch, with inexhaustible vigilance, for evidence of a similar perception in me. If I had a materialistic impulse in all this, I'm sure it was that I hoped any wife of mine could at least, in the words of America's first – and gay – Treasury Secretary, 'administer to her own extravagances'.[5]

Nina was looking for love, but she too was looking for security. Old money was also ceasing to be enough, as Nina would have seen through her Wellesley classmates' eyes, for example Eleanor Dean Acheson, granddaughter of Nina's father's great patron, whose appointment as Assistant Attorney General for Policy Development was brought about by a third classmate, Hillary Rodham (whose autobiography recalls Paul Nitze's presence at hers and Nina's 1969 graduation – the kind of galling recognition of the famous that their children invariably find infuriating). And if Nina were not assertive enough for a career of her own, at least she could, like her mother, partake of her husband's. But Nina, who had everything one might wish for from the outside, proved to have been too badly hurt readily to develop self-sufficiency and self-esteem.

After much fuss we arranged to be married in the Cathedral of St Peter and St Paul, known to hoi polloi (it was delicately put to me) as the National Cathedral. The awesome retired Bishop of Washington, Angus Dun (who had officiated alone in the East Room funeral of Franklin Roosevelt), was delegated to marry us. When we saw him, he said he had three questions: Did we love each other, did the church mean something to us, and did we mind if he used a verger during the service, owing to his wooden leg and other infirmities of age? Nina responded more immediately, and certainly far better, than I.

The Christmas wedding was several months beyond my one-year deadline for marriage, but our engagement came less than a year after my return to America. Basically, life was on schedule. I was pleasantly overwhelmed by the consequences of this match. Anyone from my professional background would have been fascinated by the ways of the rich and famous, though at times I thought them frightfully complicated. For example I arrived at the Nitze house in Northeast Harbor, Maine, for the first time, with my friend Tom Cotton, famished from a long drive, to find that we were too late for dinner, and couldn't have dined with the family anyway because seating was planned several days in advance; there was of course nothing available in the village since everybody had cooks; but we most absolutely could not go into the kitchen and fend for ourselves: 'Uncle Bob' Thayer, Nina's friendly but fussy and obsessive uncle with several gay children, was in charge of the kitchen that summer, had provided his staff, and they had positively forbad any access. We played stupid, sneaked in later and gorged on left-overs. Of course later I would see such behavior on Uncle Bob's part as a sure sign of homosexuality in him too – as it turned out to be.

One could play it as one wished, of course. The Nitzes were rather rich indeed, but they chose to live in such a way that those who didn't perceive wouldn't get the point. Not everyone, after all, was invited out to the understated farm fronting two miles of the Potomac's Maryland shore just below Washington – and those who were, and were overwhelmed, would be assured by Phyllis Nitze that things were more equal than appeared, since she didn't have air conditioning or a dishwasher in her large and historic eighteenth-century country house (one of a dozen on the property). Another ruse of hers was to drive around in reasonably beat-up cars, always avoiding if possible governmental limousines or any other pompous vehicles. Paul loved the trappings, so this could be a sore point. I routinely had friends over to the finely-appointed but undistinguished Cleveland Park house, who seemed to think they were at a cousin's – as if everyone had uniformed servants serving dinner and Impressionist paintings on the wall. *I* was most impressed by the expense of *looking* poor – for example living in that apparently average-sized house, but hiring a moving company several times a year to move the furniture out to make room for a 'small dance' costing twenty to thirty thousand dollars.

Of course it would have been cheaper to live in a larger house. Those who knew what to look for would say, to my embarrassment (because the understatement was so blatantly obvious), 'My, now you've done well, haven't you!' Even my brother-in-law Bill Nitze, about ten years after his sister and I were married, said, 'You've benefitted, haven't you . . .' and then hastened to add that Nina had surely, in her greater ambition and scope of life since marrying me, benefitted as much. In all I am struck by how many people measured our marriage in material terms, as if those were relevant in bed or at the breakfast table. They were looking at the future.

And yet, it would be hypocritical to deny the point. It *is* fascinating to live among the swells, at least for a time. Most incredible to me was the network they have: wherever you go there is someone in the local Stud Book (the ever-present Social Register) with whom one has a connection, or with whom a cousin has a connection, who puts on parties for you, gets you started with your own network, and gives you temporary membership at the local clubs. In settling up accounts for Nina and me in Bangkok and Manila, Morgan's bank, embarrassingly, gave us letters to the presidents of the two biggest banks therein, for really quite modest accounts.

And there at the banks was the biggest dividing line between us and them: *they* thought of money as scrip, something banks or family holding companies gave to you for the payment of bills, rather than something related to work undertaken and completed. I was always amused to visit Paris, where we stayed at the Ritz, not just for itself but because it was across the Place Vendôme from Morgan's, where Nina thrilled to walk in, so well turned out, and present them with a check on their Madison Avenue branch for several thousand dollars and ask for it in perfect French in francs and dollars equally; and without batting an eyelash the teller would hand her the money without even the thought of identification or clearing it with a manager. French is the language of royalty; and Nina delighted in references – in marriage announcements – to Standard Oil heirs as America's royalty.

I also soon learned that it is a myth that the rich don't talk about money: they put down the non-rich as vulgar for trying to talk with them about it – on reflection, an immensely clever self-protective tactic, since everybody, it seemed, wants money at one point or the other from them. And if you can talk about it with them, how fast the needy would make their own case! Among themselves, the rich seemed to talk about little else. I loved hearing the stories of how this particular family became rich a few generations earlier: how great-grandfather Pratt, who pretty much controlled the distribution of oil in New York, caved in – or sold out – to the general organizational scheme of one John D. Rockefeller, 'from which so many blessings have flowed', a venerable Aunt would toast with her Baccarat champagne flute.

I realized why the American upper class is successful: if the middle class knew how much privilege those above them had, there would have long since been revolution. Someone like myself could appreciate it all the more for not having been used to it – while still not having unlearned the fine art of shining one's own shoes. One further difference was in the amount of allowed emotion: the rich are more controlled. When my father died in 1980, my mother came to live with Nina and me, and not one of the large family – who shared Christmas with us – ever expressed condolence to my newly widowed mother, or to myself. There was also a two-tiered standard of living within one house, something I determined never to impose were the richer shoe ever on the other foot – and indeed I fear the generosity born of this memory did more than anything to doom my first gay relationships with men less well off than myself. I remember bemusedly discovering that I could eliminate entirely our 'breakfasts' at the Ritz in Paris, to which thanks to my running I had to add more substantial fare on the streets in any case, and thus save myself $25 per day, while Nina relished her croissants in the main dining room. Though my income kept increasing through professional recognition, it never grew as fast as Nina's, and our double standard of living widened throughout our fifteen years together.

One also had to learn an entirely new set of reference points. Poverty, it seems, was being so down and out (as one family member was for a few years) that one bought paperbacks when hardbacks were available; *that* spoke to an academic and his trade. *We* wouldn't believe anyone *ever* bought a hardback once the paper edition was available. Class, on the other hand – 'what is nobility but ancient riches?' as one of Elizabeth I's parvenu ministers enquired bitterly – was shown by the comment I heard one night after a dinner party which Nina and I put on at the Nitze house. The wife of one of the most influential men in Washington nagged her husband on the way out that the Nitzes had a twenty-four set of their plates, and she only eighteen. A Nitze woman said, in an unforgettable tone, 'She thinks she can go down to Bloomingdales and buy these.' They don't make anti-semitism must subtler than that. They were eighteenth-century Compagnie des Indes ware of which Phyllis Nitze had one of the largest and most valuable sets in America. Perhaps class to some extent is having a little man who can get them.

In any case, for whatever reasons, I had chosen the straight life and for fourteen years relentlessly toed the line. I was the sexual demandeur in my marriage and I was faithful.

The first five years were exhilarating because it was so new to both of us. I, after all, had never had a lover living with me and Nina was still at Wellesley when we married and rented a house in Wellesley Hills. I was barely aware of Woodstock nor later of Stonewall, but my civil rights efforts continued on behalf of blacks, I demonstrated against the war in Vietnam, and now morsel by morsel, began to realize how ignorant I had been on the question of women's rights. I remember significant dates in my intellectual evolution. Robert and Gloria Legvold and Nina and I were dining in the North End, and Bob socked me with the argument in the current *Atlantic* about 'the second sex' and the necessity of equality between the sexes. I took at least some of the gauze from my eyes that night but much was yet to come. Ironically, there is a long history of suffragettes in my family, including the source of one of my names, great-great aunt Frances Emma Willard, one of the most famous American women of the nineteenth century.

I may have been a Rhodes Scholar but what counted, aside from money, chez Nitze, was tennis, bridge, and of course skiing –

Paul Nitze, after all, having founded the Aspen Skiing Corporation as a very fine arrow in his quiver. It took me a long time, as a middle-class achiever, to realize how unfashionable achievement is among the swells; after all, if you've made it (meaning your great grandfather provided adequately for you) then it would be vulgar to attempt to improve on your situation. And it follows that people who did so were vulgar. I have to praise Phyllis Nitze for swallowing her pride and quite valiantly accepting me in 1968 in the circumstances. But in one of our conversations I mentioned, sort of *entre parenthese*, that while at Oxford, I had been a Rhodes Scholar, to which she replied equally *sotto voce*, 'Ah yes, you would have been, wouldn't you.' I almost didn't get her exquisite point. One by one I sought to learn these games of the rich. I was helped however by the fact that her daughter-in-law at that point was 'disgracing' her and her family by consorting with 'gentlemen of color' and heading for divorce with favorite son Peter Nitze, now a succesful venture capitalist in New York, who since the time of his divorce from Sheila McNeil has lived in a Dakota apartment which the family measured to prove was substantially larger than our 12,000-square-foot mansion in Chestnut Hill.

What I wanted most of all was children, more than wealth, professional success, or anything else – a priority that was to be tested when I had choices to make among precisely those values. Nina finally relented after four years of resistance, saying that she feared that she had to choose between getting pregnant or getting a divorce. And once she had our first child, she was the most protective and nurturing mother a baby ever had, as this first third of our marriage rounded out. Given how much I had wanted children, we now had something worthy on which to work together, as indeed we did. I could not get home fast enough in little Phyllis's first year, to see her latest progress and to play endlessly with her, as she did with me. And as the quickest on his feet in the household, I was often the one up in the middle of the night to change diapers, even when we had a baby nurse on duty with or without Florrie, for twenty years the children's beloved Irish nanny.

The second five years were the easiest. My career was looking up, more children came. We set off for Washington in 1975: I had been elected a White House Fellow and would serve as an Assistant to the Secretary of Defense. Son Nicholas was born just before we set off; he had a rough first few months, then started growing and has never stopped.

Even with (or perhaps especially with) a full-time nanny on hand, I spent my happiest hours with children in tow, at our Hadley Hill Farm in New Hampshire, at the Nitze–Thompson compound in Northeast Harbor, Maine, Christmas times skiing at Aspen, some summertimes at a family chateau in France, a music festival in Austria, or at the Nitze plantation. Likewise, there were the traded weekends with siblings, Thanksgivings at brother Peter's Dakota apartment, for example, watching the Macy's parade and meeting the John Lennons of this world. In early 1978 I wrote from Hadley Hill:

> I am on something of a high. [The Peter Nitzes and five of their children] were all here . . . and I am closing up. None of my 'problems' is solved but my problem is solved. I am happy. I think things are sorting themselves out . . . (Diary, 5 March 1978).

But it wasn't all that happy. My college roommate Tom Cotton put it to me, after a weekend at the farm, that such a 'life is too comfortable to challenge one's myths', and I added in my diary that 'I am so happy at the skin, so unsettled at the heart . . . Oh hell, I just can't keep on. I am nowhere. Yet maybe getting somewhere outside. Which is why some people get so far and then blow their brains out. The two levels are utterly discontinuous' (26 October 1977). Surely I was alluding to the Edward Arlington Robinson poem, 'Richard Cory', about the model citizen, everywhere admired and successful, 'And Richard Cory, one calm summer night, / Went home and put a bullet through his head.'

The only hint of the storms ahead came one evening in 1977, after our first dinner party at the grand mansion in Chestnut Hill, just virtually given to us: the old couple had 'agreements' with neighbors against selling to people with 'unpronounceable names' and to ensure that we would buy it sold it in effect to me for half its appraised value of $369,000; it subsequently soared in value into the low millions – of course in Nina's name, though I paid the mortgage on it for five years. Literally the most revealing and also the funniest (in no sense the wittiest) comment I ever heard on a 'class' issue was innocently made by the owner of the house while briefing Nina on the neighborhood. 'Was there a bus stop nearby?' 'Of course!' and, knowing precisely her agenda, added that it was most conveniently 'just across from the Catholic Church'. I had to walk away to hide my laughter.

In any event, a foreign service officer who looked as if he was emerging from a Botticelli painting but in fact was returning from a war zone, was searching for a contemplative PhD project through which to decompress emotionally and grow intellectually. He had no reason to know how attractive I found him during his Masters at Fletcher earlier in the decade and how much I already knew about him. My guile and wiles worked: he decided to go for the doctorate if I agreed to supervise it – little did he realize that that was my entire object. I invited him home to a dinner for colleagues to toast our forthcoming collaboration. At the end of the evening, Nina very shrewdly observed 'Yes, he's very nice indeed . . . You always like thin, handsome, finely etched, and slightly effeminate young men, don't you?' I can now add that my repertoire may have widened, but this young man fit that early bill, wrote an outstanding thesis, became a good, if always distant, friend, and still looks like a Renaissance mannerist portrait.

The last third of our married life was a slow descent into hell for four of the last years together. We had woven our love and marriage out of the shaky foundations of our shared but very different insecurities, and one by one these began to unthread as we individually got stronger. I was on the road constantly, lecturing all over the world on what we of the Committee on the Present Danger saw as the deteriorating strategic balance as the Soviets, like a runner getting a last spurt out of himself, built up their arsenal in the 1970s. And I was frequently on television, including occasionally shows like *Nightline* and *McNeil–Lehrer*. At a distinguished arms-control seminar in Los Angeles in July 1979 I correctly predicted that the Russians would be in Kabul by Christmas, and a political scientist from UCLA rose up to say I should be declared insane. The frenetic quality of my life in this period had much of the make-it or break-it pace that I attributed to the Russians. In ways the professor did not know – but could he sense? – I *was* a bit insane at this point.

As my reputation spread, especially on these strategic contexts, there spread with it, the notion that only Paul Nitze could have opened such doors for me. That a Rhodes Scholar and Fletcher professor might have achieved some of this on his own seemed hardly credible; his was a candle to Paul's finally ascendant sun. Give credit where it is due: we were associated in a great campaign, and he was the very distinguished quarterback from whom a whole team got its cues. He was, however, always the Grey Eminence unsettling senators with a few cool words, co-ordinating plays. He was not particularly forthcoming to me, certainly no warmer than ever. Edward Luttwak, the genius of our generation, made the predictably astute observation – which nonetheless almost floored me – that I was losing greatly from my association with Paul, whom I had considered only from a posture of abject admiration. Ed knew that my accomplishments went back way before I had met Paul. What I didn't know, he told me, is that people who were too scared of Paul to attack him directly would attack me as a means of getting at him; I was the designated substitute. Every king needs a beheadable minister.

In two areas I paid higher costs. In 1979 with Paul's concurrence (indeed his prodding) I went to work for the campaign of John Connally, subsequently bankrupt and now dead, but he seemed in that time of outsiders potentially the most formidable aspirant for the presidency – a brilliant Democratic governor of Texas become yet more substantial as Secretary of the Treasury, Nixon's recaster of the world economy in at least as remarkable a way as the President had employed Kissinger to rework international politics. He was more or less the official candidate of the Committee on the Present Danger. Connally made a speech in 1979 for a just settlement of the Middle Eastern conflict, and for higher strategic vigilance in the Indian Ocean – the latter a subject on which I was working that year on sabbatical at Harvard and at Los Angeles think-tanks. The former, not an area of my expertise, was something that the American friends of Israel deemed Governor Connally deeply deficient in.[6] I learned from my Jewish friends that an organized whispering campaign, to the effect that I was anti-semitic, was percolating in the foreign policy world. It was preposterous, but it was again a negative reflection of Nitze's history of favoring Nazi Germany prior to joining the US government, and a long history of anti-semitism as well.[7] Paul had been unable to get a security clearance at the White House in 1940 because of imprudent comments he had made about the Third Reich, and in the ensuing thirty-nine years he was quick to jump on any Jewish American, whether State Department counselors or friends of his children. Even identifying people as 'Jewish' was completely new to me. In creating our fraternity at Stanford, it turned out – or was pointed out – that among our number two were Jewish. This was uninteresting news to us, irrelevant to us, but not to the Berkeley chapter who pointed it out. Ironically, the Committee on the Present Danger, his most influential effort ever, which was a joining of the old conservative Wasps and neo-conservative Jewish people like Gene Rostow and Max Kampelman, was an open attempt to harness American Jews, and Israel, to American purposes – and vice versa. 'The Jews, they can fight,' Paul once said, in looking at the Soviet-American strategic balance in the Middle East. Of course it was also their recognition of the more immediate present danger – of the Republican right's rise, which they could only ride by dominating the old issue of Soviet strength, but that is the story for another book.

The other issue was not unconnected – and further relates to the growing role Paul was to play in my own career. Not surprisingly in a city of competitions, he had writhed from the start at Henry Kissinger's rise and eminence. Had not Paul dreamed from the first boyhood consciousness of capacities that he would be Secretary of State (and with every change of administration was there not a family wake when he was again passed over, or not even considered)? Had he not set out to be Washington's intellectual in foreign affairs all these years? Surely he had a right to these dreams and fantasies, considering the lesser qualities of so many of the successful aspirants. Kissinger arrived on the scene in 1957, seventeen years after Paul and about the same number of years younger, by way of a highly influential book, *Nuclear Weapons and Foreign Policy*, which Paul tried to devastate in a review in the *Reporter*.[8] Paul had no book then nor later, until some memoirs appeared over three decades later.

Above all he longed for a role in foreign affairs. 'I'd pay a million dollars to have a job in the executive branch', he often said when he was on the outside. He played an important role for the Defense Department in the talks leading to the 1974 SALT treaty, always bucking for better terms for America, and was getting to see life as a series of end-runs around Henry. The latter eventually retaliated against Paul by referring to the 'third level bureaucrats' frustrating him, which in the anthropology of office was pretty much Paul's pecking place when that missile was launched. That finally pushed him over the brink to resign and wage open war. In fact Paul's rank was far lower than the eminence he was beginning finally to attain in the respect of the foreign policy elite, but Henry had found Paul's weak spot. If as Talleyrand said, it was the lamentable weakness of Bonaparte that he had such appalling taste, Paul's equally lamentable weakness was a certain literalness about place over power – official seating, limousines, publicity. George Marshall laid it down that you can get anything done in Washington if you don't seek the credit for it. Had Paul had it in him to embrace inevitability there would have been no question of his achieving the mantle he sought, well over Kissinger's head.

Paul worked through surrogates, of whom Admiral Elmo 'Bud' Zumwalt was the most distinguished, but I was as avid. We went after Kissinger with whatever we could find.[9] Thus in December 1975 Kissinger's long-time associate Helmut Sonnenfeldt briefed American diplomats in Europe in London. Basically, the briefing called for American policy to help the Soviets put down 'organic roots' in Eastern Europe, which we saw as a sellout – certainly not a move in character with Hal Sonnenfeldt's distinguished career. My recollection is that I read it with disbelief, and took it to my boss, Secretary of Defense Don Rumsfeld, who manifestly saw its gravity. I asked him what I was to do with it. He instructed me to circulate it among those with a 'need to know'. I said 'what, a couple hundred copies?' He said, 'yeah, more or less'. Evans and Novak had it the next morning. I didn't get it to them, but Hal has a point that I was the *objective* leaker, in circulating it to people who could be counted on to leak. At one point in 1979 we found out through CIA intercepts, supplied by a true believer at the agency, that in 1977 Henry was allegedly advising the Soviet ambassador, at his Sixteenth Street embassy, on tactics with which to play the Carter administration. It could have been treachery, and in ways it looked like treachery, but was more likely simply the vanity of a man wanting a role and now out in the cold. But it embellished the notion, which Paul was propagating through us, that Henry might well be an enemy agent – a *Communist* enemy agent. Henry was damaged by the campaign against him, but at my smaller level so was I. Carrying other people's water, I learned once and for all, is expensive.

What we were dealing with was Nitze's projection, regarding Henry Kissinger's pessimism for the West's survival, from his own youthful miscalculation of the odds during Hitler's rise in Germany. Paul knew of what he spoke when he suggested treachery. His uncle, Carl Hilken, was convicted of spying for Imperial Germany during World War I.

It had been costly enough to change parties. It took me a decade, then I did it with extreme reluctance, well after Governor Reagan was elected President. I believe one can make only one switch in his lifetime without wearing the mark of opportunism, Churchill's experience to the contrary notwithstanding. Paul Nitze, after all, paid a high price throughout his career for several party flip-flops. It took me ten years to make the leap, so heavy a decision it proved, but eventually I did so to be consistent with what we were championing as the central issue of our time – defining the limits of totalitarianism. As a neo-conservative I could say, and did say, that I remained a civil libertarian and had adopted none of the conservative baggage as such on domestic issues, especially civil-libertarian. But clearly I had evolved a long way from the radical Stanford undergraduate I once was, or at least seemed to be.

There was an undertow of guilt as this wave of change crashed at the surface. My father, once a fighter and boxer, a rebel who always championed his causes ahead of their time, thus reaping none of the reward he had sowed, never tamed his own nature and was plainly dying. We had been in conflict throughout my adult life: though we were always in touch and maintained civilities, his resentment of my evolution, allies, and affiliations was beyond negotiation even were I to achieve the autonomy for which he himself had instilled in me a desire. Now, as my career took off, his life ebbed, ravaged by the alcohol he started abusing late, with a weakened, nay broken, heart. We were inching toward a loving reconciliation but it was too late; just after Ronald Reagan was elected President I was giving a lecture at a Washington conference, and a soon-to-be-appointed ambassador, Gaston Sigur, got me from the lectern to tell me of my father's heart attack. Off I went to California, though not before Phyllis Nitze could make her one comment that I must surely be relieved. Dad's death certificate, saying 'M.I., with complications from alcoholism', was a deadly warning. As I flew back across the land, a pit in my stomach, I finally understood why Freud had said that the death of one's father is the most important event in a man's life. At least I had the remnant in my heart of one otherwise painful confrontation with him, when to torment him several years earlier I told him I was increasingly sure I was gay. Not only did he not reject me, he tried to end the fight to let me know it was okay.

Before my appointment to the new administration, my teaching responsibilities kept me at home four or five nights a week, but I squeezed in considerable travel in those other days, as my children are wont to remind me. For one thing, it was a way of getting away from Nina, who no longer wanted to play. Our bedroom games and love names were disappearing, our arguments increasing, which was a function of the changes which were ever more compelling me to ask if I knew who I was. Wittgenstein once said that if a dog could talk he'd not understand himself, and it could well have been said of me. In my thirty-ninth year, I read *Seasons of a Man's Life*, which stated flatly that *all* men went through a mid-life crisis around that point, one of usually cosmic significance, however suppressed.[10] But I was reading this, right there in bed with Nina, my wife, in our Chestnut Hill home, where I played Star Wars with my son every morning at six before running seven miles with my poodle Marnier and before making breakfast for the children; surely I was on top of the world, and all was well with it within me. Could anyone have fitted together a more perfect life – with three intelligent and adorable growing children, a farm in the country, compound at the sea-shore, tenure at a major graduate school, glittering friends everywhere, and trips every few months to Europe. As Wittgenstein said . . .

## *Notes*

1. Stephen Spender, *World Within World* (London: Hamish Hamilton, 1953), p. 159.
2. *Ibid.* p. 160.
3. See Ian Hamilton, 'Spender's Lives', *New Yorker*, 28 February 1994. For a spirited debate between Spender and Leavitt, see David Leavitt, 'Did I plagiarize his life?' *New York Times Sunday Magazine*, 3 April 1994, and Stephen Spender, 'My life is mine; it is not David Leavitt's,' *New York Times Book Review*, 4 September 1994.
4. *Becoming a Man*, p. 89.
5. Alexander Hamilton to John Laurens, cited in Jonathan N, Katz, *Gay American History* (New York: Thomas Y. Crowell 1976), p. 454. This correspondence leaves little to the imagination as to Hamilton's sexual preferences.
6. Though publicly, friends of Israel on this issue couldn't fault me. See William Safire, who if quick to blame was always also quick to give credit – 'John Connally and Israel', 15 October 1979: 'The speech contained some sound ideas: Scott Thompson, a Tufts College professor, stressed our increased presence in the Indian Ocean . . .'.
7. See Zachary Citron, 'The Conversion of Paul: Paul Nitze's pro-Nazi leanings', *New Republic*, vol. 200, no. 5, 30 January 1989, p. 33.
8. Kissinger threatened to sue, and there was open bad blood flowing between them thenceforth. Nitze had accused Kissinger of admiring every totalitarian leader of history – but it was a double-edged blade. See Paul H. Nitze, 'Limited wars or massive retaliation?' *Reporter*, 17 (5 September 1957), pp. 40–2.
9. See 'U.S. National Security Policy vis-a-vis Eastern Europe', April 12, 1976, 94–2. Y4. In 8/16 Se2, MC-76-3776 LC 76-601916.
10. Daniel J. Levinson, *et al.*, *Seasons of a Man's Life* (New York: Knopf, 1978). A view somewhat contradicted, however, by Winifred Gallagher, 'Myths of middle age', *Atlantic Monthly*, May 1993.

Chapter four

# *Divorce with a Smear*

***Art is not alone in imparting charm and mystery to the most insignificant things; pain is endowed with the same power to bring them into intimate revelation with ourselves.***

● The Fugitive

MEANTIME in a quite different way, Nina's independence or at least separateness was increasing. The biggest foundation stone of our marriage to crack on the road to our catastrophe was her psychological dependence on me. She was well-off, but not so rich that to be identified in those days as the wife of an up-and-coming academic wasn't helpful, especially since she still had no particular professional aims, apart from being a part-time student in fine arts at Tufts, the kind of study wealthy women who have not set out to be State Street lawyers or physicians at Peter Bent Brigham characteristically pursue in the Boston area.[1] With a few million dollars in trust funds you could pay the mortgage and at well-bred intervals charter a yacht in the Caribbean; with ten million dollars you could begin to buy or rent seats on the board of the guilt-edged institutions like the Museum of Fine Art or trusteeships of the right schools and colleges; that was a real life – and real money, as the saying goes. 'Being rich begins at ten million,' one heard in that decade. And so when her family's Aspen Skiing Corporation went on the block in 1977, with her 47,000 publicly listed shares therein multiplying their worth by an order of magnitude over one year, she was suddenly not just well off. As she said to her financier brother in the middle of the negotiations, 'Peter, this is my one and only opportunity to be really and truly rich. Don't blow it!'

He didn't. Nina's spending potential went from two (extensive) dimensions to three as she reached the level of 'real money', and our marriage perceptibly suffered in proportion.

I contributed just as much to the slippage, rather more consciously, and every further skid down the slippery slope jostled my view of myself as a straight and proper pillar of society. It had never been easy to be Nitze in-law. Of course they were generous; everyone got the maximum $6,000 tax free in January,[2] not to mention trips to Aspen and lavish dinners. But they were what Paul Nitze called a 'we-group' in which, understandably, only blood counted. Others were made to feel like David Copperfield looking over the great wall. I had my own life and so it mattered little enough to me – that was part of the trouble: I was depriving the righteous, especially Phyllis Nitze, of their beatific contemplation at the torment of the excluded. My position was yet further strengthened now that, following through on my appointment at the Pentagon, I began to make a modest name for myself on that national stage on which I had always wanted to figure. By 1979 I was debating SALT all over the country and Bill Safire, whose *New York Times* column was at that time probably the most influential around, included me as a matter of course on his list of the young Hotspurs who would staff a new administration.[3] In June 1979 Nina gave birth to our third baby at Boston's Lying-in Hospital. We had both dearly wanted her; and so I suppose it was particularly symptomatic that as soon as little Heidi was safely delivered I hopped on a plane to debate old friend – and Carter (as later Clinton) senior official – Walt Slocombe at the Heritage Foundation on the great strategic issues pending. I was back at the hospital before Nina regained consciousness (it had been a Caesarian) but she was not amused and never forgave me.

There was the reality of the arrival of a new time of life. Carl Jung writes profoundly about the change of men and women at midlife, men releasing their tender or feminine side just as women's assertive or masculine side comes forward. That Margaret Thatcher should enter office in 1979 to do business with Jimmy Carter nicely personifies this change, increasingly manifest throughout the culture. With us my latent homosexuality – or rather the metamorphosis from latency to full potentiality – reinforced this displacement, and the women's movement advance to stage-front reinforced Nina's sense that she should raise hell and drive me to the ends of the earth. Nina's dependence upon me meant that when it came to divorce I got the worst of all possible worlds in a vindictiveness which exhibited the wounded, strengthless flailing of one who, faced by great change, could only change dependencies. I was to learn just how impersonally searing, possessing a motive revenge was.

> We might compare masculinity and femininity with their psychic components to a particular store of substances of which, in the first half of life, unequal use is made. A man consumes his large supply of masculine substance, which he must now put to use. It is the other way around with a woman . . . Very often the reversal is accompanied by all sorts of catastrophes in marriage; for it is not hard to imagine what may happen when the husband discovers his tender feelings, and the wife her sharpness of mind.[4]

The timing of these events could not have been worse – or better. 'Women's power' was showing up in divorce statistics, with 75 per cent of breakups initiated by women – but only 10 per cent of the men getting child custody even in the small number of contested cases. Women, who not unjustifiably saw their sex as having the short end of the stick for too long, were turning it around on all the men around me: like one gentle friend who, upon putting his wife through law school, found her using her new expertise to savage him and leave the city, child in hand. Nina was going into her late thirties, her behavior a little ahead of Jung's model. But it is a double privilege of the rich to buy off so much that others fear if they do not wish it to happen, or to face it earlier if they do.

By the beginning of 1982 there was slippage everywhere precisely because so much truth was breaking out. It showed up in one form for instance when PBS aired the BBC's rendering of one of my favorite books, *Brideshead Revisited*, which gave form to an extraordinary gay awakening across America, being run in bars and at dinner parties. A smart set ready to emerge was as it were legitimized by Charles Ryder and Sebastian Flyte. And in the middle of this, the most devastating thing possible: I met a young engineer a few years out of MIT, proud to be gay, handsome, sexy, and full of self-esteem.

There was now only the slightest gap between the cup of my life and the lip of political fulfillment I had spent my life seeking. I was quickly to discern that it is always at that point that the impulse to slip – indeed to throw it away – is greatest; perhaps if only because for some, life's purpose lies essentially only in the awakening quest – and to show that you can do without what you have worked so hard for.

I was certainly conscious of pressures and realities: my world, from the moment I met Mark Altbush, literally fell apart, cracking open in and by my very own hands. It was firstly in my mind; there was a relationship between the substance I had accumulated, the persona I had created on the one hand, and the extent to which I was now willing to throw away what I had always asserted was my heart's desire but which I had denied myself in the authentic world of the spirit. But as that voice of self-empowerment Rob Eichberg says in training sessions, being *in love* is to be powerless; loving – which state I had hardly reached – is powerful. I wanted Mark so badly, I was so wholly powerless, that I quickly gave it away – I keep secrets badly anyway – and Nina was understandably devastated, despite my commitment to amputate the relationship and cauterize the feelings as soon as possible, and to see a therapist about the whole maelstrom which I had released within myself. Yet I continued to function, with no nervous breakdown, no stroke, just a sense that nothing could last, that this only made sense as containment of the flood until it could meet its still unknown sea.

All this, internally so vast, was the minutest fleck on the tide of history that whirled upon my little bubble, as the United States and the Soviet Union seemed to be moving toward their final, historic confrontation. Everything related to everything. When I gave lectures and speeches counterpunching the glacierlike Soviet encroachment I was not just challenging the *bienpensant* orthodoxies of the decent sleepy world; I was tearing at the unconscious bonds of the whole universe of convention from which I was now desperate to escape.

Mark and I saw each other weekly for two months, usually at his small apartment in Cambridge, always listening to Monteverdi or New Age music, and – astonishingly for me, given my powerful libido – never once had sex. I was too scared anyway, but Mark – who had seen the house Nina and I lived in and had his own vision of what it represented in litigation, orchestrated publicity, phone calls to the 'right person', the whole deadly engine of powerful wealth pursuing him – had his own fears. And he had plenty of other suitors. Nina believed me, and in a ministerial counseling session said so later, about his and my relationship, but we both knew ours was on the precipice. At one tearful discussion I offered Nina a divorce on any terms she proposed, so pained was I by the feelings I could no longer either deny or control. Mark's death from AIDS in 1994 was both a curious proof of what I had stated about his and my relationship and – as I had long since forgotten him erotically – a demonstration of how much my feelings for him then were projections of my needs upon him.

Meantime I was traveling as never before, not only to Washington every week, but to Europe thrice in two months, organizing a session between senior officials from the new Mitterand and Reagan governments, White House and Elysée Palace, Quai d'Orsay and State, at the Villa Serbelloni on Lake Como – halfway between Paris and Washington, so to speak, as the French see these things. I wanted now to see Mark as a friend, since he couldn't be my lover, so on returning from Italy I had him visit the house openly, and Nina came home one Saturday afternoon to find us sitting on the library floor watching *Brideshead* just at the moment alas when Sebastian Flyte bared his splendid ass to Charles Ryder and the world atop Castle Howard. The race to the abyss was on.

The world was closing in. On a weekend trip to Paris in early 1982 my Tufts colleague Tony Smith and I met at the Ritz one evening and, admiring the dewy-faced hotel clerks and busboys for which the hotel is famous, discussed my dilemma. He suggested that at the rate events were moving, momentum alone would resolve matters. Nina would start the divorce, bear the onus, and I'd be off the hook. I told him he was daft; tempting as it was I wasn't even considering divorce. Anyway, I was too tightly bound up with the

Nitze family – and with Paul Nitze in particular, as permanent statesman, and Paul Nitze, father-in-law – for it to be possible.

Seeing that I had no notion of the fire and force of the volcano on whose edge I stood, Tony equally wondered if I had taken leave of my senses. 'All that is left is to pretend. But to pretend to the end of one's life is the highest torment', Pyotr Tchaiskovsky wrote after his marriage in 1877, as I too was soon to learn. And I finally got up my courage to read the only work of Marguerite Yourcenar with which I was unfamiliar – *Alexis*, a novel written in the form of a letter by a young man to the wife he has left, having discovered his homosexuality. 'With the utmost humility', it ends, 'I ask you now to forgive me, not for leaving you, but for having stayed so long.'[5] Everyone but me now saw the writing on the wall, but at least by 1982 I saw it faintly.

In late March 1982 I took Mark to Washington when I had several tickets and a suite at the Madison. One bittersweet Thursday afternoon, at precisely the moment President Reagan would be meeting with his personnel staff to sign off on administration appointments at my level, Mark and I walked through the gardens of Dumbarton Oaks, my favorite public spot in Washington, after a long talk at lunch. I had been walking on air, because a friend at the White House had tipped me off that all was well and that Reagan would be approving me for a sub-cabinet post. My lecture had gone well that morning. I was in a $500 per day suite: what else could one want?

Once again the answer was Mark. I now had committed myself; not to what 'he stood for' but to Mark himself and all he invoked in me. I thought I was two people, I was so astonished to hear my words, promising that I would leave Nina forthwith and take up housekeeping with him immediately, But Mark in the process of flying down had implicitly reconfirmed that it wasn't on. And now he was saying it without ambiguity. It wasn't on – words hard to fathom, the kind of slangy phrase with which Henry James now and again illuminates an abyss. The conceit of the straight man coming out, which confirms the lowliness with which homosexuality is looked at, is that of course the object of his admiration, presumably a fully gay man, will drop everything and accept his suit. Over and over I have seen it. No matter how many times I reiterated the advantages that could accrue to Mark if he joined me, he still said no. At what I later figured out was within minutes of the time the President signed my marching orders, Mark condemned me, I thought, to eternal misery. I ran for the bamboo thicket at the southwest corner of the great gardens and pounded my fist for a half hour into the happily yielding earth and then, being an adult, got myself together to face the real world.

Amid all this came my fortieth birthday, and Nina laid on a magnificent show – putting up a tent and hiring caterers for our ninety guests, most from out of town, while I hired a string quartet to play Bartok and a dance band. Jim Woolsey officiated at the toasts, looking more fully like the owl of wisdom he had begun to resemble even at Stanford, but also like the eagle with talons to both sides, as he would require when the need came, as soon enough it did, to demonstrate his implicit loyalty equally to his old friend and his powerful patron. And from that powerful patron I got a full cup of adoration and admiration, to be my last from him: Paul Nitze rendered an account of my life in the form of a mythic enumeration of the lectures I had given, articles written, books undertaken, as if it could all be schematized into some great and unending productive and public enterprise.

Sitting there in the tent, watching everyone drinking some of the last of my 1961 and 1969 Burgundies, I knew an era in my life was about to close: at least it was rounding out in style. Surely not without some degree of intent, all the Nitzes, and all the swells from Chestnut Hill, were on one side of the tent. All my old friends who gathered from almost anywhere else were around me: Geoffrey Kemp (from the White House staff), Janne Nolan (Brookings), Arthur and Karen Elliot House (Connecticut politics and the *Wall Street Journal*, soon alas to split); Bira and Rampi Kasemsri (Thai ambassador at the United States), Ken and Cal Adelman (deputy US Ambassador there), Edward and Dahlia Luttwak . . .

When we went to bed Nina's look told me that it was all over. The spiritual faith I had always had told me this only ratified too long drawn out an ending; it meant more, or could come to mean more, as a beginning. My moral and physical exhaustion was such that I no longer could try to stop the waves from crashing. I made arrangements to move to Washington, realizing that it made things easier all around for both of us. The old world had to give way before I could find the new one.

Almost immediately I was named Associate Director at the United States Information Agency, a sub-cabinet job at the Assistant Secretary level, with wide responsibilities for policy, publications, co-ordination with the White House, State and Defense Departments, and a staff of over eight hundred. It is not the job I had originally targeted, and in fact that the high command of the administration had targeted for me at the administration's start. That was to be 'SP', or Policy Planning at the State Department, a job at the same level but one which had always been held by men of great stature – including, not coincidentally, my father-in-law, whose finest hour was there. By a fine irony, when my name was put up for SP at the appropriate White House conference, the new Secretary of State, Al Haig, demurred amidst dropping jaws because I was 'ambitious'. I didn't mind that (true) charge, even from Al; I minded that he had been so friendly as a guest in my house, and had so willingly accepted my assistance in pursuing the presidential nomination that in his memoirs he denies he had been interested in, and now was unwilling to follow through on a commitment.[6]

By the time I got my actual appointment, my personal world, deeper than any public life, was beginning to come apart, and I realized to serve at USIA would be less demanding in the areas where I was by now vulnerable; I had enough stress and didn't need the kind of conflict one must hourly meet at State. At USIA I really had my own little empire of magazines, policy guidance, speakers to be sent abroad, embassy program development, and so forth.

The only downside was that as number three I reported to number one, Charlie Wick, eminently qualified as husband of an intimate of Nancy Reagan and thus, to all intents and purposes, unaccountable. Charlie seemed psychotic on the job – viewing anything less than instant compliance with his every wish as an indication of a vast conspiracy against the true faith as held in Beverly Hills. Indeed, I had been appointed in part to offset Charlie's problems, and to enable the agency to cope with State, Defense and CIA. But Charlie's bullyboy tantrums and his ideas, though sometimes amusing, usually had to be given quiet, swift, dignified burial before le tout Washington heard of them. Of course we had double-entry bookkeeping for dealing with his 'Z-grams' – Charles Z. Wick had been born Charles Zwick, and apparently had heard of Admiral Bud Zumwalt's reform-oriented 'Z-grams', the real thing – half of which if acted upon would have put his friend the President in quite interesting trouble.

We spent much time distracting Charlie. Once he wanted my shop to send out to every embassy a peculiarly tasteless compilation of anti-Soviet (and anti-Russian) jokes. My blessed colleague Jock Shirley, the agency Counselor, who was nobly earning his future ambassadorship, called him in his limousine in Paris – limousines always made Charlie more secure – and hornswoggled him into signing off an instruction to send the compilation 'on background' in such a manner as we both knew would consign it to an immediate dustbin. It took a day, but at least the government founded by Washington and Jefferson didn't have to sign off on offensive nonsense. Such is life in a large part of the United States government.

I lived chez Nitze, since Paul was negotiating in Geneva, and entertained frequently, with my splendid tapes playing Haydn or Springsteen in the background, to the amusement one night of former student Rick Burt (prior to his departure as Ambassador to Germany) and Jim Woolsey. But 'Darkness on the Edge of Town' wasn't entirely funny, whatever it was juxtaposed with. I had a thousand new ideas a day, but for the first time I had a splendid instrument for doing something with them; and finally the self-confidence with which to justify such public trust had emerged, who knows from where? I worked hard at getting to know the civil servants on my staff, since I knew they could undercut me or go around me if I did not show trust in them and make good use of them. We built a team.

These were the best months of my life to that point, except perhaps early fatherhood. The dam holding back the roiling waters of the heart's deep troubles – Nina's as much as mine – hadn't burst, and I was fulfilled professionally for the first time in my life and confident that I was going to find my sexuality without paying a price for it. Rather soon my secretary buzzed me that there was a noisy man named Mr Casey on the line. Smart people in Washington often call directly, so I wasn't really so surprised as elated that the breathy and indistinct director of Central Intelligence was calling. He asked me to join a small dinner group that met every two weeks to plan 'action' to get Reagan's plans through. I was bidden because I had horses, so to speak – an open capability to deploy money, people, channels, whereas everyone else in the group was covert or lacked funds and the will to use them. Whatever people think, power tames far more power holders than it energizes. Our goal: disrupt the Soviet Union, something I had long thought possible and had even 'agitated' for through a small non-governmental institute of which I was an adviser, the National Strategy Information Center.[7] In 'The Group' our main focus was finding ways to make it intellectually credible that the Soviet Union could indeed explode, or, more likely, implode. In retrospect, that that gigantic monument to ill-faith should last even to the 1980s is startling. It comprised Leninist tyranny without Leninist purpose, revolutionary slogans with reactionary policies, a system which could only be justified from day to day, let alone decade, even in Lenin and Trotsky's time resting upon profoundest resentment and demoralization – the whole atmosphere for years had been that of a long-drawn-out 1789 or 1917. The Faustian arrogance that at least had an idealist streak was replaced by a gangster bureaucracy that could only conquer or bully its way out of its societal failure by exploiting the industrial democracies. To borrow Paul Anderson's phrase, a robot was walking with corruption beneath its armour – and that armour of nuclear weapons and bombs to kill Afghan children which so fascinated the peacemakers, the don't-let's-be-beastly crowd of the 1970s, made it more urgent to see that the Soviet Union was dead.

This all was a metaphor of my life at this stage. We were trying to do the impossible on a gigantic scale, just as what was being done to me, and what I was doing, was in its way on an impossibly gigantic scale. But that part I did not yet know.

In September 1982 Nina and her siblings held a grand golden wedding party for their parents. It was held at the New York Botanical Gardens – all of them, that is – not because Peter Nitze's eighty-five-foot Dakota ballroom was too small, but because, as I had finally learned, to those sufficiently endowed, diversity of venue becomes a challenge. Nina assured me that I was 'invited', but I knew it would be a bad idea to go, so I remained, of course, at the Nitzes' in Washington.

The next morning, with his usual sixth sense for catastrophe and his yet more customary loyalty to a fault, Jim Woolsey showed up on the doorstep about nine, having flown in from the party the night before. Jim has long perfected the disarming but directive gesture that lets you know both that he cares but also that he knows what medicine is in order. He simply ordered me into his car and took me to his house in Chevy Chase, where he and Sue did what they could to be helpful. But I couldn't dissimulate. I had known Sue since our freshman year too, and she meantime (*inter alia*) had won a PhD in psychology from Harvard and forged a career whose distinction matched Jim's. 'I know you love her, Scott . . . but do you really *like* her?' she asked – and she had become a good friend of Nina's. I couldn't say, any longer, that I did, but the implication of that still wasn't completely clear to me.

I had been going home to Boston every weekend, and every weekend things were worse. I had completely broken off my friendship with Mark and wasn't even in touch. It was too late. I knew by now that if I had to make a choice between a job that was exciting me more than anything in my life and a marriage that, aside from the joys of the children, wasn't working, there wasn't any doubt that I'd choose the former. At least it was something.

Meantime I was supervising the dissertation of Janne Nolan, soon to become a friend of presidents and one of our best political–military analysts. The range of her admirers extended beyond the Oval Office and included numerous gay men. We would talk about the development of her thesis, and then find ourselves venturing onto dangerous territory, avoiding gender when I spoke of Mark and the forces that he had unleashed within me. With patience but persistence, Janne led me to see that my choices were narrowing, and that I now had the worst of both worlds, without the aid and comfort of the world I would voyage to eventually, or of the world I was inevitably leaving behind. For one brief terrifying period I seemed to be between two worlds, one dead, the other powerless to be born. Janne was calling me to realize that strength which I had been unconsciously mustering.

One night I had a group of friends over to Cleveland Park; looking at me lost in contemplation of an Impressionist painting and watching my friends drink the last of the wine that I had laid down in the 1960s, she whispered, 'There is life beyond the Nitzes . . . Anyway, your parties before you married Nina, I gather, were much more fun. And there are much better Monets at the National Gallery . . . You can visit it anytime you want.' My debt to Janne is unrepayable.

After eighteen visits to Boston things had gone from bad to intolerable. We saw our minister, and Nina committed to a reciprocal eighteen meetings with a professional counselor in Washington. Significantly, she admitted that the problem was not the crisis of sexual orientation I had been going through (after all, I had never failed in my husbandly duties). Most of the gay men I have come to know who were married for many years report that they had such a complete lack of sexual interest in their wives for most of their marriage that this was the prime engine forcing divorce. In our case that was not true, right up to the end. Our crisis was in most senses deeper and started with her own lifelong crisis of confidence and self-esteem.

In any event soon thereafter something set her on a different track; on my next visit, en route to Washington from an official conference in Bonn, she looked like a death mask and refused even once to see the counselor we had obtained for the eighteen sessions in Washington I had proposed. She showed up for my formal swearing-in – as indeed did her entire party-loving family,[8] to crown and dissolve this phantasmagoric relationship – but as she had aborted my attempt to buy a house with my money, a wreck in Dupont Circle whose restoration was to proceed *pari passu* with my own recovery, I had no place to celebrate. Jim and Sue Woolsey as usual filled the void, and we had a party for about a hundred of our nearest and dearest in their house in Chevy Chase, their hospitality seeming effortless as always. Nina had seen lawyers in Boston and wouldn't discuss our marriage. I came to realize finally it was over, and had that most painful feeling there is, when no matter who is to blame, one spouse determines to end the family as both had known it – and the other is left with an emptiness beyond belief in looking into the black hole of a failed enterprise.

Finally, several months after she first went to her attorneys, I saw one. He told me my figure of $5,000 for the whole thing (which I figured I could borrow from somewhere) wouldn't get me out the front door; his services, he claimed, were $200 an hour, so we were spending almost a grand up front. He could have said a million. I didn't have a nickel at that point, since I was pouring my entire salary into restoring my house, and bringing the children to visit in Washington – though his later revelation under oath that the top corporate billing rate at the time was $160 makes clear how fine a Nitze divorce could be expected to be for a law firm. I was surviving at mealtimes by gorging at diplomatic functions; and when there weren't any of those or when I was too busy, I had to depend on the free hors d'oeuvres at the Metropolitan Club. Ultimately I had to give Nina a lien on my half of our farm to get her to sign the Dupont Circle contract as a spouse must, separated or otherwise – even though I had been paying the mortgage on the great house in Chestnut Hill which didn't even have my name on the title – and of course there I had signed everything else the family had suggested.

It was a long, cold winter. My two charming and loyal personal administrative assistants, Fred Knecht and Andy Walworth, and I drove all night in a rented truck with our respective worldly goods from Boston to Washington; they were doing everything they could to keep the situation under control and to buoy my spirits, which since they were starting out their own professional lives was rather a tall order. I loaded up from our houses a tiny fraction of what I could claim as my share of our property – indeed only a fraction of what I had paid for myself – in hopes that my 'material sensitivity' in the area of Nina's greatest anxiety, money, would calm her. When we stopped off in Darien to dine with Andy's mother, he and Fred drugged me so that I could get some sleep during the fourteen-hour drive before a big day. We arrived in Washington barely in time for my welcoming breakfast at the White House with the President. Rick Burt, than whom no one in Washington ever was more to the point and who was there to be welcomed as Assistant Secretary of State for European affairs, said I looked like a cadaver. In fact, I weighed under 130 pounds. I usually weigh at least 155 pounds.

I am sure that I got through all this because of a substantial health margin, so to speak, and continuing vitality. Of course fitness, nothing new for the young, was something new in my generation, and I had pushed myself to the far edges of it. That too started in the gay world, and undoubtedly it was my unconscious attraction to its source which drove me to improve both health and appearance through marathons and light body-building. In 1982 I had started a diet without any fats or sugar, and was at my best running weight ever. The race I ran in New York in October, for which my seven-year-old son flew in to help, holding the spare set of running shoes for me at mile seventeen near the 57th Street bridge without which I would not have been able to finish, was my best ever – three hours. I well recall lying on the floor of the tent near the start-up point of the race listening for three hours on my Walkman, over and over, to Vivaldi's *Orlando Furioso*, not surprisingly the evocation of a stirring figure driven mad by the world's demands. Being able to run in the top ten per cent of a great marathon, at age forty, showed stamina, an intangible power of resistance to mental anguish and moral destruction grinding at every edge. Of course I would not even have attempted a marathon until Father died, two years before, lest I gave him the satisfaction of the athletic accomplishment he had always sought in me.

One gets through stressed periods like this with the support of friends, who don't even have to say anything. All of mine were mystified about the four-story town house I had bought for a song near Dupont Circle, crudely split into ten junky apartments. The state of its heating, plumbing and electricity required that we gut the house while keeping all the splendid Victoriana that had miraculously survived. I invited all my friends to come by on a given Sunday when the children were in town, to help get going on it. I got a ton of pasta from Sutton Place Gourmet, and Walt Slocombe, my Balliol friend (now Undersecretary of Defense), rehung twelve windows, saving me hundreds of dollars; Ed Luttwak elegantly discerned the secrets of the house's utility systems and destroyed old partitions of tiny Arab apartments; Jim Woolsey brought a hammer and ripped out old fake walls, and another forty or so found incredibly useful projects that got me started, saving the thousands of dollars I no longer had. But the effect on my soul was worth far more than that.

My personal and public life were constantly ricocheting at one another, and the shrapnel from either was enough for one life. One noontime Strobe Talbott, now de facto Secretary of State and then a well-known *Time* bureau chief who was writing a biography of Paul Nitze, came up to me at the Metropolitan Club, and not knowing of my domestic distress, alluded indiscreetly given the circumstances to the treasury of government documents Paul was slipping him, with the obvious intent of projecting the Talleyrand-like magic which he so hungered to air for contemporary posterity. Everybody knows how newsmen get their stories in Washington, but this was on a somewhat larger scale – and manifestly Paul had his rewards, if a little too obviously.[9] Strobe must have been appalled when he got wise; in any event from then on he was distant and cold.

Strobe's biography of Paul illustrates another point of the times. We did feel we were up against the wall with the Soviet Union, and in retrospect the peril looks even greater, because their walls were so near to cracking as to terrify them to potentially extreme measures. It seemed by the early 1980s that the Europeans were beginning to hedge their bets and take out insurance with Moscow in variously disquieting ways, and thus the question of our installation of new intermediate range missiles in Europe became extremely important; my job was to set up the selling job in the swing NATO countries, particularly Germany, for which I was practically commuting to Europe for some months. If the missiles didn't go in, the Europeans would have the already-installed Soviet intermediate range missiles staring them in the face uncounterpoised. Nitze's position – and it was his portfolio – was that we had nothing to bargain with and would have to seek the best deal available; we saw that as a sellout. Richard Perle thankfully sold Reagan on the 'zero option', namely that we would put in zero if Moscow would go back down to zero. And if they didn't, we'd install – as we did to their horror, in what was the first great dissipation of the Soviet shadow. The Russians knew perfectly clearly that where we had the will to move ahead, we'd bring far more threatening and powerful missiles – or anything else for that matter – than they could deploy.

In the middle of this debate Georgii Arbatov, head of the Institute for the Study of the USA and Canada, addressed the Council on Foreign Relations. No one had ever been more of an apologist for any position of the moment that the Kremlin chose to advance, so the Establishment turned out in full force to get the real word.

It turned out that Arbatov wasn't the only apologist present. Strobe presided over the auspicious occasion, and introduced Arbatov, to us the evil in the empire incarnate, as an ally in the good cause – he and his people in league with Strobe and his people against us terrible Reaganites who were stirring up the Cold War, long since healed by reason and the common thrust for peace. I was so appalled at the message Arbatov was sure to get that I wrote and circulated a letter of protest, and made certain Arbatov saw it too, making clear that with most of us at least, discussion of foreign policy stopped at the water's edge.

So, the public issues immersing me were grave enough: indeed Strobe went on to lambaste me for calling in senior officials to tell them we were moving into a 'post-containment era' and were going to 'take the struggle directly to the enemy, on his own ground'.[10] Oh yes, he was right, he didn't know how right he was, even when he says as a result the Soviet Embassy became convinced that our goal was 'doing in' the Soviet Union. We did, we won, and I was proud to have played ever so minor a role in that glorious dismemberment.[11]

Difficulties never ceased. In the middle of all this, one cold midnight at the end of January 1983, my new administrative assistant, Robert Kiernan, who was staying at my house, and I were listening to a Handel cantata at midnight when the electricity went out. Bob cautioned me against going down to the basement fusebox; minimizing the risk (not even grasping his point), I got two candles. His instincts were right, though he followed loyally. When we had groped our way down, we saw something silver in the air; and Bob told me, 'There's somebody else here.'

It was too late. Guns slammed against our heads, we were tied up for several hours while three men ransacked the house. Bob was far calmer than I; at least in retrospect, I thought that his remonstrances to the robbers not to take his watch because it had his mother's initials on it was an appeal to their sentiment. He wanted to try to break out of the little closet into which we had been jammed, fearing they would kill us at the end. I overruled him less as his boss than as his landlord, reasoning that if that was their intent they would have done so already; while the odds of making it out alive were slim even if we managed to get our hands untied. Finally I was right about something; the robbers soon left, with $80,000 of valuables. Then we ran for our life, and spent the rest of the night with the police, notably with a skillful officer named Detective Queen, who caught them within a few days.[12] They had taken the entire étagère of antiquities – such of my collection of mainly Sung Chinese porcelain that Nina had not already appropriated – all the jewelry, and what would lead to their capture through a pawn shop, all the electronic gear. Strange how practical extremity makes us; I was rather hard up for cash to finish the renovation, and was mumbling at Bob through my gag during the ordeal that the no-longer-needed baubles' insurance would translate into new sinks, beds, stoves, and bathroom tiles.

Life was such at this time that, after one hour's sleep at the Metropolitan Club, I took the affair as just one more little misfortune, going to my psychiatrist at eight and our staff meeting as usual at nine in the Deputy Director's office (with of course a great new war story), and keeping a luncheon engagement at my club with Congressman, as he was then, Les Aspin, to discuss Project Democracy, my agency's high-profile program which had already led to the President's epochal address at the Palace of Westminster and would eventually take substantial form as the National Endowment for Democracy. Les thought I was daft not to be licking my wounds, and my psychiatrist warned me that I would feel aftershocks for at least six months. He was right; it was two weeks before I could bring myself to review the desecration.

But greater tremors came that same week in a cruel letter from my father-in-law, turning down my written request for a meeting to discuss ways of calming the marital crisis in the best interests of the children. Some hours later, I left for Honolulu to stand in for Vice President Bush before the Pacific Telecommunications Forum, shaken doubly as never before. At a stopover in Denver, my friend John Milstein found me barely coherent. At least Honolulu, where I had some delightful letters of introduction to charming young men, and saw Clare Boothe Luce, who told me my boss was a nut, improved my spirits.

Money was tight. I did not easily make the transition from a world of unlimited funds to one where every dollar counted. I thought I was merely returning to a world I had known all too well. Friends told me otherwise. I sometimes even worked evenings as a caterer's waiter – this while in a sub-cabinet job – to pay for the children's monthly air tickets. Once I was sent to a house where I had often been a guest, and the hosts, the John Bross's – close Nitze friends and sometime guest of Nina's and mine as well – recognized perfectly who their knowledgeable butler's assistant was, but played it as if they didn't know me from Adam. In a very real sense, they no longer did.

Then, in early 1983 Nina stopped the children's visits. She submitted a public brief to the court that said the whole problem was my homosexuality – a response in the strictest sense at the least gratuitous and legally irrelevant. This was, my lawyer and I both immediately realized, more than a tactical legal maneuver; it invoked what my friend Timothy Dickinson called a 'sacred horror', and a warning shot across the bow: legal action was for them, not for me. After all, society had protected me and my secret – and now the wheels had turned and Nina and the house of Nitze were calling for the alien blood. I turned cold with fear for my cherished career. Her lawyers wouldn't have submitted such a brief except as a fully-considered and fully-authorized lunge for the jugular. We got the brief impounded, we regained access to the children, but now I knew what was in store; sooner rather than later I would have to resign and return to my university, where I had the security of tenure. My war with homosexuality had been, up to now, wholly within me: now it would pass into the fields and streets. On that spring day of 1983 in the Norfolk County courthouse I think I knew in a small way what good Europeans experienced as bombers spewed out their explosives on the centuries of civilization below – the life we had contrived for ourselves as a team and the children, and individually as well.

Nevertheless, even I was not in principle unsympathetic to Nina's underlying position. How could anyone fail to sympathize with someone who felt that she had discovered that the love of her life was incapable of loving her in all the ways she had desired, or as fully as she had loved him? I was always to wish, however, that she were personally in charge of her legal team and of her father – rather than giving them full rein to do as they wished with my career, my person, and my relations with our children, using tactics of which she could not possibly have approved. But how much did she know or want to know? 'We do well not to know how dinners, and our Constitutions, are made', said a worldly Frenchman. Most of the rich, individuals or nations, economize on knowing how their wealth was made, or is preserved.

Not for the first time when in distress, I called Jim Woolsey, then practicing law in Washington, but already a junior statesman, and he offered to drop everything and come right over to meet me at the Metropolitan Club. I showed him Nina's document, desecration of house rules, which forbid the circulation of papers at a 'social' club; he asked me for a dollar – a far greater impiety but which valuable consideration established attorney-client privilege. He always had been a trusty keeper of secrets, and a career of that appropriately rewarded him with the CIA as the first of his positions of great eminence. No one in the world knew both the Nitze family and me so well; at that point he had worked for, and with, Paul off and on over a dozen years. Jim looked at me gravely and gave his most serious advice. In effect, he said, take what you've got and run. He agreed they were out to get me and that the further away from it all I was the better. Maybe I could get some access to the children, and maybe if I were lucky I'd get the farm in New Hampshire, of which I was half-owner (and full-maintainer) already, but I shouldn't even think about more.

It was the ghastliest – and frankest – advice anyone had ever given me. We spent vacations together at that farm, his three and my three children of like ages crawling around at first,[13] then trekking the woods, swimming in the nearby lakes. Now we were talking about the end of my material world as I knew it, and wondering whether I'd be able to salvage my relationship with my children. I made one simple vow at that point: nothing would separate me from the kids – they would be my only, and absolute, priority.

Between the emotional pulls on me, my emerging homosexuality and my desire to remain in, and benefit from, the world of conventionality, the children unwittingly reinforced the latter. I delayed at least two years coming out after splitting with Nina, and even got engaged to another woman, until my parenting patterns were established beyond challenge, especially in the children's minds but also in the courtroom. I was not conscious of this, but so it looks from this distance in time.

Another point was just dawning. Everyone in theory can of course hire a lawyer, except the very poor for whom the state provides counsel. But the difference between a salary-earner like myself and a rich person, went to quality not quantity alone. I had to save every minute of time that might be billed by my lawyer and to avoid all court action not absolutely necessary. For all that, Paul Pearson, my first lawyer, ran up a bill of almost my annual academic salary in that first twelve months. Nina unblinkingly incurred at least thrice those expenses for starters, and didn't have to lie awake at night thinking how to pare down the hours and then how to pay for them: she could lie awake at night thinking of new ways to *use* the lawyers to press her pain, her hurt.

The rich contestant goes 'to law' not only calm but intrinsically on the offensive; the poorer person enters court already in such deep fear of his lawyer's bill – if he has a lawyer, and I often didn't – that he has cut his objectives by half, then half again, lest he not even be able to endure to the smallest sweet victory.

In a system that, as Edward Luttwak has so colorfully demonstrated, is dragged down, nearly drowned by the legal profession, the litigation system is simply an inexorable force requiring one's attention whether one is rich or poor, a juggernaut grinding its unwilling votaries under, unless they can muster one hundred thousand dollars or thereabouts (for starters) for a reasonably routine affair.[14]

All this warfare was going on despite the fact that, now that Nina had made clear that the marriage was over, I was free to have, and was having, an affair with a sprightly (female) former student of mine, while avoiding Washington's gay world like the plague. The Nitze connection never does anything lightly. I simply wasn't going to give them a sword.

But it seemed they were looking for one anyway. Most years since 1968 I had spent the second weekend of September at the annual conference of the International Institute of Strategic Studies, a prestigious London-based center of the best strategic reflection and application. Most years Paul had gone too, and some years we had taken our wives. Therefore he might have noted my name on the advance roster for the 1983 conference in Ottawa, which he was also gracing. I was on the lists, and there on time in the flesh. What the list did not say was that I would leave early, hopping Richard Perle's Defense Department jet.

I let myself into my town house that Saturday afternoon, my ears ringing with in-flight news of Paul's latest European and extraordinary indiscretions, to hear movement upstairs, though (unusually) there was to have been no one visiting; I had turned on the security system and locked the gates. But this was unmistakable. So I picked up the phone to call the police, keeping a beeline clear to the open door in case the intruders came downstairs with guns. Well, someone had jammed the phone electronically – an unusually professional touch, more like intelligence types than the big-city burglary crowd. I got courageous and yelled for them to get the hell out. Commotion. I yelled out to a passerby on the street to call the police. Papers were rustling. Grabbing an umbrella I willed myself upstairs, but as I did so the intruder crawled out by the one neglected security hole, the roof skylight. As I scampered after him I could hear his clatter down the neighboring roofs then saw a figure plunge through an empty renovating house at the corner.

Back in the house, a quickly-arrived police officer and I found nothing disturbed except papers – divorce documents and diaries – from a second floor closet and my bedroom, now strewn all over the floor. It was evident that much was missing. Astonishingly, cash lay on the mantlepiece undisturbed as did some important office papers on my desk. No piece of electronic gear was touched, including some new small and valuable ones.

'Are you going through some legal proceedings, sir?' the detective asked.

'I sure am, Detective.'

'Well, don't you think that's what explains it?'

I did, but was more interested in what he proposed to do about it. Unfortunately the more I told him about the case the less he seemed prepared to pursue my visitor. He had figured out that I was probably gay, if only from the location of my house. When I mentioned who else was involved, he downright backed away and suggested that things just might sort themselves out.

I was ready to make literally a federal case out of it, since not only my private papers (luckily replaceable) had been stolen, but my most personal musings and thinking, covering decades, which I thought were not. To my astonishment, I found the next day that, on his own initiative, my assistant Bob Kiernan had xeroxed all those diaries and had stashed them elsewhere, and this cooled me down a lot. Bob as usual was street-smart about what might happen.

By January 1984 I was just about at meltdown. There had been the armed violation of my home, my friend and myself the previous winter, all the tension over the children's visits, then Nina's refusal to submit a divorce agreement, knowing that the longer she held out the more desperate I would be – and the more willing to settle for a pittance from our legally joint funds.

Paul Pearson, my lawyer, had originally assured me that the courts would ensure not too great a disequilibrium in living standards between the parents, in the best interests of the children, and that meant at least a 20/80 division of assets, and more likely 30/70; in Massachusetts, marital assets were divided according to eighteen variables, ranging from who worked, who needed more later, what each had contributed to the family, who stood to inherit what and so forth. Where the main pot of the money originated was one variable among eighteen and the only one that favored Nina. Pearson now urged me to take essentially nothing – about two per cent of the joint pot – and run. I fired him, and never paid him the $30,000 owed. I was indeed to come to the conclusion that client's should always inspect lawyers' bills with care, and where conscious inadequacy seemed apparent, or gross overbilling, refuse to pay the full fare.

The gay issue creeps in at every chamber and corner of our society, from cellar to attic, and gay men know precisely what to expect whenever courts appoint officials to 'look things over'. It became clear that my lawyer had not taken me seriously – because I was, he presumed (or knew the charge would stick), gay, and thus 'unserious'.

It turned out that the bane of my life was not only a rich and powerful family, willing to spend upwards of a million dollars to try to destroy my world by breaking my ties to the children and my access to positions of influence; but agents of the state, court officials openly colluding with them. When I went to court to regain access to my own children, we asked that the court appoint a *guardian ad litem* (GAL), that is a spokesman for the children, on the assumption that anyone looking out for their best interests would surely want them to have access to their father, irrespective of their mother's wealth. Indeed, when I thought about it, how could that even enter in, among civilized people? Yet it turned out to be the received wisdom that it was precisely my relative impoverishment that one young heir and two heiresses must be 'saved' from. When we learned that Judge Keville had appointed his 'friend' Ms Ruth-Arlene Howe, of Boston College Law School, as GAL, we thought we were home safe, or at least I did. She is an African-American, and I had committed to the black civil rights movement as early as my teens. Surely she would sympathize with my desire to parent.

It took me a long time to understand how innocent I was; a member in good standing of various branches of the American élite, I assumed treatment in the court system at least no worse than anybody else's, whereas a born minority-member would expect judicial discrimination. I simply hadn't recalculated: I was now *entering* a minority and committing to it, a despised one, and had no notion of how rough a playing field any legal process was for gays, or *anyone* for whom the playing field is not configured. Nor had I taken into account the kind of power – private power – that need not justify itself to Senate committees or enquiring journalists. What Ruth-Arlene represented was someone tame, precisely *because* she was black. She knew what she was supposed to do. It did not have to be spoken: it was to hack me to shreds. Before Ruth-Arlene was through, she had proposed to have me committed to an insane asylum, and cut off virtually all access to the children until countered with the threat of publicity and court action at the highest level.

No one on my side ever doubted how I loved and cherished the children, and that they were getting from me what their mother eventually graciously conceded – when they ran off with top prizes from their secondary schools – namely much of their intellectual inheritance. Indeed, precisely to preempt her concerns, my therapist advised me to hire another, and therefore distanced, therapist just to monitor the children's interaction with me – which meant there would be six psychiatrists and psychologists examining the unquestionably healthy participants! At our second meeting – seven consecutive hours of negotiation on the lawn of her law school – Ruth-Arlene conceded albeit with great bitterness that I should have some kind of role in my children's upbringing; she made it clear at the start that Nina should have sole custody and I virtually no access – and that on Nina's bitter sufferance.

As the wretched encounter wound down she unmasked her guns: 'Why didn't I just *go* – and go quietly?' meaning leave them behind, forget them forever – hinting that if so she'd argue for a fatter payoff. It took me half a decade to realize what she meant. *She* had figured out that I was gay, and thus deserved no role in bringing up children whose genes were fifty per cent mine. She still hadn't noticed that the children were the most important part of my life then as today. I simply refused to leave until she gave in, the best technique available to a weaker side angry and committed enough to put everything on the line – had not the North Vietnamese said they would sit at Paris 'until the chairs rotted'?

Ruth-Arlene wasn't impressive and formidable enough in the end; Paul was operating through too many cut-offs and John D's money was at last running into the sand. But children grow up quickly, and if she had read me out of their lives even for a few years, it probably would have been forever. Within two years I was winning.

Ruth-Arlene went to the level of sending me a proposed visitation schedule for one spring vacation *after* the vacation had already begun! Which meant that I legally could not see my children during the first week, and making it financially impossible to see them over the second because the schedule came too late for me to get APEX discounted fares. Well, Ruth-Arlene knew that I couldn't possibly afford full-fare tickets.

Of course her most powerful weapon is one which divorced, particularly gay, fathers always see used against them. They are the ones setting up a new household, having to learn many new skills, often emotionally shattered; three-fourths of divorces these days are initiated by women. If one assumes with Ruth-Arlene that the father has no intrinsic right to parent, then it is always possible to find evidence that he is doing a lousy job of it; and where there is no evidence, the pressures of innuendo and prurient investigation can be increased until he is rattled enough to make mistakes. But after the first two years I simply avoided those traps – and by then the children had their monthly visits very much plugged into their schedule and expectations, and we could have a ball and Nina and Ruth-Arlene couldn't do anything about it. As it was, my two younger children, the ones in school in or near Boston, agreed to testify against Ruth-Arlene, which had a lot to do with her coming to terms and agreeing to withdrawal as GAL after those eight years, so painful to me, so lucrative to her: her billings had come almost to $100,000.

The argument had nothing to do with the merits of men as opposed to woman as parents. It had to do with homophobia. Ruth-Arlene could not stand to be in the room with me. Queen Elizabeth had managed on several occasions; Pamela Berry (Lady Hartwell), the greatest (female) parlor intellectual of England in her day, had befriended me for my four years at Oxford; a variety of fine women loved me, and Nina and I shared a bedroom for fourteen years, but Ruth-Arlene was utterly determined to 'save' my children from their faggot father.

Now the most cruel moment of all. I gave notice on my job, to return in 1985 to the security of my tenured teaching position. The day I said goodby to my job at USIA – a very sad one indeed for me – Nina's lawyer George Kidder called me. George, with all the considerable offensiveness he could muster, opened by saying that I had better sign their proposed agreement, whereby Nina got sole custody and about ninety-five per cent of the joint assets. If I didn't sign, he and Paul Nitze would see that I'd never see the children again, could never again get government employment, and that all the world would know that I was a 'faggot'.

My housemate Rick Lewis was within hearing. Asking him quickly to get on the other line as a witness, I requested George to repeat himself, and he very considerably embroidered his threats, the legal implications of which the reader may ponder. And the long and short of it is that, with a few cosmetic changes, that is what I signed: I had hepatitis B, was working against doctors' orders, indeed starting a new job at a foundation to make a little money in a money consuming time before returning to Fletcher. My spirit was cracking. I, who had to get on with my life, had no lawyer and no money to get one. The only thing that mattered was the children and it was clearly going to be tough to maintain contact.

For the lawyers wanted not just war – parties to domestic litigation can get that pretty much without their attorneys' encouragement – but dirty war. Nina was not a knowing party to the skullduggery her party was undertaking, but in her very dignified and determined way, she did want war.

What it amounted to is what every gay man, until very recently, routinely encountered. Even if he hadn't come out, even if his homosexual encounters were scanty, even if only the faintest smoke was visible, as it was in my case where the smoke – of my friendship with Mark Altbush – was purely attitudinal, anyone could use that to browbeat you into just about anything and they did. That's what gay men have always put up with, that's what the straight world has been able to get away with since the human race learned to hate.

In March 1993 a court finally recognized the peculiar vulnerability of gay married men. The case involved a scoundrel who videotaped his seduction of a married man and then blackmailed him for $16,000, which drove his victim to attempt suicide but finally overtook him and led to his arrest. The court noted that all blackmail victims have a secret, but that some secrets 'are a good deal more painful than others'. And, it went on, in targeting married homosexuals, as George Kidder had, there was a 'malevolent focusing in on a particularly susceptible subgroup'. But reasoning most germane for this book runs as follows:

> To the argument that government ought not use the criminal laws to protect the privacy of people who engage in conduct that rightly or wrongly is an object of social reprobation . . . it is a sufficient answer that the law against blackmail proceeds upon virtually the opposite premise.[15]

As my health improved slightly, with the hepatitis lifting, my friend Mark Sullivan, later General Counsel to the Treasury, advised me to try to improve the agreement; even though coerced into signing it, I could still try to improve it on the margins without conceding its legitimacy. He recommended another lawyer, whom I hired on a contingency basis. As a new man on the block he could expect to get a few concessions, especially since I was now showing some resistance even to appearing at the divorce court. If I were to work within the existing legal framework, I had to choose between money and the kids, he thought, and since there never was any choice, there was at least the clarity that imparts determination.

Now we played a legal game, with Kidder convinced that I was doing it for money. In fact we held out for joint custody – only the children mattered although the financial settlement was utterly preposterous and the lowest percentage agreed to by a spouse that I could find in the Massachusetts annals. But I made clear that if we did not share custody of our kids I'd renege on everything I'd signed. They gave in – on that alone. The character of the imposed agreement is illustrated and symbolized by the fact that Nina kept all but just exactly two of all three hundred-odd wedding presents, and one of those two she waited five years before returning, since it had monetary value. Out of the two ample houses we maintained, the Nitze family managed to find less than one room's worth of furniture, and nothing of value; when it was found that a painting given to me was very valuable, it was of course kept. All this gave me the mind-clearing (if self-serving) pleasure of knowing I really was starting from scratch in my new life, with no debt whatsoever to the past.

What the settlement revealed was the respective bottom lines of the two parties, which they both achieved – though mine was a 'minimalist' threshold and Nina's a 'maximalist' one. Mine was joint custody of the children, which the court bestowed. Nina's was simply that I was to get none of her money, no 'real' money, that is, no more than what I would probably be able to demonstrate was mine by right or origin in court. And the number her lawyers were using – my half of the farm in New Hampshire plus a bit more – came approximately to what Walt Slocombe had said I might use as a guide: what I could reasonably calculate I would have minimally accumulated in the fifteen years had I *not* been married to Nina. So apart from the children, I ended up pretty much where I at the very least would have been, had events joined me to a young woman without estates, or perhaps even to a man, with his own career.

But just as the court did its messy business for the Nitze side, my health returned. I saw another, tougher, shrewder lawyer – Jacob Atwood, who looked at the agreement and told me I'd thrown my life away. He advised, as my visiting arrangements were nullified, aborted, bent out of shape or canceled by the GAL and Nina, that the only way I'd ever reestablish a relationship with the children was to try to break the entire agreement, during the process of which the GAL and Nina wouldn't dare prevent my access, lest they provide proof inescapable to the sleepiest court that they meant to renege on the key aspects of the separation agreement. We probably wouldn't actually break the agreement, but at least I'd establish in the children's minds during the period leading up to the trial their right to be with their father and their right to visit him routinely in Washington. Which is precisely what happened.

We did go to trial – strictly speaking a hearing as to whether to have a full trial, 'my day in court', now that I was healthy again. At least we had four days of argument. It had surely been a most exciting moment in August 1984 when Nina and Paul Nitze came down to court in Dedham from the grand compound in Northwest Harbor, to hold forth *in propria persona* the many reasons which must keep me from our children. At the end of it, my lawyer astonished the judge by saying he was throwing the whole thing open, presented both Nina and Paul with various legal demands and briefs, along with subpoenas for depositions, and asked the judge for a hearing as soon as possible (when of course in fact we wanted it as far away as possible).

Nina and Paul went scarlet, less even with rage or horror than at the impiety of it all. The courtroom was theirs, after all, because the system was theirs, and they looked at me as an imposter with at best contingent rights – soon enough to be proven hollow and fraudulent – as the rich seem always to look at adversaries in the law. If there was some truth in the old adage that 'the man who marries wealth works the hardest for it', I was finally getting at least some psychological return on the investment.

Our whole game plan was to seize the customary tactics of wealth and drag it out as much as possible, getting at least three child 'visitations' (which, to the GAL's continuing annoyance over eight years, I insisted on referring to as 'parenting' or 'parenting occasions') to Washington before the verdict; and if we lost, another four or five before the appeals court could rule. By then the children would be eleven, ten, and five, and plenty old to demand the rights to which they had become accustomed.

We deposed Nina and Paul: Nina to her horror had to sit alone at the midpoint of a great table in Jacob Atwood's Victorian mansion-cum-law offices, while he coldly and routinely reminded her at every turn that she could no longer hide behind George Kidder. She conceded her adultery, with an oncologist who had left his wife; she admitted virtually everything Atwood put to her. She admitted that her mother was an alcoholic, and conceded that her sister Heidi was gay. As Atwood bore down on her to the time at which she determined our family had come to an end, she was reduced to tears, and the acrid excitement of seeing the long struggle for once swaying my way had to be offset by the most intense feeling for someone long loved.

But to me, the payoff came on one question. Atwood told me that without exception all women who take the initiative in breaking up a family go off and buy a gold necklace after they do the dirty deed. I told him he was daft. Nina would have felt impossibly guilty for that. He crept up to it, sneaking a glance at me from time to time as he neared the kill and then asked: what had she done in the immediate aftermath. No, where *precisely* had she gone, he demanded. When she said to a jeweler – and had indeed bought a gold necklace – and he sneaked me a victory grin, I knew I had a brilliant lawyer.

Paul – surprise! – was a trickier number. Confronted with Nina's admission of her mother's alcoholism, he simply said that Nina 'always overreacted' and had no valid judgment in such matters – giving much away, but of no legal interest. He conceded her adultery, saying he approved of the gentleman in question but he denied, somewhat disingenuously, that his other daughter was gay.

The issue of homosexuality underlay everything for both sides, even though it was technically, certainly legally, not at issue. I had lived at that point for well over a year with Richard Lewis, the graduate student at Georgetown University I introduced earlier, who worked off his rent by renovating my townhouse. His sexuality was evident to me from the women he had in the bedroom above mine, whose rattling heating pipes loudly advertised what was going on most nights. A most attractive man, he never initiated sexual relations with me or gave any reason to think they could be available. But we were intimate in the true sense, and bonded. He was my children's new elder brother, loving them as they loved him. He chose to attend the trial, if only because, having witnessed the telephone conversation with Kidder, he would surely be my witness. So, we drove up to Boston, stopping in Connecticut to see his psychiatrist father and psychologist mother, both to become friends of mine.

To my astonishment, Atwood chose not to call Rick. The fact that Kidder never even denied my description of the telephone calls was sufficient, he thought. The reason Atwood didn't take Rick's testimony was simple. In the old Irish judge's mind, the only issue was homosexuality, the one Kidder had painted the town yellow with. Was I or wasn't I? – even though the substantial and real issue where law met ethics and was challenged to give it form was (as our case put it) extortion, and the technical question of whether, in pronouncing the divorce the judge had asked (which he had not), the division of assets was fair, as had just become required by law. Sensing this, my lawyer was convinced that whatever the merits, the judge would believe Rick was my young lover, and hence my foresworn witness. Better to have him sitting there with my references to him, than to swear him in.

There were a few circuses. Nina called her star witness, Jill Tarlau, the former wife of my close friend Peter Magowan, who had not long before ascended to the leadership of Safeway. When they had split, as Jill admitted under oath, I divided my visits to San Francisco between them, rigorously, even matching every phone call to one with one to another, even though my friendship started with Peter at Stanford.

As it happened, Jill had visited Nina and me early in 1982 in the agony of her divorce aftermath, when I was getting to know Mark Altbush. In deepest confidence, one witnessed by my own sympathetic warnings two years before her marriage was giving way, I unfolded my confusion, and said I was 'ten per cent gay'. I thought she would like Mark (their New York and Jewish background gave them much in common). Now she was brought back to Boston to repeat the conversation. Of course, ten per cent is, as we got out of her elementary school arithmetic, a little less than ninety per cent, but she made her point, and sold her friend down the river, for how many pieces of silver I know not, though Nina from then on treated her as an equal and visited her in her rather splendid misery in Paris; now Jill was at least someone Nina wasn't ashamed to be unhappy around.

The trial of course showed who were the first class citizens and who were not yet fully enfranchised, and the judicial process itself showed all the farce of law on an unequal playing field. We of course lost in the immediate and technical sense. Indeed, six years later, when Nina out of some unknown frustration went to court to get sole custody yet again and was refused, she got her revenge by suing me for the court costs which had never previously come up. The agreement that was worked out will in effect keep me paying this vastly wealthy woman for the rest of my life.

It is the best money I spend every month, because had I not done so Nina, Ruth-Arlene, and an irretrievably corrupt judicial process would have definitively cut me off from the children. Those who assert that a gay man, or one simply with the smoke of homosexuality circling around him, could get domestic justice in the courts then, or for the most part today, are ignorant to the point of callousness. For homosexual men, this aspect of life and its adepts are still the South before the constitution got there.

## Notes

1. She completed her PhD thesis at Boston University, on images of *fortuna* – or luck – and poverty, fittingly, in Bocaccio's Incunabula, in April 1994.
2. To be increased, with the widening of this tax loophole in 1982, to $10,000 apiece, rather than the $20,000 permitted. This showed the limits of Nitze wealth – and underlined the point often made in the family that you knew how rich people were not by how they lived,

but how their *children* lived. The Nitzes, however, were uncommonly generous in passing their fortune down the generations and often stretched the tax laws to transfer their capital.

3. 'The new-boy network', *New York Times*, 7 June 1979. 'The N.S.C. staff, which should once again become an exciting place to be, would include Prof. Scott Thompson of Tuft's Fletcher; Kenneth Adelman . . . '
4. Carl Jung, 'The stages of life', in *Modern Man in Search of a Soul* (1933).
5. Curiously, Yourcenar, the first woman to join the Académie Française, lived her adult life in Northeast Harbor, Maine, thanks to the ties there of her lover and translator, Grace Frick. The wealthy summer residents had no grasp whatsoever of the distinction of this fine woman, with whom I had innumerable conversations during my Nitze summers in that village – all in sharp counterpoint to the cocktails and sailing conversation that otherwise prevailed.
6. I had offered to put together an evening affair at our house in Chestnut Hill for Republican notables while Al was still SACEUR (Supreme Commander) in Europe, late in 1979. Even then Al was denying interest – but his staff, on taxpayers' money, called me at least once a day for six weeks to make certain that every single delegate, notable, influential was invited – and coming! See his memoir, *Caveat: Realism, Reagan, and Foreign Policy* (London: Macmillan, 1984).
7. I had also tried to use scholarly channels to raise this possibility, something that was unthinkably incorrect in academe. Thus for example in the second edition of my book *The Third World* I commissioned an article on the 'third world status' of Soviet Central Asian 'republics', as a way of opening them up to outer influences.
8. I for all intents and purposes never saw any of them again, aside from frequent sightings of Paul, who had the same habit as did I of eating lunch in the (substantially cheaper) buffet room of the Metropolitan Club.
9. See Strobe Talbott, *Master of the Game* (New York: Knopf, 1988).
10. See Strobe Talbott, *The Russians and Reagan*, p. 73.
11. The role of the Reagan administration in 'bringing down the evil empire' will be debated for years to come. See Peter Schweizer, 'Who broke the evil empire?' *National Review*, 30 May 1994, for an accurate inside account of the steps taken to weaken the empire's will.
12. They were sentenced to fifteen years to life, which I took to be a minimum of fifteen years. It wasn't. They were out in a year and a half. I learned a great deal about the criminal justice system: each

had an extraordinary file of letters attesting to his good character from ministers, counselors, and the like.

13. A classic picture of Phyllis Thompson and Robert Woolsey, aged six months, shows them inspecting the huge *Washington Post* headline of 9 August 1974, 'Nixon Resigns'.
14. See chapter 8, 'From Law to Legalism', in Edward Luttwak, *The Endangered American Dream: How to stop the United States from becoming a third-world country and how to win the geo-economic struggle for industrial supremacy* (New York: Simon & Schuster, 1993).
15. Cited in Lisa Keen, 'Court singles out crimes against married gays', *Washington Blade*, vol. 24, no. 34 (August 1993), p. 13.

Chapter five

# *Keeping Secrets, Having Enemies*

***. . . there were no abnormal people when homosexuality was the norm, no anti-Christians before Christ, that the opprobrium alone makes the crime because it has allowed to survive only those who remained obdurate to every warning . . . by virtue of an innate disposition so peculiar that it is repugnant to other men . . . than certain other vices which exclude those qualities, such as theft, cruelty, breach of faith, vices better understood and so more readily excused by the generality of men . . .***

● Cities of the Plain

BETWEEN the time I left the Reagan administration and came out – over one year – I thus lived in a shadow zone, trying to protect my privacy, trying to figure out my options. I was not in good shape.

A series of developments opened in my professional life parallel to what was going on between Nina and me. Just after I left the Reagan administration, I became involved in a scandal, in effect as the accuser, which is alas in many ways a less advantaged position than that of the accused, especially when one is pitching uphill. And the gay issue underlay it throughout. In the summer of 1983 Charlie Wick removed my immediate boss Gil Robinson as number two at USIA, and appointed on White House advice Leslie Lenkowsky of the Smith Richardson Foundation. I thought that was fine – we'd known each other for several years – and had no problem reporting to someone younger than I with no experience of government. He certainly had a network, as head of a conservative foundation in New York, which had given grants to all of us at one time or the other; I hadn't even expended mine fully when I entered government, and he had been wholly understanding. There was every reason to believe that Les thought well of me; it was therefore striking upon his arrival how enthusiastically he endorsed various job prospects for me outside government. Although only on interim appointment, whenever introduced as 'Deputy Director Designate' he corrected this to 'Deputy Director'. People look up when you publicly insist on rank in Washington.

Les had made a real mistake. Infuriated that his writ didn't instantly run throughout our large agency – he had lost two and a half years of Reagan-time in New York, having been passed over for several jobs for which he was well qualified, including mine – he was set upon immediate results. Finding that one of my programs, 'Amparts', which sent speakers abroad, and had fifty-odd professionals responsible for it, wasn't invariably responding to his memos and taking his suggestions of speakers from his Rolodex card-file, to replace those they had long fished for and assessed, he rather unfortunately cast his Rolodex into the scales to outweigh their entire body of work to date, just as investigative reporters began suggesting the existence of a USIA 'blacklist' of speakers. I suggested to him afterwards that we might want to spread the word that such was merely a pleasantry, since it otherwise might go directly to the *Washington Post*; in Washington, that is the way the permanent government reins in political appointees. Let it, said he. The fat was in the fire and he wasn't yet confirmed.

Of course almost the next day the *Post* ran a story on the so-called USIA 'blacklist' – a misnomer, but a plausible ring to it since such as Coretta King were to be displaced by Les's neo-conservative friends from his card-file.[1] Now certain Hill staffers, not uneager for the first chance to fry a senior Reagan nominee, did some research, took some affidavits, and came reasonably enough to the conclusion that they could cook Lenkowsky. They had him on what was now routinely referred to on the front page of the *Post* and occasionally the *New York Times* as the 'blacklist'. They ridiculed him for his line 'I stand by what I meant to say', and accompanied it with the *Post*'s highly unflattering cover picture of him with his large stomach seemingly still more bloated. If you don't befriend the journalists in Washington you don't survive.

They also had him on his boast that he had 'fired' me – a serious charge in Washington, I *in medias res* having left USIA. He hadn't, he hadn't even the power to do so, but he claimed it in Senator Zorinsky's office, thoughtfully adding a few lines everywhere he went about my sexual orientation.

I didn't wish to testify, with all the implicit overtones of disloyalty to the administration: especially since if I did testify before the United States Senate I was not, under any circumstances (I told the White House), going to perjure myself. The truth would be most unpleasant; so I went to Williamsburg on vacation with my children, but the Senate Foreign Relations Committee issued me its first subpoena in many years. Such a show of power obviously made it easier to do the necessary – against White House wig-wagging and all manner of well-meant private advice. What had started as an 'inside the Beltway' story was now bloating into a fairly serious national topic.

My friends who found the story growing tedious from my lips now wanted me to up the ante. Walt Slocombe put partisan advantage aside and advised me to take counsel up to the Hill, and Jim Woolsey, after a Council on Foreign Relations lecture, treated me to dinner and advised the same – telling me also to slow down the train I was on. But I only had to tell the truth. Taking an attorney would make it look, as always, as if there was something to hide or finesse. Mark Sullivan, another prominent lawyer friend, agreed with my instinct.

And then good Charlie Wick decided he had finally better try to bail Les out. I invited him to the Metropolitan Club for lunch, to which he invited Ed Feulner, the powerful and brilliant president of the Heritage Foundation. Charlie first apologized for the canard that I had been fired and cleared that up once and for all in front of Ed, then wondered why Les and I couldn't get our stories together. I pointed out that I had offered to get together three times. He plainly felt that he was on top of the world and considered that getting help from me would show weakness. Ed said that if I were serious, he could deliver Les to his office in half an hour, even if he'd refused a thousand times in the past. I chuckled: that was one offer Les just couldn't refuse – the Heritage Foundation was every conservative's safety net in Washington.

Ed was right. Les came, fuming at me, the perceived source of all his troubles and insisting that he had the Senate eating out of his hand. Confirmation problems? Nonsense.

'Fine', I said, once more. 'Then there's nothing to talk about, is there?' He didn't need to cut a deal whereby (as I proposed) I would go public with a finely-stitched joint statement about any past disagreements, one which would basically obviate any question of perjury on Les's part.

There was a certain unexpected auspiciousness to the hearing. The word had gone around that some principles were involved – blacklists, for example – and that the Democrats might get their first confirmation hit up front.[2] Right off the bat Leslie gave the senators a sword: his veritable first line was to correct Senator Cohen's English. One doesn't correct the English of senators who are passing upon one's fitness to serve the republic. For that matter, one doesn't correct the English of senators in any circumstances. And so it just went from bad to worse, until three Zorinsky aides testified that Les had said what he'd denied under oath saying about me, and that was the end of that. A couple of Republicans joined in defeating the nomination, and the 'Deputy Director' had to bowl his Rolodex back to New York.

It was obvious at this point that Leslie was going to burn in hell for a while, and he did.[3] But what astonished me was that we were going to burn together, like conjoint sinners in Dante. Of course, as far as Washington was concerned, we were partners in one conjoint sin – embarrassing the order of things.

So Leslie would pull me into a common flame, and in a city which operates on the most principled prosecutors' axiom – get one wrongdoer in the crosshairs and a chain reaction of incriminations true or false can detonate outward through the fabric, destroying as it goes – my homosexuality neither criminal nor relevant was nevertheless excitingly destructive. At least it was a fact. But by an important secondary rule of the game, at least one such falsehood should ignite. And in an atmosphere so intensely charged now with stigma and counter-stigma, there was a ghastly logic to an imputation of antisemitism. The first I heard of it was when I was helping out in Governor Connally's ill-fated presidential candidacy, more or less on behalf of Paul Nitze, as we saw earlier. I saw the campaign against me after that as just a general part of the obstacle course to office in the forthcoming conservative administration, or so it seemed at the time. However frequently used, this was a really vile lying tactic, and how do I know? Because some of my best Jewish friends are Jewish. I set out on my first two trips to Europe with Jewish friends – as I in time found them to be – and sought out other Jewish Americans in schools because they were so often the people who were different, and I was fascinated above all by difference. It is true that on occasion I disagreed with the tactics of some Jewish friends in office, including on matters involving Israeli interests; but such disagreements were just that, a matter of tactics.

The deep lesson to be derived from both outcries, is that a nigger can't be an accuser. Lawry Chickering, a good friend close to us both, warned me presciently that if Les and I didn't come to terms it would destroy both of us. Indeed Ed Luttwak, who had planned a huge gathering of kindred spirits about this time to honor my departure from government service, was lobbied so incessantly by Les's friends (and by Lawry, for the very different reason that so visible an event might push the temperature beyond the boiling point) to drop the party, lest it destroy neo-conservative harmony in Washington, that cancel it he finally did (but characteristically held a dinner in my honor at a superb Italian restaurant for twenty of the most distinguished of the guests).

Such was the background noise of my life for several years, but there was a foreground as well. I recall some time at the start of this interminable tumult seeing a stress chart, in *Newsweek*, as I remember, which posited a sound barrier of about three hundred points of emotional and external crisis. Rate over one hundred, you were in pretty bad shape; over two hundred you were surely already in a strait jacket. Death of a parent, divorce, major illness, change of job, each of these was fifty points or so. I had them all, I had many more, three hundred and counting. As I reread the diaries of this period, I understand a little clearer why I didn't make more of my life than I did. Stress showed itself in nightmares, burst out of guns literally at my head, snarled letters from lawyers tearing at my simplest paternity, and showed up in a dozen score of revolts of a body even more shaken than the spirit it carried. Oddly enough, most of the time, I hadn't even conceded that I was going through a trauma. It was to get worse.

> As each day spreads out a new low, a new bottom in my exterior life, I grab harder for something inside. I then find – or rationalize – that some of the exterior losses aren't so bad. I take comfort from some of what I have . . . But I don't yet find the inner strength. It's as if I have to fall yet lower, fully expunge my ego, arrogance, so that I can do something about the other side of the coin, the low self-esteem . . .
>
> . . . Obviously all the props [of the past] stood in the way . . . [but] they were sought precisely to prevent that self-confrontation – the farm, the mansion, the whole works. It's as if I have to lose everything, literally everything, before I can, must, face myself. I hope I can stop half way . . . (Diary 2 April 1985).

At that point, however, as 1984 moved into 1985, consistency required that I live a straight life and put aside temptation to the contrary – and put down rumours as to my sexuality. Of course there is disingenuousness in insisting on your heterosexuality when you are increasingly aware of your gay side, but society allows no in-betweens; and if doubts persist you must persist.

My problem in Washington was the enmity of one great man. Outside the beltway, Paul Nitze was never well-known, maybe breaking the barriers a little in his eighth and ninth decades with the 'walk in the woods'. Inside it, the higher up one got the more deeply he was admired, feared, and chronicled; his chairmanship of the group that authored the critical strategic document NSC–68 in 1950 alone entitles him to an important place in history. The 'silver fox', as *Time* called him, had been around a long time, had allies throughout the bureaucracies of Washington as well as on its social ramparts, and at all times commanded respect. He had been passed over so many times for the highest posts, the posts on the nation's lips, for which he was at least as well qualified as the ultimate recipients, that he rightly took his position very seriously and did not take slights lightly. Indeed the persistence with which he had sought the brass ring, over a generation, and failed to get it, is notable. As it happened I came into the Nitze outer circles just after he was once again passed over for a cabinet job, this time Secretary of Defense, leading his wife to give him two white canaries whose chirping, alas, continually reminded the family of the humiliation.

For Paul good taste was a weapon, a glittering shield, that protected him when he was out of office. Having a Monet, after all, was worth a bit of deference from the more exalted. And indeed, if he seemed when out of power a bit ghostly in his air of confidence, it was because he seemed the same when in power; he evened things out with his air of confidence in permanent power.

My naiveté about Paul knew no bounds. When I first saw a divorce lawyer I told him how sometimes Paul forgot his daughter's name, how I had worked closely with him professionally,[4] and that we saw each other often socially as family members. I added that he sympathized with my family position after all – had been son-in-law to the awesomely rich and influential former Congresswoman Ruth Baker Pratt . . . But of course I hadn't told him my deeply held secret, the enormous implications of which it took me five years to ingest, that Paul Nitze and I had something far more basic in common, as we soon see. I was afraid if I said anything the gods would reach down from Olympus to strike me dead: but so long as I kept silent, he'd basically leave me unharmed. My lawyer said, 'You'd better run for cover. He'll be playing catch-up ball.'

The lawyer was right. The minute Nina said 'divorce' Paul drew the line and cut off all contact, making clear to all our mutual friends that they could not be friends of his *and* mine; in retrospect, reasonable enough, if not the way I would have proceeded. At the time I had no place to go, since Nina was refusing to sign the contract on my town house, but eventually she relented and an angel in the form of a realtor lent me a little house on 16th Street to live in until I settled on 1729 Q Street, a ruin of a townhouse but ready for restoration to the Victorian glory in which the famous architect Schneider had framed it.

Subsequently Paul coordinated very closely with Nina's divorce lawyers and was always at her side in court proceedings, finally coming to terms with her as she reached thirty-six – though hardly even then coming to understand her. This was penance, from the man who once told me that her only problem was being a product of only one parent. Now I began to hear echoes of his unmistakable gracenotes catching the right ear along the corridors of power. I feared that if he succeeded I would never get another position in Washington. My friend Ann Kovacovich Bingaman, now the very famous Assistant Attorney General for antitrust, a one-time girlfriend and classmate who had become an immensely successful lawyer, provided me with her partner Joe Onek, who did some investigation and advised me to sue Nitze for a substantial sum. He prepared impressive papers to that end.

Nina's father was worried enough to go big-time; I had hit a raw nerve. His habitual lawyers at Covington and Burling (indeed Dan Gribbon, a senior partner) got nowhere trying to twist the *Post*'s arm out of commissioning a series about my lawsuit against Paul. So he went to his old friend Edward Bennett Williams, possibly the most famous practicing attorney in the world at the time. I again had confidence, because I knew Williams slightly, since we worked out at the Metropolitan Club gym side-by-side from time to time, and he had seemed friendly enough.

That briefly worked in my favour. As I was to learn over and over, big people, serious people, didn't engage in fag-baiting, nor did they encourage vendettas against anyone, especially parents of one's children, as a useful foreign policy. Williams went down to Onek's office, itself quiet remarkable, and suggested a settlement, one in which all the claims would be rolled up in one renegotiated contract. This in itself was an enormous victory, if we could just get it to paper. Williams said that it was beneath the Nitze family's dignity to be going after me, and he was advising them to stop the nonsense and make a once-and-for-all decent settlement.[5]

Williams was also lawyer to the *Washington Post*, and I had reason to think that he was thus aware that Sally Quinn, the wife of the paper's then legendary editor Ben Bradlee, had already interviewed me twice for a series on my proposed lawsuit. Sally, a brilliant and tough journalist-novelist, was just waiting for me to press charges formally before striking. Williams may well have presumed that such a story in itself was not good for a rich family like the Nitzes, who always shied away from publicity, and that this series in particular might, as Seymour Hersh, that remarkable tunneler, put it, have weighed much in my favor. Sy, who had his own sources at the *Post*, told me *en passant* that I was going to be rich, for whatever that was worth – but I couldn't stop thinking about his last words, 'Boy do you have some powerful enemies.' Looking back, the threatened lawsuit concentrated their minds – but Sally's prospective series in the *Post* galvanized them.

But when William's advice got back to Boston, Nina's lawyers stonewalled. The deal was off, we were back to their one-way war. And the reason wasn't money; clearly, it was that they wanted to destroy my credibility, since I simply knew too much about them – from a rich and telling family tradition on how to deal with income taxes to chronicles of sexual deviation up and down the family tree, which had got fuller as we spoke. The war, they had obviously concluded, was well within their dignity. Any more money paid to me toward a fair settlement would be, they feared, just a war chest which I would use against them, and they were now holding the keys to something I wanted badly and so they could get away with this too. That was to link their position to the modest, but meaningful, presidential appointment, for me to be on a new presidential commission, which part-time appointment was pending. I do not know how they found this out (though such prior knowledge was typical); perhaps one of Paul's protégés was now at the White House. But as a result they were able to offer a green light for me to go to confirmation in exchange for my libel suit.

In this case, I was only too happy to trade a bird in the hand, which would bring modest and partial political redemption and perhaps even some income, for the two in the far distant bush, which I could only reach through searing litigation. And thus far litigation had been the most stressful experience of my life. How they did this in practical terms I do not know: the way things happen in Washington is usually mysterious, though inevitably it involves the tacit trade of favors. The head of presidential personnel bawled me out for being so stupid as to have taken on Paul Nitze. 'Don't you know how this town works?' he asked.

Paul was developing an additional reason for his undertakings. The year Nina and I married and settled down, I got to know Paul's beloved friend Sidney 'Spiv' Spivack, who died of cancer not long afterward, his devoted roommate in early 1930s New York. Indeed on my way down to my wedding I stopped in Far Hills to spend the night with Spiv and Dot, herself daughter of the legendary billionaire financier Clarence Dillon (through whom Paul got his financial start) and sister to the former Treasury Secretary Douglas Dillon. Aside from numerous and splendid gifts to all the Nitzes and a Ben Shahn lithograph for me, Spiv gave me lots and lots of advice. He had spied into my soul and understood my story better than I realized, in fact better than I did. He assured me I could stay the course amid so much ambiguity: after all, Paul Nitze had prospered doing so in like manner in far stricter times. Spiv had figured out that I was gay.

It took me years to unravel Spiv's history and advice, and then to put them back together. In the first place, Spiv was, despite his late marriage, gay, and unambiguously (if not openly) so; he was also schizophrenic. He and Paul had long been roommates in New York before Paul's marriage. It was the style of the time to cover up even an openly gay man's sexual orientation, as Edward 'Freddy' Warburg does half a century later in his remarkable privately published biography of Spiv – turning two nubile naval ensigns whom Spiv brought to the Nitze residence during World War II (and about whom both Spiv and Paul had separately told me) into women, for example, in contradiction to what even Paul himself had admitted to me, and through which I have a detailed description of them. Paul did not fill in any details for me about his own behavior, but made clear that Spiv at least had a roaring good time on the third floor of the Cleveland Park house with the gorgeous young men.[6]

Paul had a terrible problem when he met Phyllis Pratt, a Standard Oil heiress who fell instantly in love with this very handsome and otherwise eligible young man. For an ambitious fellow in New York, this was nirvana; Phyllis was to have trusts worth $6 million at twenty-one, but that was just the start. Her mother, moreover, had been a Congresswoman for the Silk Stocking District and was infinitely well-connected, including to the President of the United States, who once came to dinner at her Fifth Avenue mansion when Paul and Phyllis were present. But Paul was, as Phyllis was wont to tell intimates to the horror of children and friends, impotent with women (though 'not impotent' Spiv assured me, significantly), and thus had to turn down her much advertised proposal of marriage; he wasn't the marrying type. But she assured him all would be well in due course if he married her, which is the way it turned out. And since Paul worked for Clarence Dillon whose daughter was Phyllis's close friend – and Dillon had to take the wider interests of the fatherless Phyllis into account – Paul was under even greater pressure to go along with Phyllis Pratt's suit. And since Spiv smuggled himself onto their ocean liner so that he could be with them in Europe for their honeymoon, we see his continued interest in Paul's development.

Of course from all that a rather banal suspicion arises, but in fact it was Phyllis Nitze herself, fifty years later, who articulated the by now fairly obvious missing point of this book which took me so long to grasp, when she accused her younger daughter of 'driving Scott to homosexuality . . . whereas she herself had *saved* Paul from homosexuality' – a charge I am happy to absolve my former wife from, though *mutatis mutandis* I cannot logically say the same, or at least cannot say it to the same extent, for the elder generation. For I do not believe one can be 'saved' from homosexuality, in any event. But surely this explains much of the underlying rage and war in the tale, and makes the Nitzes, for me at least, far more sympathetic. Specifically, Paul emotionally couldn't deal with my being gay, while professionally he dealt with it only too deftly. The more I thought about it the more I realized that it was his latent homosexuality, largely suppressed from the time he so advantageously committed himself to Phyllis Pratt, that was the underlying force driving this war, and that the real divorce going on was between him and me.

The issue was not that I was gay as such (he dealt with gay family members, after all, as a matter of course, with courtesy and duty, as long as they were not open about it), but that I had acted out what he had suppressed in large measure throughout his adult life, at least after 1932. Whether Paul acted out his homosexuality after 1932 is largely speculative. He was known never to have had affairs with women, for obvious reasons. Given his wealth, charm, and drive, it is hard to believe he didn't avail himself of opportunities with men, for example when he was living in London during World War II for a long period. In addition, Nitze was perennially attached, sometimes passionately, to the causes of a sequence of fairly young, tall government officials, all men. His attraction to young men – for example all my friends in Washington, whom he generously included in the Nitze circle, and even backed financially at times – now was obvious to me, and they were always of a type. In his dotage he fell prey to a much-married far younger woman precisely because he had to prove his masculinity all over, and in the minds of some, was being driven to death by her incessant demands with which he was only too quick to comply.[7] By one report she bragged one night of his tennis game that day – passing over lightly that it led to a heart attack.

As Paul was eventually able to learn, I prepared a paper for delivery to several fora of psychiatrists and psychohistorians, a psychohistory of his life, the basis of a larger biography forthcoming. The essential part is the link that became obvious between Paul's impotence with women in his twenties and his need to press for big missiles on America's part for the duration of his career – along with his denial that we ever had enough, that ours ever counted, and that we could ever stand up to the Soviets. Whence of course his central participation in the creation of the infamous 'Missile Gap Crisis' of 1960, which Kennedy was happy enough to forget once it had done its work and he was installed in the White House, but of which Paul continued to believe a version.[8] As late as 1983, when Richard Perle had brilliantly and courageously stood by the 'zero option' position, by which neither side was to have any intermediate missiles in Europe, Nitze was saying (as we have seen), and, extraordinarily, being quoted in the press as saying, that this position was not realistic, that we could not counter their already installed missiles with the threat of our undeployed missiles, in other words undercutting our own position.

In fact of course Nitze on this as on so much in this arena, turned out to be wrong (and, to his humiliation, a far younger – and Jewish – official was vindicated). Historically no one turned out to be more off in his assessment of the Soviets overall than Nitze – indeed he wanted them in the 1980s to remain in power, ironically perhaps to avoid the awful judgment of history on himself. 'Good God!' he would say. 'The worst possible thing would be the end of the Soviet Union. Then you'd have total anarchy.' And of course, in some senses he is turning out to be right, if not relevantly to

American interests. But that his angst over his own missiles and his continuing concern for the nation's were connected can only be denied with blatant ignorance of the connection between the psyche and one's politics.

The bottom line is that homosexuality was a very bad issue within the Nitze household, especially ironic given the disproportion of gay people among the 'G' branch of (the maternal) Pratt family. One was categorized among the Pratts by one's distance from the family founder, Charles Pratt, first president of Standard Oil. His children were A through H. Phyllis Pratt Nitze was G-4 (the fourth child of G), whereas I was G-4-4-S, or sire of the fourth child of the fourth child of G. Not only were there one or two gays in the immediate Nitze family, but next thereto: Uncle Robert Thayer (G-2-S) openly scoffed at his two gay sons, one of whom grew up in the Nitze household, throughout their lives. And then papa took on, in his late seventies and after the death of his wife, Phyllis Nitze's sister, a young male lover, a charming Australian artist, to whom he willed his chateau near Beaune – where Nina and I had spent much time, and to which I alone was able in due course to go back, with, triumphantly, a male lover.

Sexuality ought never to have entered into any of Nina's and my legal problems. Nina and I were divorced, period; the reasons were no one's business. But social attitudes prevailing made a person going through a sexual identity crisis a sitting duck for anyone who wished to fire at him. At a higher level the war waged between Paul and me had significance for my whole being. It was a titanic struggle between my two sides, that represented by my late father, an altruistic and idealistic educator and a conscientious objector who never saved a cent and often did give people in need the shirt off his back; and my celebrated father-in-law Shadow, who acquired not only a fortune but a network of powerful people to do his bidding, yet who for all his brilliance and successes always lacked the courage to be his true self – whether by resigning from government when he differed from it on issues of principle, by letting those around him be themselves in an atmosphere of respect, or most importantly, dealing with his suppressed inner self honestly and coming to terms with the conflicts that had driven him throughout his life. Many though his accomplishments were, they did not bring him the satisfaction to which the less driven world watching him thought him entitled, because there were always the vaulting expectations: to redeem himself in the closed eyes of the father he had let down; the failed statesman he felt himself every four years when he wasn't appointed secretary of state; and the failed man he has been throughout his life in his own eyes – so unsparing of others – because he did not act out his true soul. For in all events and even for such two-dimensional giants as Paul Nitze, there takes root and flourishes no ending and adequate self-esteem; what must do duty instead is an endless series of transient self-confirmations, cast on the clouds of passing events, and dissipating with them. Enormous were his professional achievements: but somehow they never knit the great metallic career into a green life.

Small wonder that the splendid little novel Kaguro Ishiguro's *The Remains of the Day*, chronicling one man's discovery that his life-long duty left a wasted shell, so touched Nitze that he sent several dozen copies to friends. And small wonder that he was both admired and criticized for his frostiness and disdain; what better protection for a man scared that he would be discovered? His most revealing comment to me was during the Carter inaugural, when Mr and Mrs Vance were staying at his house; Nina and I thus stayed with Chet and Saone Crocker, but picked up Paul and Phyllis to go to one of the inaugural parties. Paul went on at some length about how stressful and painful executive office was for Cy, given his back problems, as compared with his more leisurely and remunerative law practice in New York. I asked then why did he take the job of Secretary of State? And Paul replied that he'd never known anybody 'in this game' to leave it of his own volition, that is to say no upper-echelon player would ever leave the perks and gratification of (external) office. As it happened, it was precisely Cyrus Vance who resigned three years later over an issue of principle, the use of force in the Persian desert.

This interim was one of continuing warfare between me on the one hand and Nina and Ruth-Arlene Howe on the other. Thus spring vacation 1985, with the children, then receiving a threatening letter from Howe's lawyer, on the assumption that, if they couldn't in the short term prevent me from having the children, they could at least try to make my life miserable while I was with them. But then at other times my resilient spirits would bounce back, especially when visits with the children went particularly well, as increasingly they were doing. I also, with the immense enthusiasm of the children driving me, expanded our living quarters: first by adding decks up the back of my Victorian townhouse and on its roof, where I experimented with my new love of gardens. And secondly by acquiring a Virginia farm, on the way to the Blue Ridge, which was the opposite of every residence they were accustomed to: informal, open, 'child-friendly'. We even got busy designing and having built a 'children's house' where they and their pets – Siamese cats and Irish Setters – had free rein.

But somehow as the pressure to come out built up, I developed as an argument for the defense the notion that life wouldn't change, that I could have it both ways, that I could square the circle. Possibly my denial was so great about what would happen that when the winds blew against me once again, the denial was ready and waiting. I was also building up my reserves.

## *Notes*

1. I was accused reportedly of anti-semitism precisely for referring to his card-file list of 'New York friends' – that being, I was told, a code-word for Jews; but it wasn't I who proposed use of the list. I was twice in his office when he so insisted.
2. Ernie Lefever had already lost confirmation as Assistant Secretary of State for Human Rights, but he at least had got to a full Senate; the Democrats wanted to knock an appointee out at committee level and had not yet succeeded.
3. See the thorough, indeed exhaustive, Senate examination of the whole affair: S381-26 *Nomination of Leslie Lenkowsky*, April 5, 11, May 9, 15, 1984. 98-2. Y4.F76/2L S, hrg 98-960. MC 85-2584. LC 85-601035. Lenkowsky, a person of enormous resourcefulness, resurrected himself within a few years, turning up as head of the Hudson Institute.
4. I edited a volume, a sort of geopolitical lightship for the Reagan campaign, entitled *From Weakness to Strength: National Strategy for the 1980s*, of which Nitze was a leading co-author, though in fact I wrote over half of his essay. I also played amanuensis and sometimes silent co-author in various of his essays of the late 1970s, when his time was tight but the need for his crisp logic was everywhere; see for example 'Deterring our Deterrent', *Foreign Policy*, vol. 25 (winter 1976–7), pp. 195–210, my expansion of a

simple brilliant oral outline given at his Maryland farm. Much of his substantive argumentation was, of course, taken from T. K. Jones's brilliant Boeing studies of the strategic balance, still largely unpublished, other than under Nitze's authorship, as it were. See for example, 'Assuring strategic stability in an era of detente', *Foreign Affairs*, vol. 54 (January 1976), pp. 207–32.

5. Williams' biographer, Evan Thomas, has a completely different version of these events. But the inaccuracy is given away by the fact that it refers to a lawsuit by a son-in-law claiming damages for 'alienation of affection' in 'breaking up the marriage of [Nitze's] daughter', and says that Covington and Burling urged Nitze to settle while Williams with phone call caused the lawsuit to vanish. The lawsuit was for slander, and the position of the law firms was in reverse, as the record shows. One suspects that Williams gave out his version in confusion with another case, and in any event as a very minor matter indeed. See Evan Thomas, *The Man to See: Edward Bennett Williams, Ultimate Insider, Legend, Trial Lawyer*. (New York: Simon & Schuster, 1991), p. 383. In correspondence, Thomas accepted the corrections.
6. Edward Warburg, *Spiv*, private publication.
7. Including a $2.6 million Kalorama mansion with all new furnishings, jewelry incessantly, and lavish trips and vacations. Her new swimming pool even required special District permission. See Stephanie Mansfield, 'At 87, an old flame burns bright', *Washington Post*, 13 June 1994, for a devastating portrait of Paul and Leezee's marriage – the sort of publicity Phyllis Nitze spent her life avoiding, and the trap by which Leezee thought she would vindicate herself.
8. His line to me was always that, although the estimates on which the missile gap was derived turned out to be in error, in fact the more important part of the estimates, on tactical missilery, were even worse than that at the strategic level. The evidence is simply not there to sustain his position.

# *Part Two*
# *Resolution*

Chapter six

# *Coming Out*

***But the infinitude of love, or its egoism, brings it about that the people whom we love are those whose intellectual and moral physiognomy is least objectively defined in our eyes; we alter them incessantly to suit our desires and fears, we do not separate them from ourselves, they are simply a vast, vague arena in which to exteriorise our emotions.***

● The Fugitive

BY the middle of 1985 the pressures were becoming unbearable. 'Sally', my fiancée, a beautiful widow in the media with two young children, was writing longer and longer letters urging why our relationship had to work, would work, if only, if only . . . and increasingly I knew it couldn't work and wouldn't work. My actions were loud enough but my words were insufficient. I could not bring myself to break it off when it seemed to mean so much to her, when I cared so much about her, when she was so stunning a person – and, I suppose, when the relationship was so convenient to me – a calculus deadly similar to so many gay men's in marriage. But I kept being haunted by Jim Woolsey's question to me at BWI airport the previous Christmas, as we packaged our respective children off on vacations: none of these reasons mattered – was I in love with her?

I knew the answer. For other things were happening, crowding such psychic room as I had available to give scope to love, for it is the practical possibilities of loving which determine its reality, however unquenched the will and energy to give love in general. How often had I faced this in the past. My diary wearily recalls how

> The value of the currency of acceptance outside has declined dramatically, and the value of that of internal acceptance has increased even more so. The desire thence to be held, to hold, to be loved, to love . . . has become almost an absolute, an absolute like that of getting married, having children seventeen years ago. (2 April, 1985)

In September I went as usual to the annual meeting of the International Institute for Strategic Studies, held that year at the Hotel Intercontinental in downtown, still-divided, Berlin. The whole experience of that city of edges and extremes at this stage of my life was as briefly mind-bending as to Isherwood, Spender and Auden in the 1920s; it was Cabaret, it was Weimar, it was the Kurfürstendamstrasse, and above all, it was the Dahlem, where I saw for the third time – but first since I had bothered to prepare my mind and spirit for what my eyes offered – the world's most evenly high-quality collection of paintings. When I saw the Saint Sebastian of Botticelli, so tellingly undervalued a work, something almost burst out of me. The shimmering sensuality of the almost naked Roman soldier, its mindful sensuousness nevertheless harmonizing with the beatific expression on the exquisite face, began to unveil something very basic about the very structure of my feelings. I paced the eight kilometres back to Berlin as if on a cloud; and just before reaching the hotel encountered a group of beautiful young men coming out of what, on consideration, seemed to be a gay sauna.

To go in or not to go in? Good God, the proprieties! What was I contemplating in my respectability? My former student Rick Burt was actually the American ambassador in this country and I had just visited his Berlin abode the night before. It was one thing to come out to an EST seminar, another to affirm it almost publicly at a bathhouse next door to a gathering of my peers. But I recalled Sainte-Beuve's comment that some people's clocks stop at a certain point in their life and, resolved that I wouldn't be one of them, but traumatized, I said it was now or never. Shaking all over, fearing the entire world was watching, I entered while looking over my shoulder. My anxiety luckily was busted by amusement – at Germanic thoroughness: firstly, the concierge handing out condoms on entry, several years before such was common at home; secondly, these forever disciplined Germans carrying bottled hospital soap around with them. Thirdly, it seemed as if Hitler had won the war; these blond and muscular boys and men were the epitome, the caricature were they not so beautiful, of our image of young Nazi manhood, the youngsters singing in *Cabaret*. I was well taken care of by two of these alternately, and then luckily met a somewhat less compulsive but equally gorgeous Cuban-French dancer who took me off to his cubicle and assured me that I would make it in the gay world, though averred that I'd do better when I calmed down, and not by just a little bit. But we spent most of the night together and I hoped I would see him again.

I returned to Fletcher, which I was now back at full-time, commuting from Washington, trying to keep steady a world which had been thrown even more off balance. I was reeling from the changes that had assaulted me, and more importantly, that I had summoned up from within. It was hard enough to admit the defeat of returning to the campus before conquering the capital, although there were many reasons at that point for making a virtue of necessity, not the least that it enabled at least weekly visits with my children, in addition to the monthly ones they made to Washington; I had seen my youngest child Heidi so little in her early years that I really owed it to her to be at her side as she grew up. And like most third children, she welcomed the chance to dine with a parent alone, as we did every Tuesday evening for four years after her older brother and sister left for boarding school. I note too that my first divorce therapist, Justin Frank, had told me I should return to Fletcher just for the sake of my children. I thought this was daft in 1982 when I was riding high but at least I took him seriously; I am fortunate that events, and my better instincts, ultimately drove me back.

Nor did my external world calm down. I had another quick trip, to the Austrian countryside, for a conference organized by the writer John Marks and 'Search for Common Ground', his path-breaking institution that exists to bring contrary types together, in this case Sandinistas and Americans. They simply hadn't bothered to invite anyone representing the Reagan administration until the last minute, typical of the liberal dispensation, but I was delighted to go and make the acquaintance, so shortly before his death in his nineties, of Carl Rogers, founder of the Rogerian school of psychology, and with whom I had a spiritual time and brief correspondence thereafter. This kind of experience, however, made me think disparate types *could* work together, and by now that meant gays and straights. I all but came out at the final quite emotional plenary; for me it would have been gratuitous and intrusive but not out of the spirit of the occasion or of Rogerian psychology. And everyone had figured it out in any case, I learned later.

At this point, I needed only one more Berlin-like epiphany, but one that denial couldn't put aside on return to reality. No sooner was I back from Austria than I had to turn around and go to Turkey for a NATO-sponsored conference on the Bosporus. There I met a sophisticated Capitol Hill professional with whom I seemed to have a lot in common; we both hung around the hotel's massage and steam rooms, though nothing was said. But he looked at me knowingly. At dinner he mentioned that he knew the same doctor I was using, who had a largely gay practice in my (largely gay) neighborhood. We talked about AIDS ('SIDA', since we were speaking in French with our Turkish table-mates). I was sure Bob was gay, but I had never before carried through such an identification by medical allusion.

Our Turkish hosts then bore us off to Izmir to see the NATO base, and the glorious Greek ruins, most sensationally at Ephesus, misty Stanford memories became miraculously stone. After the first night's dinner Bob suggested, I thought with a certain street-smart look, a walk along the seafront. We said little. The moon was full and my spine tingling at the possibility of danger and excitement. We saw two young men, of perfect bearing, wearing Turkish Air Force insignia. Bob motioned for me to open a conversation. One was Bulent, very tall and gangly, the other Adnan, shorter but six feet, with the most perfect body surely since Praxiteles' models of the fourth century BC (who may after all have been his ancestors), with a countenance to match. Bob flicked out a coin, and motioned for me to choose head or tails. I didn't even have to ask: we were gambling for Adnan, but in fact for much more. I lost, but now I knew my destiny. Not inappropriately, I had planned to read Somerset Maugham's *Of Human Bondage* for the evening. At this point I would have much rather done that than come out by way of Bulent; fate had closed in on me and there was no going back. We all returned to my hotel room for beers and cokes. I explained to Adnan and Bulent how and whom we had chosen, emphasizing we each adored both of them. 'Mais Scott', cried Adnan, 'Je t'aime . . . et Bulent, il aime Bob . . . ' Well, you couldn't fight 'love', and Bob knew when he was beaten. There was a special fairness to it; Bob was leaving the next day, I had another four days, and it seemed reasonable that in the circumstances I should have the living Greek statue for my coming out.

And come out I did. Adnan stayed with me each night, and if our linguistic skills sometimes faltered, he rapidly taught me different but still communicative skills in which I was plainly inexperienced. What this young man wanting me did for my self-esteem in four days and nights would have taken years of psychotherapy.

From the novel I drafted too close to the middle of its own action, but which at least caught the emotions engulfing me:

> Eric was overwhelmed. It was all a joke. How had ['Bob'] known he had wanted it . . . Known what? Did he want it, would he admit to himself he had been a liar for how many years? No, damn it, he wasn't a liar. He had been what he was then, he would now be what he had become. And he had shifted gears into full rebellion. How better to show his contempt for the whole corrupt, rotten system . . . than to stand up and rebel . . . All the roads behind him were closed. Only honesty was left, honesty to himself, of himself.
>
> Why had this most gorgeous of boys . . . wanted him?
>
> It didn't matter. Six times during the night [the Turk] crawled back on top of Eric and taught him yet new, ever more wonderful things. Why had he wasted all those years, he had found what he wanted, and for the next six days [their] bodies were entwined.
>
> Eric returned to America and sent Helga a letter and a present. She deserved better, he wasn't available, and it was over. Like a mantis praying or a crab crawling sideways, Eric phoned in an ad to the *Boston Phoenix* and placed an ad for a

housemate, starting with the initials GWM ISO GM – 'Gay White Man in search of Gay man' – 22–35. 'Must be loving, sharing. Am interested and interesting. Come live in my lonely house in the Southend. Open your heart to me.' Eric was now *contra mundum*.

I would be gay, I would be honest, I must throw caution to the winds; because I *was* gay, I had found something truly beautiful in the brief affection between Adnan and me. I arrived home and mustered myself to write Sally that she deserved something better, that I couldn't give her what she wanted and that we must both move on with our lives. When I didn't hear back I knew that she understood.

In the same period I wrote:

> Oddly just as everything in the literal sense is falling apart . . . I feel more comfortable about everything especially myself. Obviously the one key area of self-deception hindered the development of a feeling of self-esteem throughout my being. I no longer feel (or at least think I will come not to feel) the need to be discovered, the need to be understood: I would give less away because I am surer of it. (Diary, 6 November 1984)

More accurately, of course, life was finally coming together; I was still at that point insisting on seeing the world through the mainstream eyes.

At least my actions were honest. Fatefully, on my return home I placed my first ad in the gay community's weekly, the *Washington Blade*. A young physician responded: our first visit was three hours of talk: I fell so devastatingly in love that I determined to subordinate everything else until this man was safely part of my life. It was not indeed to be the most prudent of moves – but quite possibly at that stage if any psychopath within my template of visual acceptability had ventured in I would have fallen in love. As it happened Jeff was smart, fairly tall, attractive, and obsessed by control. He knew what he wanted, which was to go up in the world, and I knew what I wanted, which was him. I invited him to one of my periodic chamber concerts at my house, scheduled for November, but it was Christmas before our busy schedules permitted a real live date, and it was early January before we become completely intimate, the interval of most exquisite pain and anticipation of my life, as I waited for him.

Meantime I came out to my friends. As most gay men find out, for real friends it's either no surprise, or a big relief to discover a great cause of anxiety in a friend, though in my case they all cautioned me as to the political effects. Only one friend took it hard, as if I were not only throwing away my career (as all agreed) but surrendering to all the mighty evil forces I had withstood hitherto. And admitting 'they' had been right about me. I wrote him asking what my successes thus far had added up to in my 'fifteen minutes'. 'It repositions me, perhaps, for a sub-cabinet position – but with the same anxieties, neuroses, hates, and uncontrolled passions. With the difference that now one could make bigger mistakes, perhaps hurting more people.'

> What I now know life is about is simply, and only, emotional growth, which I see as a progressive freeing of oneself from his ego: call it developing a relationship with God, a Higher Power, or just taming one's soul, it's the same. Most of the pain of my life is post-1982 – hence most of the growth as well. . . . [but] whatever, I will need my real friends more than ever, though less now for my own *internal* survival – since that is where I have performed major constructive surgery – than to help me protect myself and my children from the effects of what will certainly look to many as destructive external surgery.

People's feelings about their friends' transitions are of course proportional to the extent they can identify with them: and in this case, I believe my correspondent's undisguised pain at my coming out expressed an anxiety much closer to home.

But everyone warned me, over and over, don't do it even if it is psychologically right; you'll lose everything, there will be no more political career, everything will go up in smoke. But I felt that everything had gone up in smoke anyway. There was nothing left to burn. In the ashes were some glowing embers of the real me.

There was, for all the joy I felt in coming out, a heavy shadow over it. I knew no one with AIDS but had discussed numerous theories about it with physicians, psychiatrists, and clinicians. I had met Dr Caesar Caceres at the house of the enigmatic, somewhat sinister lobbyist, Craig Spence, at whose parties one met cabinet members and ambassadors. He eventually destroyed himself with drugs under the relentless homophobic persecution of the *Washington Times*. Caceres advanced the thesis that AIDS didn't really exist; it was just NIH types hyping old sicknesses to get new research funds. It was just gay men with a bad lifestyle dying of other things. I wasn't convinced, but at least it was a ray of hope for some. So as I prepared to come out I went to his offices, only several houses down from my own, for an HIV test, which had only just then become available. Life had been so lousy for so long that surely it would make little difference how the test came out, and it was the proper thing to do, before hopping into bed with people. But I was scared, precisely because everything *had* been going so badly. Immediately before going to get the results I lunched with Sid Blumenthal, about the smartest student of American politics and now the *New Yorker*'s Washington voice, who noticed I was upset about something, and wished me well as I went off to the clinic.[1] There was no doubt that this remarkable judge of character knew what was on my mind, since he knew just where I was coming from.

And indeed there it was; Caceres gave me the HIV 'positive' results with a whimsical chuckle, telling me not to worry, there was no such thing as AIDS, and to come to see him often – one paid (and one paid generously) at the door as one entered; a decade later he was singing the same song. It didn't occur to me to have a second test or other opinion. In a sense I felt liberated; the end crowns the effect. The fit outcome of this interminable ordeal was to be not redemption but death; the test of the whole struggle would prove to be given by how I faced a powerless end to which I had not been able to impart significant form; let us consult what reinforcement we may gain from hope. If not, what resolution from despair. I at least knew how I was going to die. It is the kind of certainty that is valuable in hard times, though in this case the certainty was a special, sealing part of the hard times.

My attitude toward my HIV status, like so much, found its expression in Proust.

> The happy years are the lost, the wasted years, one must wait for suffering before one can work. And then the idea of the preliminary suffering becomes associated with the idea of work and one is afraid of each new literary undertaking because one thinks of the pain one will first have to endure in order to imagine it. And once one understands that suffering is the best thing that one can hope to encounter in life, one thinks without terror, and almost as of a deliverance, of death.

I had numerous necrofantasies, planning my funeral, especially the music thereat, and imagined a modest version of a pre-funeral like Charles V's, one that I could enjoy, at which the Monteverdi Marian Vespers would be performed and all my friends could join me in a celebration of life made the richer by its impending termination. I wasn't concerned with death as such but rather how I would live with – and deal with – my friends as I declined.

In those days, there was no hope of a cure for AIDS – no AZT or anything else – but on the other hand it was also thought that only about half of those infected would go the whole deadly route. So I hardly thought it fanciful, given my vigor and energy, to hope that I would be among the survivors. I took to sleeping longer, eating better, and all the other steps that seemed to separate victims from potential survivors. There was much evidence, though, of Yourcenar's truth: 'Suffering turns us into egotists, for it absorbs us so completely; it is later in the form of memory, that it teaches us compassion.'[2] I doubt I was the easiest person to be with in those days, as I lulled myself to sleep nightly with false data and desperate hope.

One early spring day, a year and a half later, I saw an NIH ad in the *Washington Blade* to test Interferon therapy on HIV+ men in excellent health. Having recently run a marathon in just over three hours, I guessed that I fitted the bill. The only downside was that those not on placebos were going to endure much nausea, and I didn't like the thought of spending summer being sick. But it offered a hope, and at that point I was ready to try anything.

Several weeks later, however, I got a message from the nurse at NIH who had processed all my papers and drawn blood several times, that Dr Fauci himself wanted to talk to me. My knees started shaking. It could only be bad news. I couldn't reach him before having to leave for New York. I spent that evening at a dinner given by two wonderful Thai diplomatic friends, seated next to Peggy (Mrs David) Rockefeller. Dredging my mind for all the good and happy things I could come up with to talk about, I landed on Sotheby's, where I had that day managed to buy a substantial wooden fifteenth-century statue of Saint Sebastian, whom gay men like to consider their patron saint. After dinner David Rockefeller joined us to tell of his bidding for a Vuillard, that same day – at a level just two orders of magnitude higher. It was the same process, and the same appreciation, an invigorating conversation that got me through the evening.

Back in Washington, I shakily tried the NIH again, only to get the great man directly on the line. 'Professor Thompson', Dr Fauci said in his crisp, no-nonsense voice, 'I have to disqualify you for the test.' Bad news, all right. My heart sank right through the floor. 'You're not HIV+, so we can't use you . . . we ran the tests three ways twice.'

'You can't do this to me, Dr Fauci. It's my only hope. I've run a marathon recently . . . I'm . . . '

'Professor Thompson, you're not listening to me . . . You're *not* HIV positive . . . and that's why we can't use you.'

Caceres had run a bad test, and now I no longer knew how I was going to die. I walked into the spring sunshine reeling with anxiety and giddiness at the same time. My immediate appointment was lunch at the Metropolitan Club with that man of extraordinary charm, wit, and probity, Ambassador Kim Kyong-won, whom I had known since his days in Seoul as National Security Adviser to President Park. But I scarcely thought a Korean diplomat could quite understand what I had just gone through, and I sat glassy-eyed throughout listening to his brilliant exegesis and prognosis of the riots just then tearing his country apart – and, in the vent, putting it back together in far better form. Just like me. The news around me was forever a metaphor of my soul.

Meantime I was discovering other costs of being gay. I was encountering – and we must consider – the 'flakiness' of gay men, something much derided, particularly among gay men, before people of the straight world can comprehend the rest of my tale. The issue is a serious one: I long for the certainty of my straight days, when, at least, if you invited someone to dinner and he accepted, you could take it pretty much for granted that he would show up. Recently I gave a noon luncheon party at my farm: eleven guests accepted, all senior professional gay men of Washington. One called at noon to say his friend wasn't coming because he had a business appointment and my friend didn't wish to make the hour's trip alone, but *might* come (but wouldn't advise me) and of course didn't; our friend with whom he was supposed to come of course didn't call me to say he wasn't coming. But he came another time and told me he had been there before – as the accomplice of an ex-lover who was reportedly investigating the farm for stealables. Another very senior official of a major Washington institution didn't come (and didn't tell me) because his young lover wanted some help moving. Another couple arrived at three for a noon invitation – a good example of Gay Time. When I returned to Washington, a person whom I was supposed to meet failed to show up at all.

Then there is the amusing issue of how gay people present themselves, especially through third-party mechanisms. Many gay men use ads in the gay press (and other city newspapers) to seek partners; so do straights but nowhere near as much or so exclusively. I have done so and have had a man correctly describe himself as 'cute' and '26', but leave off the minor and sad detail, with which one was otherwise bound to be sympathetic, that he was paraplegic. Routinely gay men meet through an ad, make love, insist they will soon be back in touch, and never talk again. Or they leave mid-way through an assignation; an ex-lover of mine was stood up at the ballet during intermission. Another blind date drove fifty miles to look over someone and, finding him, apparently, wanting, said he had to finish parking his car and left. Gay mores and *politesse* barely exist among singles, since there are literally no traditions or institutions of society that apply to them – it is they, *contra mundum*. A Washington lawyer came out to my farm and wanted to be tied up and whipped, and then, not surprisingly, was embarrassed at pressing so much so soon; and ultimately left in a whine. Sometimes the ads work (I met my two longest-time lovers through ads); but I am appalled at how many lies seem to be told in getting there. Gay men don't think seriously enough about what is involved in sexual contact even in the days of AIDS – nor of the eventual costs of dishonesty which always catch up.

More serious is the moral issue, that verges so often on sociopathology. In the straight world, in the circles in which I had always moved, there was a presumption that if someone told you something he was up to, it might even be true and generally was. In equivalent gay circles, life isn't so simple. When devastated by a breakup and by the incessant lies I had been told about Jeff's absences, and fearing the worst regarding his accumulation of expensive paintings, rugs and toys, I visited my friends Dahlia and Edward Luttwak, the great student of strategy and military history; Edward, who grew up in Sicily and knows about such things in people, made the startling observation that gays feel they have to lie to protect their identity in the straight world, especially on the job and not just in the military, but then must erect strong barriers between that compartment of their lives and all the others, where truth is appropriate. Many do not make those barriers very high. I regret the continual pillage of my house by guests at parties, who from time to time have helped themselves to small antiquities, pen sets, pieces of silver, ultimately making me hide much stuff whenever I entertain on a large scale. One day I was having a chamber concert at my Washington house and my lover of longest duration asked me, with respect to a professional associate attending, would I please not reveal that it was I who had bought our new house at Rehoboth Beach, indeed that I was even involved in the purchase. I said, with heavy sarcasm, 'I suppose she thinks this too is your house', which we had also bought with my money. 'As a matter of fact, she does . . . I have always lied, I will always lie, and I am proud to lie.'

We remember the Houyhnhnms in *Gulliver's Travels*, who have no word for lies, and refer to them as 'the thing that is not', just as Cardinal Newman does. Lies have lives of their own; the gay world shimmers with falsehoods. In the gay world promiscuity is rife and everyone is ready to protect everyone else. Lies float around. And Sissela Bok reminds us in her excellent book that there are few circumstances where, in any ordered moral logic, we are entitled to lie.[3]

Of course sometimes the impulsion to lie is professional necessity; Paul Monette, in *Borrowed Time*, his moving account of his lover's death from AIDS, writes of lying about the illness almost *en passant*; 'in fact we couldn't tell anyone, for as soon as word got out, Roger would lose his practice. AIDS was that extreme a stigma. The losing of jobs was a foregone conclusion, since everyone knew or at least assumed that once the secret was out, Roger would have to quit his job as everyone else to that point had had to do.'

The film *Philadelphia* revolves around that premise, where the protagonist, played by Tom Hanks, is in fact fired, of course on a trumped-up charge. At other times it is from the stigma with which one is confronted; J.R. Ackerley, in his splendid memoir *My Father and Myself*, tells how he 'disliked lying', though 'got used to it now in the course of years', and once had a chance to come clean with his father about his sexuality. But the latter had asked him if the Maharajah, a principal of his book *Hindoo Holiday*, were 'a bugger'. 'I was romantic about homosexuality then, "bugger" was a coarse, rude, objectionable word I did not care for and never used, except as a joke. I could not allow it to be applied to myself or my friends. I said no, and closed the door on him.'[4]

There may well be a biological explanation for gay promiscuity and the tolerance gay circles show for it among their friends in relationships. And that is that gay relationships are men–men, without the yin–yang of male–female, without the still greater solidarity of women–women relationships, the least promiscuous of all. Men are, after all, the biologically aggressive sex thanks to hormones, enzymes, and neurotransmitters; the more susceptible to abuse of drugs and alcohol, the ones who enjoy fighting and competing.[5] It is in the male nature to go out and find new conquests, and men do. In other words it's pig–pig. Given the relatively small percentage of gay men actually in monogamous relationships, which is itself partly a function of the lack of institutional support in our world, there is insufficient structure to restrain men in relationships, little incentive for them to settle down. And if AIDS is certainly a danger, pregnancy is not.

But wait! There *is* a reason for gay flakiness. It is not the gayness that explains the sociopathology, it is who has a stake in the system. My experience around marginal straight people is quite the same. I prefer a person to tell the truth, but I hardly give a rich mountebank moral credit as such for telling the truth when the whole system works for him and rewards him for telling the truth. There is seldom such a reward for the gay man to tell the truth. The parallel is to the gypsy. In the film *King of the Gypsies* it is made explicit that gypsy children are taught to steal and we watch them do so, including one who swallows a huge diamond in a ritzy jewlry store – and then expels it back home to the amusement of the doting family. For gypsies are not only at society's margins, like gays, they have institutionalized their marginality and have made a virtue of necessity.

Edward Luttwak on another occasion provided further explanation of the gay propensity. Like members of some ethnic minorities when they are still discriminated against, they take invitations – and the demands of proper behavior – lightly with respect to their own we-group. These people don't matter, after all, in their own estimation. Invite them to a proper Wasp function: and they'll be on time and quick with a thank-you note. The suggestion offers a little solace at least. As, one might add, Dr Johnson's observation that the Scots are a fair people: 'They never speak well of one another.'

When we can marry, when we are rewarded by merit on the job even when we're openly gay, when we have as much a stake in society as straights, does anyone seriously think gays will behave, morally, substantially differently in these areas from straights? It reminds one of the 'black' issue; long ago one heard of 'CPT', or Colored People's Time, meaning they were always late; and why not, given that it wasn't their system! Literally the same can be said of the high incidence of black crime; African-Americans in the same socio-economic strata as whites have crime levels roughly the same. And I might note than in all my sexual comings and goingswith men over eight years, no black man ever 'ripped me off', but numerous white ones did. When I bring a street person home for a meal and a good night's sleep, he has absolutely no incentive to respect my home and property unless he wishes to be invited back. But he usually does have some values, which come quickly to the surface as he fights with himself whether to rip me off. Few do. A person with a job downtown, with a stake in society, would never even consider taking something from my shelves. He has far too much involvement in the system even to consider it; the issue of morality would only arise at a far higher level of temptation. But this illustration makes a very important point.

The point about marriage is of particular importance. I note a substantial and significant difference between gay men in stable relationships and single men – far greater than the range between the similar straight comparison. Because 'married' gays quickly find both the road to fulfillment as well as solace for past pains in their homosexuality, their behavior swiftly comes to resemble their counterparts; they become reliable, they tend not to steal, and their word becomes good. The single gay, however, is not in a comparable position with his straight counterpart; he has no assurance that he will or can find what he wants or that if he finds it he, or they, can have it, given societal attitudes and constraints. The stable married ones, after all, are the small percentage that found a way and made it stick. So the single man soon sees himself as a law unto himself and acts accordingly. The best thing our society could do for the gay world would simply be to legalize relationships as one form of marriage, whatever one wishes to term it: all those straight people claiming to have problems about homosexual behavior would soon have no basis for complaint, I am sure.

There are amusing consequences, of course, to being on the sidelines, as a man coming out, formerly at the center, surely will see himself. Andrew Harvey, the now celebrated Anglo-Indian mystic, says his homosexuality 'gave me a very acid understanding of the hypocrisy of those in power . . . I think it made me a spy very early on.'[6] A friend since Oxford days, Georgetown's man of letters Timothy Dickinson, said I had previously existed as a sketch of myself, a blueprint, rather than a whole person; something, he knew not what, was missing, back then, until he saw me at the somewhat infamous Craig Spence's Kalorama house among gay and straight men in the early 1980s. As I came out, in other words, I could begin to supply from within those parts of myself that would fill out the blueprint.

There was another dimension to it, one Jim and Sue Woolsey referred to in their affectionate inscription to a six-volume biography of Disraeli, presented to me on my fortieth birthday, in which they expressed their 'conviction in the positive effect, in the long run, of [my] *heilige Unruhe*'. That 'unruly spirit' or sacred discontent might have survived within me in a wholly accepting society, but my guess is that it was a direct function of the suppression of my gay side.

There is another side oft-times to the gay man which showed up over and over in me, in parallel to the *heilige Unruhe* – the two sides of the personality reflected in one's chosen associates, the successes, the superego reflections; and on the other hand, Jung's 'shadow' or other side, usually being represented by those on the margin. My choice of ushers at my wedding gives sufficient indication of the public success and present distinction from the first category, a promise that all wore plainly while still in their twenties: Jim Woolsey; Peter Magowan; Bob Legvold, the distinguished former head of the Harriman Institute at Columbia; the Rev. Marston Price, a prominent Episcopalian priest; Maynard Toll; Jonathan Small, partner of a major New York law firm; Jim Wood, Caracas business executive; Bill Butler, the well-known environmental lawyer; Lawrence Chickering, founder of a very influential San Francisco think tank; Dr Ken Nies, my brother-in-law and sometime professor of medicine at UCLA; and Tom Cotton, Stanford PhD and Rhodes Scholar and the only one with whom I have fallen out of touch.

But I always also walked at risk to my safety on the other side of the street; seeking Proust's 'intoxication of danger' – it was a way of linking myself to an unknown sexuality, to the danger it presented to my ambition, to my desire to tempt the universe – to be found out as *whatever* I was. Being found out is the most certain and economical form of declaration. But it was also a means of testing things, a symptom of guilt; it was a stimulant, but also an instrument of bewildered enquiry; and it was something to make the world more real as its instability made it seem less and less so. A

Rasputinesque student at Stanford, one Mike Bell, whispered of murders committed in Texas and emotionally seduced several of us into believing, briefly, that we were under his power. During *coups d'état* in Africa, as later in the Philippines, I pressed terribly near the fire, literally in one case risking my life to liberate government documents from conflagration, as officials of the collapsing regime sought to immolate the more entertaining records of their endeavours on which I partly built my PhD and shared them with several other scholars. On such passions is learning built. In every city I have sought out the poor – and usually dangerous – section, to see what 'they' live like – courting destruction, admittedly in running shoes, with which I have so far always been able to outrun external trouble. The one time I was mugged – cutting across an unusually dangerous zone of Central Park at night – I was in coat, tie, and leather shoes. As long as I suppressed my basic sexuality, I was ever searching for a dark side outside me, in fascination and to distract myself from a discovery of my real self.

When I found my sexuality, these tenebrous fascinations wouldn't leave, but only changed their form. Camille Paglia says that 'Male homosexuality, pushing outward into risky alien territory, is progressive and, overall, intellectually stimulating.'[7] I should know. Proust wrote of homosexuality's levelling effect: 'for in this romantic, anachronistic life the ambassador is a bosom friend of the felon, the prince, with a certain independence of action with which his aristocratic breeding has furnished him, and which the trembling little cit would lack, on leaving the duchess's party goes off to confer in private with the hooligan . . . '.

I had other shorter visits on the dark side. Concerned in the plight of the homeless, I was bewildered that our rich society could have created – and tolerated – the phenomenon (for example by redefining mental illness so that the institutions were depopulated whereupon the streets filled up). But my Good Samaritanism was usually self-serving, since I brought home only the good-looking young male waifs. Invariably they purported to want to go clean, needed just a good bed, a little money, and were willing to give, if not real affection, what seemed real appreciation. Maybe I lost in the trade, at least at market prices. But something in me wanted this, and maybe it did a little good.

I had to take a number of tenants to court because they abused my indulgence on rent or everything else – one indigent family for virtually an entire year owing to my unwillingness to toss out a young couple with a baby; and of course I lost there too because the destitute have no assets to attach. True, some of this continued, for the first prolonged time in my life, my father's passion and lifelong work for the underdog; it also showed up simply in wanting friendships with groups marginal in status, minorities like Jews – from among whom came so many of my friends – or African-Americans, groups that had a bondedness in their marginality which I admired, and which the gay world has not learned how to duplicate in kind (except to cover lies of someone in the closet).

Jeff, my first lover, who had fallen into my life upon my return from Izmir, turned out to be a sociopath – at least so diagnosed by a psychiatrist we consulted, though a medical specialist himself in one of the highest professions. While I tempted fate, he flung himself at it. For three years I was held in thrall by what he would attempt – and invariably get away with, both in playing with other human beings' lives and in defying ordinary and basic laws of society. I was after all frantically searching for the ideal love both to make up for twenty years in the desert and to compensate for my more catastrophic recent losses; there is also the conceit of the man coming from the straight world – which shows so revealingly the belief in the gay world that anything over 'there' is superior to anything on the fringes – that he, the straight man, can have anything he wants out on the margins, given where he's coming from (as if that had anything to do with it!). This conceit of the power exercised and favor conferred by the real (straight, white, male, Christian, great-power, whatever) over the less real other is basically human. Perhaps humanity is among other things about the dissolution of this idea in itself.

We were at different stages, alas. He was in academic medicine but wasn't suited for it, and his restlessness affected every dimension of our life together. Though we had committed ourselves to fidelity, Jeff could conduct several sexual affairs at once, right under my nose in our house, taking a frightening pleasure in exploiting the knowledge that most people are truthful and faithful. He needed lots of people over whom he could establish control: and throughout these years the moment I had gone to Boston, he would have 'young things' to the house, some of whom were employees considering themselves sexually harassed; invariably failing to tell them he was in a relationship, and then usually succeeding in inducing them into what could only be called plumbing exercises; I know because at the end a self-actuated tape recorder furnished a gruesome record. And throughout the next year as I dated potential replacements I had the eventually amusing experience over and over of learning that my date, or dinner guest, had already been to my house and knew his way to the master bedroom: 'did you buy this from a doctor?' they would ask.

He would 'obtain' vast quantities of material goods, convincing me until near the end that they were spin-offs of medical favors or the like. If I'd gone on believing for another month I could have believed in beards and reindeer for the rest of my life. The auctions which we attended, which for me were my only opportunity to buy antiques and paintings of the quality to which I was accustomed at prices I could occasionally afford, were just covers for him to infiltrate the back rooms while I paid for my goods up front. A psychologist friend said he must surely have been horribly hurt as a child, enough to propel him into Emergency Medicine, where he could have the gratification of sewing people up at the same speed as he tore them apart, as indeed he did.

On the legal front much worse was happening. I was finally taking advice from several lawyers as to how to protect myself from the world's crushing down should my lover be caught by one of the taunts to fate whose iridescent, shifty intensities he substituted for a life of growth, a life of the emotions, and a life of the mind.

Well, we put on a good show. We entertained frequently, with my old china and our new Baccarat or Venetian crystal bought together in Europe. We had intimate and precious times in Italy sipping espresso in ancient unchronicled little villages, and planned to get rich together, using my small capital to build a real estate empire. I felt as had Henry Kissinger toward the Soviets; I would use these entanglements to web him in so he couldn't get out, and would never want to. And like Kissinger, I was betrayed by the splendors of my vision as much as by my *vis-à-vis*.

I was out, I had come out, but by my choice of lover I had chained myself to an emotional roller-coaster for three and a half years, that postponed any serious work, or any serious effort to understand my gayness and to develop my life in the gay community. I lived in the unreasonable anticipation that one more house bought in both our names from my funds, yet one more trip to Europe to visit my friends usually on my tickets, one more season of being together eliciting the possibilities of our gardens and houses, would bring about some common emotional growth. It was never to be. He was a Richard the Third in a perpetual season of discontent, in his own eyes crippled not bodily but sexually, inflaming him to prove himself superior to mere domestic love in the name of unanswerable power. What mattered the joys of our life together if he could have it and undercut it both?

So of course the relationship blew up as painfully as my marriage – indeed more so, since the divorce from Nina was, as I had come to realize, an inescapable part of my karma. I had decided to get off the train when he withdrew a pain-killing prescription from a friend for the crime of not inviting him to a dinner party: the friend had to fly crosscountry with his back in agony. So the break with my lover was something my mind knew had to happen, but nowhere in accord with my heart's play. I set a trap: one time too many he accused me of paranoia in suspecting infidelity, so like Hamlet I summoned players, in this case in the film *Gaslight*. When Ingrid Bergman began to turn literally sick from her husband's absurdly manufactured accusations, Jeff got nauseous, turned off the television, threw out the videotape, and stormed off to bed. So I made the breakup happen just as I had with the previous divorce; on 18 December 1988, I gave him a written ultimatum to clean up or get out. Of course he left, to the universal hurrahs and toasts of my friends, but I, at first jubilant, once again echoed Marguerite Duras's 'lover', facing 'the desert that would be the rest of my life'. It took all of a day, however, to begin to face forward, if painfully, to look for successors; I quickly found at least temporary sustenance, never to beg that man's favor again.

But it wasn't over. Once it had all come apart – when the evidence of sociopathy was too overwhelming for me and his own triumphant high too far up to coast him back to earth – he did something so fascinatingly evil that I gave into it. Of the four houses I had bought in both our names with money made in the stock market – notably from a shortsale killing on 1987's Black Monday, and in previous real estate deals – he now wanted the greater part, though he had put up only trivial equity.

I was then up at the White House for reappointment to the board of the United States Institute of Peace, an increasingly visible organization with whose foundation I had something to do. He simply pointed out that if any of the places he had looted caught him, he'd make restitution and in all likelihood they'd be satisfied (as proved to be the case when in April 1989 I forced him to return some things – fine nineteenth-century paintings, old Persian rugs – I could positively identify to a Virginian auction house). Whereas for me, I had riding an appointment worth surely a hundred thousand dollars in fees and far more in honors. Were he to tell the White House that I had lifted some of the loot, I might disprove it ('Do you beat your wife?') but that just wouldn't matter; such fellowship with wrong-doing would sink me instantly into the frozen hell of those who cannot judge their associates.

In a prodigious leap of self-revelation he presumed that the typewriter I had borrowed from the Institute (to edit its first book) was stolen, so he took it as additional leverage, but acknowledged the deed on an answering tape datable by the inaugural activity it described, thus producing not leverage on me but evidence of theft from the government on his part.

Of course I should have gone straight to the police now that I had his own admission, but my devastation at love lost fused with the incarnate evil of his mindbreaking game to down me, just as he knew it would – after obtaining a few concessions. I gave him the two houses he demanded. The day I called him to account for only some of his behavior I was so manic and fearful that all I could do was cruise for tricks and have sex off and on around the clock. And of course I had had a powerful lesson about love, having projected in my mind what Jeff was from my desires and not the reality, having called into being a Jeff of my needs and desires – and, dare I say, my ideals? – a beautiful Pygmalion, not the uncultured, often mean and always heartless raw force which did exist. Proust said it so well:

> That Albertine was scarcely more than a silhouette, all that had been superimposed upon her being, of my own invention, to such an extent when we love does the contribution that we ourselves make outweigh – even in terms of quantity alone – those that come to us from the beloved object. And this is true of loves that have been realized in actuality.[8]

His problems were compounded by homosexuality, as with almost every gay man I know. He had a lively circle of gay medical friends, but was not out with his family or at work. Answering the phone in the middle of the night to find his mother on the line seeking medical advice, I instinctively said, 'oh, he's right here.' He almost hit me – and indeed his mother, much later, confessed that from that moment she knew her son was gay. His problem was anger, anger that he had grown up bright, ambitious, aware how others lived, in lower-middle class circumstances almost stultifying to his real capacities, his probing spirit, rage at his sexuality, fury at everything that held him back; but then he was angry lest the results of his own anger, which he vented upon everybody in his path and which deeply affected everyone's perception of him. But since, as with so many physicians, 'all the world's a nurse', there was no one whom he could hear to tell him so. The period from our breakup until the following fall, nine racking months in all, witnessed some of the most spectacular fights ever (and equally spectacular make-ups, usually in bed), as I began to reassert myself and as he began to realize how much he had thrown away.

But those who substitute rage and flight disguised as aggression for self-knowledge are chained to a chronic round of repetition. His subsequent lover, Mike Bucci, had identical complaints after two years, though he hadn't had the leverage of capital and trust funds to head off the most cyclonic of the doctor's temper tantrums. But he was able to give me pictures he had taken of various objects that he knew our mutual friend had removed from my property (among others) after we broke up, including a bronze Italian statue that had been cemented to a pillar in my Tuscan-style garden. They had fittingly hidden it in a closet whenever friends of mine came to the house off Dupont Circle I had given to him in our 'settlement'. So now, several years later, I told him that, at least for a moment, there was only one sour subject that still had to be raised, and that was the statue. He told me I was materialistic, he'd already denied he had the statue, so why was I spoiling a dinner? I took the picture out, and in the middle of the sentence he switched voice and accused me of greed: 'I'm going to make you take it back this evening.' But when I told a psychiatrist friend of the incident later that night, he said it was a perfect illustration of the 'fallback phenomenon' in sociopathology. After all, if explanation the first isn't true, why not have explanation the second on hand just in case the first fails – and how curious that the lawyers have the same technique, but call it alternative pleadings.

Though my lover's problems transcended homosexuality, the root problem was with his denial and cover-up of his sexuality, which became the pattern for all his other behavior. How much denial was he practicing? 'Enough to power Chernobyl', but of course it was unconscious; 'that's why it's called denial', Paul Monette so usefully puts it.

There was also the difference that Nina and I grew apart over many years and indeed started with the difference my bisexuality endowed me with; my relationship with Jeff blew up almost overnight with a violence such that no one experiencing it could ever be the same: one had to grow an alternative aspect, not to pretend to heal the unhealable wound (or, to follow Fitzgerald, the emotional amputation). Finding the one he loves so powerfully in the grip of vices and others whose existence he had barely suspected is another step in that long journey of discovering the twisted world's insubstantiality which is part of the journey of life. A character in *Mark Rutherford* never gets over it when she read in Swift that 'happiness is a perpetual state of being well deceived'. One only gets over it by reconstructing happiness.

And of course I ultimately had to ask myself what else the two traumas had in common. Although from the point of view of the heart I was in opposite positions – Nina's love for me was purer than my love for her, while mine for Jeff was purer than his – the two relationships had in common the impossibility of intimacy. Nina's distance, played through her Germanic character or class distinctions, had the same effect as Jeff's grinding millstone heart, for he was equally threatened by the traumatic notion of someone finding out who and what the real person inside was. I was also in the middle of the trio in personal power; Nina liked her dependency, until in divorce it was an embarrassment that had to be alchemized into crippling advantage won by others: whereas Jeff visited his 'power', which meant my will to submit, in rage, abuse and bullying. But I in the middle had chosen two people with whom I could not expand our shared space.

The one area where I was fairly advantaged compared to so many gay men of this period was on the job. Tufts University's faculty's vigorous tone has long been set by a provost, Sol Gittleman, to whom my homosexuality was so little a threat that he could send me fliers coming his way on new gay literature – and took the time to do so. I returned to Fletcher in 1985 just as the weakest dean in its history, a Boston Brahmin, was resigning in odd circumstances. For over a year, the acting dean, the late John Roche, was a homophobic colleague whose malice I chose simply to ride out; he went after me on enough grounds as not to make gayness particularly special. In the summer of 1986 there arrived a tough new dean on the scene, a lawyer and former Ford Foundation official in Africa. He paid courtesy calls on all of us in our offices (an old trick I'd used to good effect in the government). When he came to mine I casually mentioned that, as he probably knew, I was gay; he said, equally casually, that he couldn't care less; which meant, I was soon to learn, that he *did* care, in the vital sense, of ensuring that the frontiers of civil liberties weren't neglected at Fletcher. Although my social life was in Washington, I never hesitated to 'intrude' my gay friends into my Fletcher life where relevant.

My problems on the job were at two levels and always manageable. Literally the only open hostility I ever experienced in eight years was from another gay man, an advisee coming out, who needed a scapegoat for the sense of guilt he was mastering very unimpressively. That aside, an administrator, at least mildy homophobic, denied me access to the guest suite in the student dorm when I didn't wish to drive many miles home on bad nights or was working late, on the transparent grounds that such proximity of (gay) faculty and students was inappropriate. And when I remonstrated with the model of Oxford, where faculty residence in the colleges is considered highly desirable (and has gone on for over seven centuries) she replied, 'That's precisely what we *don't* want here.' This usual happy crossroads of student-faculty interchange was blocked out of blatant prejudice. She took subsequent steps to obstruct further avenues of contact with students, but always in ways difficult to protest; in fact, not even worth protesting, because so routine in most of society.

There was a problem at a more structural level, still harder to pinpoint but so general throughout society. I had stated openly that I was gay on return to the school and took at face value the general assertions that such wouldn't matter. Slowly I realized how much people gossiped behind my back about how odd this was. It went beyond gossip. I got called on the carpet once for doing yoga and meditating in my office, because a cleaning woman had walked in on me and *she* was embarrassed – but I was the culprit; anyone living my level of stress needed outlets and maybe straight teachers do not so avail themselves. If they did, I wondered, would the whole administration of a school bring itself to bear on the errant contemplator, as it did in its entirety this time? Then, I again got called on the carpet because one of my advisees said that, although I gave her excellent advice, my posture suffered while advising, and she doubted I was paying full attention – this at a graduate school. Her presumed wounded narcissism at my lack of erotic interest in her has parallels throughout gaydom. Ultimately I had to tell my administration colleagues that as much as I appreciated their theoretical support, they still didn't 'get it'. The precise parallel is to civil rights in the Kennedy administration. One recalls the famous encounter between the Attorney General with black leaders at his New York apartment, where the former was overwhelmed by the sudden realization that the clichés and rhetoric the administration had bestowed on the black movement were gratuitous; action was in order. I minded far less the obvious absence of promotions and other such recognition that were so routine before I came out (because this is everywhere and routinely the price of coming out) than the attentive prurience by those purporting to be my friends.

Coming out had been a necessary, but not a sufficient, response to my problems. My life had been centered, even if falsely and to my real self untrue. Now, like any man who comes out, it had lost this carefully contrived center of gravity, wherein the centrifugal and centripetal forces were roughly in balance. I might well become a far more integrated man – but not for a while. Even while tied up by burglars – and thus for once with the time to think – I had an idea of where life was going. Now however I was on a very slippery slide, one which had started very high up, but down which I had already progressed a fair way. Having reached a new level or self-honesty, what was my alternative? Not to have proceeded, even down this scary slope, would have been more destabilizing: let us say one would have frozen, there on top of the mountain, rather than encountering mogul after mogul skiing down the mountain, including some that caused some painful spills. I often thought of my children's term for a crash on Aspen's slopes – 'Wipe out!' – but the metaphor was now rather more encompassing.

The extent to which the man coming out is upended can hardly be overstated. His life's values, the institutions to which he has been bound, the course on which he has long been set, everything, suddenly, is up for grabs. One looks at himself and says, well, I still eat Special K at breakfast, I still run, I still function normally as a mammal, I can still reason these things out intellectually. In fact that person might as well be thinking these thoughts in the eye of a great snow storm, which is where he is. He confirms his rationality as he skis over a precipice. Reason is what you do with what you see. It doesn't necessarily give you a new pair of eyes.

In my case I had a wall – four stories thereof in a Victorian townhouse – to pound on at all hours of day and night, at least until my neighbors complained at my using a sledge hammer at three a.m. A useful index of return to health: when I moved into my townhouse in the fall of 1982, I was averaging two hours of sleep. A chart on an old wall showed me back to my ordinary six hours the fall of 1985, having advanced by an almost methodical quarter hour every two months. Still laboring under my HIV diagnosis, I was medically recommended to sleep eight hours instead of the five I had so far achieved, and began to take sleeping pills. The house was progressing at about the same pace that I was, and by this time looked quite presentable – not that I had ever hesitated to entertain there on small or large scale.

About this time my close friend and legal adviser, John Milstein, recommended me for a post in these terms:

> I treat the next period delicately. Scotty by 1984, just as he had found his high ground, felt the need to bring his heart into relation with his senses . . . as his otherwise fabled and extraordinarily lucky marriage careened on the mid-life crisis of the two partners. All of his friends warned him that the change he contemplated would destroy his career. He made it clear that, now that he was in full knowledge of himself, his own honesty and decency were of far greater consequence than his career, and he set out on a new path with courage – almost alone, largely giving up the wealth, great house, and jet-setting life he had enjoyed for fifteen years. Characteristically . . . he largely put aside the fights over the division of marital assets in order to gain joint custody of his children; indeed I calculated at the time that he would have had an additional half a million dollars in the deal had he permitted his wife sole custody . . . on a shoestring budget, he put together two gracious houses where students, colleagues, and friends gathered for brain-storming or celebrating the good life.

So we lose our center in coming out, the illusory center which church, school, family, and societal values have geometrized us towards for our lifetime bearings. Even in the smoothest of transitions, gay men sail near shipwreck from these inner storms. Hitherto we have lived dual lives, accepting 'their' values while knowing they do not relate to our essence. Only with difficulty do we find a program for living that squares this unforgiving perfect circle. Now we proclaim that we will live by *our* inner dictates, our *prime* dictates, and expect miracles overnight, as if a lifetime of Pavlovian conditioning to outer stimuli will disappear, as if we can construct a program for living without all the familiar markings, way stations, and rules to which we are long accustomed. And in this we gay people are again a beacon of our society, the quintessence of a civilization that itself has lost its bearings and moorings, and is trying to find new values and structures that restore its meaning.

And just as 'pop culture was homosexualized' in America, 'it was only logical that the political culture would follow suit'.[9] And so too, the 'homosexualization' of America's healing culture.

But perhaps the ultimate commentary of this remains that I had mixed feelings even about discovering I would live, when Dr Fauci gave me the stupendous news. Whereas Paul Monette, in his memoir of his lover's death (*Borrowed Time*) goes on at length about the immense anxiety they lived under for several years, before tests were available, wondering if they carried the virus and would die from it – and then of the horror upon his lover's all too real diagnosis at about the same time I had my phony one. What a reflection of the false Eden gay men had lived in for several years! In that same period my life had been such hell, that my HIV+ diagnosis was a partial release. When Dr Fauci subsequently sentenced me to life I wondered if I could stand it; it took another few years to regain my taste for it and the *joie de vivre* for which I had always been known.

But what were the alternatives to working through these problems? On Erik Erikson's death one was reminded anew of the importance of identity and centeredness – the word he used so memorably on Thomas Jefferson. Can one imagine a closeted homosexual as centered? Isn't a false identity the opposite of being centered?

## Notes

1. We had become acquainted when he did a full-page profile of me in 1981 for the *Boston Globe*. See 'Portrait of a Defense Intellectual', 8 February 1981.
2. Marguerite Yourcenar, *Alexis*, trans. Walter Kaiser (New York: Farrer, Straus & Firoux, 1986), p. 48.
3. Sissela Bok, *Lying: Moral Choice in Public and Private Life* (New York: Pantheon Books, 1978).
4. J. R. Ackerley, *My Father and Myself* (New York: Poseidon Press, 1986), p. 147.
5. James Q. Wilson, *The Moral Sense*, chapter 8, 'Gender' (New York: Free Press, 1993).
6. Laura Leivick, 'The merry mystic', *New York Times Magazine*, 3 October 1993, p. 36.

7. Camille Paglia, *Sexual Personae* (York University Press, 1990), p. 24.
8. *Within a Budding Grove*, pp. 917–18.
9. Frank Rich, 'The Gay Decades', *Esquire*, November 1987, p. 92.

Chapter seven

# *Making Peace: The President Appoints a Gay*

*. . . the true paradises are the paradises that we have lost.*

● Time Regained

I was always on the lookout for redemption of my political ambition. More urgently, 1985 found me looking for a way to come out of the closet without losing access to the children. Had it not been for Nina's court challenges and her family's shadow war on my reputation, I would have come out at this point or even earlier without fear of political repercussion. President Reagan himself was hardly hostile to gays; after all, he was from show business – and was, as Timothy Dickinson has put it, in the 'warrior-king' tradition which can afford to tolerate homosexuality.[1] And many of his wife's best friends seemed to be gay. Charlie Wick, my former boss at USIA, had told me that he didn't have a problem with my being gay if I was – this when Paul was lobbying him to fire me on these very grounds. It turned out to be the redeeming blossom on Charlie's barren stock. Moreover, in a move whose importance was little appreciated at the time (though without direct application to political appointments) the State Department earlier in 1985 had taken sexual orientation off its list of criteria in security and personnel investigations. I had noticed this first when, suddenly, the gumshoe boys interviewing me about my students were no longer asking indirect questions about lifestyle, 'odd' or 'off-the-wall' dress, gestures, and all the other little codes for gay. It followed that the White House needed better reason than was in sight not to do likewise.

Meantime I found both the symbolic token of redemption and, soon thereafter, the possibility of coming out with the word made flesh. This was (with respect to the former) through the passage of legislation for a 'United States Institute of Peace', the brainchild of Senator Jennings Randolph and a host of people who would bill themselves as the 'peace movement'. For which reason there was much opposition to the proposal from two constituencies – those usually most liberal institute heads or academics who feared the competition of a federally funded entity and who considered that conflict resolution research could easily be handled through existing channels, especially theirs; and conservatives, like President Reagan himself, who had said to someone that he didn't want to see a 'Jane Fonda Institute of Unilateral Disarmament' come out of his administration and was therefore sitting on the whole thing for a while.

A group of us thought it a canny piece of legislation, however, which could help some good causes. The communists – it is hard to remember that so recently they were still around – had corrupted the word 'peace' and turned it to world-wide propaganda use against us, to the point where it had become anathema in conservative circles even to refer to 'peace' as such. My thought was, we could repossess this noble word, precisely through the vehicle of this Peace Institute; I hadn't been the administration's chief of foreign propaganda for nothing.

I suggested to my Stanford fraternity brother and friend Bob Tuttle, Reagan's influential White House personnel director, that we could put together the bipartisan slate for the board that was statutorily required but which would have Jane Fonda's hair standing on end: starting with a stand-in for the Defense Secretary's position, Richard Perle, known in 'peace' circles as 'prince of darkness', and a Democrat at that. Richard is probably more responsible than anyone in America, other than Reagan, for dismantling the cold war.

Reagan bought our proposal. Our list included conservative Democrats like Evron Kirkpatrick, who long had run the American

Political Science Association but whose health was declining and had in any case in recent years been overshadowed by his wife Jeane; and old-line conservatives like Ambassador William Kintner, both of whom I had known for a long time – along with a number of distinguished younger folk. In the event Tuttle saved *me* from being knocked off the very list I had helped to contrive. Pat Buchanan, that hero of the gay world, had campaigned against me inside the White House, along with (more surprisingly) kindly, unassuming Bud McFarlane, National Security Adviser to the president, but Tuttle's support was powerful and prevailed. Besides smacking his lips over my rumoured homosexuality, Buchanan urged that I had 'left the reservation' over Lenkowsky's confirmation struggle. Freud would have found it interesting that Buchanan thought that his movement lived on a reservation, the contemptuous leavings of the wronged and defeated: this may explain his bluster more than any claim of patriotism.

But Buchanan's opposition was enough that Bob thought it apposite to call me in to the White House to read me the riot act. 'When the Board wants one thing and you want another, Scott . . . '

'I'll stay silent, Bob.'

'The hell you will. You'll stand up and join them and support them!'

I got the message, and was forever, I hope, a team player on the new board, what, forever? – Well, almost. And the real point is that conservatives for the first time in similar circumstances had beaten liberals to the crossroads of substance and propaganda in the search for peace.

There was only one hitch for me at this point, late 1985. Confirmation was taking a very long time. A friend at the White House tipped me off that there was trouble in the FBI investigation; I had had nightmares about that possibility for the half of my life that I'd been subject to security investigations, of the little men asking the wrong questions in Chestnut Hill or tracking gay cruising grounds. But at this point I just couldn't let it bother; I wanted the appointment but I was close enough, I knew down deep, to coming out – this is before I went to Turkey – that the issue was in the hands of the gods. I helped the gods out a little, however, giving the investigators a list of an additional thirty friends, including a number of women whom I knew well and some with whom I had had affairs relatively recently, and suggested they interview those in addition to the fifty or sixty on the list I had provided six months earlier.

I quickly saw the system at work: as soon as the gumshoe boys started their job, friends around the country called me to report on their conversations with them. Everyone wants credit for a favor, and some of these knew they were doing a big favor in stressing just how very straight I was. I knew there was going to be laughter with some and pained irony with others when I called them in a few months to say that I was, after all, gay. But the investigation underlines how much the world had changed – a silent preparation for the more public changes President Clinton would usher in. Five years earlier, even the questions the agents were asking would have disarmed some and cost me some of my friends. The Yahoo presence in public affairs is always enough to scare off the weak-hearted.

The next nine years were to provide the most exciting intellectual–political challenge I had ever had, but it wasn't all peace-making; it was something of an armed truce between us and the 'Peace Movement'. The Institute was controversial, but since it had money and the imprimatur of the US Government, indeed of the White House itself, I knew it would be less and less so as time went on if we spent the money wisely. It was a matter of standards, and I was the only teaching and tenured social scientist and student of conflict on the board; though our chairman, John Norton Moore, was a distinguished professor of law. I had a heavy responsibility or so I saw it. There were ideologues in our number who felt that since the big foundations had always rejected our (individual) submissions because we weren't of liberal persuasion, we should repay in kind.

Our chairman and I felt strongly that we simply had to fund the best efforts around and let the ideological chips fall where they may; otherwise, at the least, when the liberals got back into power they'd make the Institute over into their own image, without reservation, and cut us out far more than we could ever cut them out, since they had the media and the whole liberal establishment behind them. All our discussions were taped and transcribed, and the record shows that Congress not only never harassed us for obscure or misdirected 'pork barrel' grants, but substantially increased our budget in this financially constrained period.

More importantly, we wanted the institute to have an integrity apart from political persuasion, to stand on its own feet and to be looked to as a standard-bearer and benchmark for the best research and work on peace. So John Moore and I were allies in countering anything that smacked of ideological one-upmanship or retaliation. We sought to build firm and deep foundations for peace, to help educate America to the need for structures of peace, rather than the often illusory paper treaties as a substitute for peace.

So when the distinguished Yale political scientist Bruce Russett made a vicious ideological attack on our board at a conference in autumn 1986, saying he would never take money from such a reactionary lot, I was able to arise much more amused than hurt, to counter that hitherto he had always been far more empiricist than ideologue, and to challenge him to submit a grant proposal and see if we were prejudiced in one direction, as the foundations with which he had always dealt were in the other. He did so submit and we gave him a grant, as we did to numerous others of the received wisdom – when they came up with worthy proposals. Our offering and their accepting was also a way of indicating that the tide was running out for them.

Our first project, which I chaired, was to create an 'intellectual map' of peace, a project which allowed us to show our respect for the 'peace' movement while making the point that there were many roads to Rome. We held hearings in California, in Boston, and frequently in Washington. It led to the institute's first book, which has had some healthy influence.[2]

My appointment to the board in the fall of 1985 and its commencement of its work in early 1986 coincided with my coming out, as I foreshadowed above, by hooking up with my first lover. He had refused to live in my Dupont Circle house, on the grounds that it was too near his hospital – though after we broke up he subsequently moved into one nearby which I also owned, so I suspect it was the possibility of getting his name on a grander title that impelled him. Whatever, I was happy to accommodate and was led to a house on Rock Creek Park, of extraordinary architecture, with seven garden terraces and the great, tree-arched Broad Branch curving round the bottom of its hill. Alone of great capital cities, Washington permits professionals without great fortunes to live in fine houses with finer grounds, within minutes of the government's center. He found it, I bought it, but we both fell in love with it, and for three years it was itself a veritable actor in our life together.

At our first board luncheon I renewed my friendship with a new colleague Dr Dennis Bark, Senior Fellow of the Hoover Institution at Stanford, a classmate from days past and influential in conservative circles; and in the process I came out to him – not that he felt any problem, having gay friends from the San Francisco area. We were allies from then on, and I blithely assumed my other colleagues would be similarly relaxed.

In summer 1988 the issue of reappointments to the USIP board came up, since those with four-year terms – dating from well before we really got started – would be out in January 1989. There were four of us eligible for reappointment. The other three were Evron Kirkpatrick; Dennis Bark; and Allen Weinstein, president of the Center for Democracy. Then there was I – but when the list came out from the White House there were only three names.

I called our principled and distinguished board chairman and told him that I had had my fifteen minutes. I had accomplished with the intellectual map project much of what I had set out to do; it was the price I had to pay for being who I was. I would finish that project and then go quietly, but would be supportive of him and the rest of the board until my replacement was sworn in. I fail to understand why I was being so timid, given the changes taking place in Washington; it was surely the effect of being beaten down for so long on the issue of sexuality that it wasn't obvious I could start the fight of a lifetime.

John Norton Moore, who more than anyone deserves the credit for the institute's strong foundations and direction, is an international legal scholar with an awesome reputation for integrity wherever he goes. He was silent for a minute. I was sure he knew to what I was referring, though the issue had never come up between us. Then he said, 'Scott, you have to fight this. It will dog you the rest of your career if you don't. Besides, we need you . . . Call Morry and get advice.'

Morry was of course the incredible Morry Liebman of Chicago, fit holder of the Presidential Medal of Freedom and the instigator and guide of more good causes than anyone else. He was the heart of our board. Morry was pushing eighty at this time and looked dead-on for Yoda in *Return of the Jedi*. To sit with Morry at the Madison Hotel lounge was to have waiters bringing phones so that he could take calls from the deputy prime minister of Israel, to have the deputy attorney general stop by for a drink, and to have Henry Kissinger ask if he could call later for advice. I had known Morry for twenty years, for he played a role in all of the conservatively oriented, but broad-front constructed, national security organizations. No one knew how Morry kept track of all his commitments and honored them so meticulously, but he was surely our board hero, and I got on with him famously. My house is set deep in the woods and finding it stupefies all first-time visitors without neigborhood knowledge. At the first board dinner at my house – these were to become a regular feature – Morry's car was very late. He had everyone in stitches in his first toast – 'We've come, we've spent too much effort finding you and getting here, Scott, we're not leaving. We're staying for breakfast, lunch, and tomorrow's dinner too . . . '

Morry offered to provide me with his own advice, and to get one of his Washington lawyers for me on the best terms available. I knew even that would be far too expensive, so milked Morry of such advice as I could, which distilled into 'Wear them down.'

So I requested that the FBI explain just what was going on, and had two lengthy sessions with several of their agents. With extraordinary disingenuousness they replied that there were several unresolved issues obstructing my appointment – for example a $400+ bill owed to USIA from my days there four years earlier, the first I had heard of it. I gave them names of people who could account for the return of equipment and books allegedly kept by me after I had left, but in the end I simply said, let's get on with it, I'll pay. There was no evidence that I had ever been billed; in the new computer age, records survive to the next age or vanish at the press of a button. It was obvious that someone was getting full revenge for a bad Officer Evaluation Report or whatever; it didn't matter. In Washington government is king, and when the king asks for meat, you provide steak. I wrote a check.

It went on like this for several months; newer and ever sillier issues would crop up, I would settle them, and something else would take their place. Meantime the clock was running against my chances, as someone knew it would.

By chance I learned that anyone designated for a position but not subsequently cleared by the White House had the right to see the White House Counsel's office. I acted quickly – it was now October 1988 and Congress was about to adjourn, which would have killed my chances once and for all. I saw the deputy counsel, who had that Reagan-era Sunday-school-teacher appearance and dress, all moral and pedagogic in righteousness, more worthy of the Bush administration than great Ron's. We faced off in his West Wing office and sparred for half an hour through the sandstorm of vindictive trivia.

I finally put it to him. 'The real reason you are doing this to me is that I am gay, isn't it? Shouldn't we stop beating around the bush?'

'Well, I am glad to be candid about it. No, it's not. That's not allowed', he admitted and how right he was by this time, at least technically, as we have seen, from 1985. 'It's probity.'

We both were quiet for a minute. He had a real issue – and one that was murky, gray, and unanswerable. 'It's that you said you were *one* thing three years ago when this office investigated. Now you say you are *another* thing . . . Anyway, would you *really* want me to send *this* folder up to the hill?' He fingered an enormous file, obviously the FBI interview reports, as if it were Valjean's dossier.

By this time my guts had volatilized into hot steam, molten iron and red rage. 'Well', I said, trying to be relaxed, 'as far as the file goes I'm not going to pull your chestnuts out of the fire. The people on the hill who might find anything objectionable in it are *our* people. The other side, well, lots of the Democratic staffers are former students of mine and they'll find nothing surprising or objectionable. I think this would make an *excellent* public issue in fact, if it came out, say, in the *Post* or if I wrote it up for the *Atlantic Monthly*', in both of which I had published in times past. 'Now as for the probity issue, are you *aware* of human evolution? Are you *aware* that people evolve over time, that I went through a horrible divorce and over a period of several years determined that I was gay and would live that life openly and with dignity, unblackmailable by anybody? And your two investigations come on either side of that decision, which was the product of a thousand smaller decisions, and you want to stop me in my tracks because of this fortuitous and bad timing?'

He leaned back and folded his arms. 'Ah, yes, I see. Very convincing. You've *evolved in your sexuality*. I grasp it. I'll send the appointment up to the hill immediately . . . ' though the cynical might have suggested that this Christian servant of his republic took as his sign in the sky some vision of an *Atlantic* cover rather than any appeal to the works of Darwin.

'Everyone evolves, Sir – though yes, I certainly evolved', I said. The larger point is that America was evolving. This I thought self-righteous savant was prepared to change.

Came a funny aftershock. There were now four USIP board nominees, Congress would shortly adjourn, and who knows when the new one would get to us in the Bush or Dukakis administration (were it the latter, of course reason would have been found to replace our names). But Bush had just smashed Dukakis in debate, the election results looked foregone, so I called my friend Peter Galbraith, now ambassador to Croatia, whom I hadn't seen in some time, but who like everyone in Washington was willing to pick back up on a congenial tie; one of the brightest and most respected staff contemporaries on the Hill, enormously influential on US policy in South Asia. I asked him to help out and get Senator Kennedy to put our names through. I told him that, after all, two of the names were Democrats. 'Who?' he asked. 'Evron Kirkpatrick . . . ', replied I.

'Evron Kirkpatrick, Democrat', Peter said to the room of fellow staffers. There was raucous laughter. 'Who else?'

'Allen Weinstein (the distinguished historian).'

Peter again turned to repeat this; the laughter grew even louder and more contemptuous. 'Allen Weinstein, the name dropper!' We were sinking fast.

'Peter, do it for gay liberation!'

Then there was silence, as Peter contemplated the irony of helping a neo-conservative from a Republican administration on the grounds of his sexual orientation. And then: 'Done, Scott.' We were confirmed the next day without so much as a hearing. Amusingly, the other almost boringly uncomplicated three nominations owed me for their quick and timely passing. The staff at least had the satisfaction of doing what they probably were going to have to do but for a more delectable reason.

Now I was the first openly gay presidentially appointed, Senate-confirmed official, a 'PAS', Presidential Appointment, advice and consent of the Senate. And sworn in, early in February 1989, at the Supreme Court by the very conservative Justice Scalia, as the rest of my newly contrived world caved in around me, with my lover Jeff threatening what was left of my career – another part of the price of being gay – if I didn't surrender two-thirds of our little real estate empire to him to consummate his trashing of our three-year relationship.

But meantime George Bush came to office, and, counter-intuitively, this much more Eastern and more polished – if not necessarily more sophisticated – leader set gay rights sharply back. Reagan had nothing to prove to the religious right – or to anybody else for that matter – and thus could be his Hollywood self on such matters, but Bush, on the defensive, set a nasty tone for gay civil liberties from the start; and one wondered what this said about the confidence he reposed in his masculinity. I was astonished to overhear some of the most senior of his officials in spitting contests with each other – and in one case at least in one direction, a middle-aged unmarried adviser to the president, accusing his enemy, a ranking official outside the White House and a married man with children, of being gay.

But it was also in this atmosphere that the *Washington Times*, perhaps not coincidentally singularly close to the South Korean government, saw fit to run an utterly scurrilous campaign against Craig Spence, an agent of influence, who made the mistake, among other trivia, of taking some marine-intendeds for a late night White House tour and grabbing some souvenirs, for which the paper crucified him.[3] Craig had been the kind of man who could gather the Attorney General, Roy Cohn, and Jeane Kirkpatrick under his roof in one night – along with several hundred hangers-on. He wasn't out, but little was left to the imagination; we talked with complete candor of our world, in which his search was for straight and hunky marines, whom he could degrade (as they saw it) into sexual activities in order to confirm his own low self-esteem by dragging them down – indeed he took one he was impassioned over to Venice and treated him to the Gritti Palace. There was also ample evidence of call-boy activity, not surprising, not illegal, but unpleasant to the public. The *Times* had a new headline almost every day, each one thinner than the one before, and eventually Craig killed himself at the Ritz-Carlton in Boston. In any event he had AIDS, it turned out, but it was a tale to set the teeth on edge. Craig wasn't the most admirable person I have known, but few have ever deserved as bad as the *Times* gave it to him. But small wonder: the signal from the White House was loud and clear.

Of course in such an atmosphere, the spitting could also go from the outside to the inside. In 1989 some Pat Robertson newcasters came to interview me with alleged gossip about one distinguished Bush adviser, Chase Untermeyer, whom I had known since 1970. Chase, who was about as close to Bush as anyone could be, had sacrificed his personal life to politics and hadn't at that point married. Although the issue had never come up I had always considered him straight, and anyway was appalled at the malevolent presumption of these interviewers, who in effect were offering me 'protection' if I would out Chase, as if I cared about my own reputation at that point. They claimed to have Visa stubs for call-boy activity, a concern derived from the investigations of Craig Spence. I only saw the men to draw them out for Chase's benefit, but it turned out that they were running on hearsay, so I got rid of them quickly – and promptly called the White House. Chase informed me that the Secret Service had been through all his records and, not surprisingly, could find nothing. He rode it out, and soon his life quieted down enough for him to get happily married. It was an atmosphere of little witch hunts.

The road of a gay man through Washington politics is however much rockier and often tougher. One of the first things he develops antennae for is whether there is hostility towards him solely on the basis of his sexual orientation, or whether he is being singled out for special treatment of any sort. In the summer of 1990 I joined a delegation of members of our board and several distinguished historians, including Arthur Schlesinger, Jr., John Lewis Gaddis, Dick Pipes, and fellow board-member Elspeth Rostow (who brought along her husband of Vietnam war fame, Walt Rostow) to Moscow, to discuss the origins of the Cold War with an even higher-level Moscovite team at Meshcherino, the foreign ministry's dacha – a splendid manor of Catherine's time assigned in Stalin's day to Kalinin, nominal head of the Soviet Union.

Any gathering that lasts long enough produces a bad boy or bad girl. If only because I was younger and quicker on my feet, I ended up playing literally the role of negotiator on our team, when one spouse continued to misbehave, and I could jog back and forth between the main house where she sat with the delegation and our Russian hosts, whom she did not wish to pay the tariff we were all assigned, and who were in a distant building. I was also the one chosen to try to persuade our team chairman, Allen Weinstein, to shorten his twenty-minute introductions of people like the foreign minister, Eduard Shevardnadze, or Gorbachev's adviser, Eugeny Primikov, so that we could hear *them*, rather than about the unusually full list of heads of state with whom he was close friends and about whose views he was willing to enlighten us. But I chanced to overhear one conversation from which I deduced that the delegation, by and large, took me as some sort of a freak or curiosity insofar as I was an openly homosexual man. One famous member of our board reportedly thought it utterly inappropriate for one to 'be' gay. Small wonder that I spent most of my time making friends with the Russians, one of whom, I quickly surmised and later confirmed, was a closeted homosexual, in a society where the penalties for openness were still orders of magnitude greater than in ours.

There were other anomalies. Sam Lewis, whom we as a board elected to the first full term as the Institute's president, had an awesome record as America's tough guy in Tel Aviv and Jerusalem, whom the Israelis respected for straight talk and whom Washington knew would not knuckle under in tough negotiations with our most relentless allies. He had also distinguished himself in other diplomatic incarnations.

Nonetheless, a sizeable minority on the board, including me, opposed him for the presidency, despite Morry Liebman's stern support for him. Basically, we the Board of Directors had been running the institute to a large extent, and we knew that would end if Sam took over. I had an additional reason. When I interviewed as a White House Fellow at the State Department for a position there in 1975, I had seen both him, as deputy to the Policy Planning Chief, and Winston Lord, the chief; the latter had been courteous and thoughtful, the former acted as if I were an intrusion. He was smart enough to realize, after all, that I wouldn't end up in the position for the simple reason that I was Paul Nitze's son-in-law and Henry Kissinger would never allow even a small fox in his chicken-yard. So, I guessed his attitude, why waste his time. And, unlike Winston Lord, he didn't.

Nevertheless, when Morry drove a ten-ton-truck over our opposition, we decided to make a virtue of necessity and throw the same weight behind Sam. I settled with him at a lunch at the Metropolitan Club, explained why I had opposed him and proposed to give a dinner in his honor for senators, high executive branch officials, and the like. Sam made a real effort to work closely with me, since I was most of the time by far the most active member of the board, and, as he no doubt saw it, would be quite capable of retaliating if ignored and I had come to admire him enormously.

But one problem was not to be overcome. Sam made faggot jokes in my presence, until I sent word indirectly that it was intolerable; some day soon it will one may hope be grounds for dismissal. Of course in context such crude talk showed that he was one of the boys, and I was well used to it. But as stigmatized groups grow in self-respect, what was tolerated or even tolerable becomes unthinkable.

There was the related problem of double standards; when we had a board retreat at Wye Plantation, since everyone else was bringing spouse or friend, I announced to the organizer that I would bring mine. I got a call from Sam himself saying that he was doing me a favor in saying no, that he simply wanted to protect me and the institute from raids on our budget by the likes of Jesse Helms – 'public funds paying for sin on the Eastern shore' – though of course, I would have been paying, like the others, for my friend's entertainment. I caved in and took it in stride, while muttering for God to save me from my protectors.

The next incident was more serious. A close friend of mine, a Belgian national named Alain Rouvez, who had been my student when I was teaching at Georgetown while working at USIA, applied for a USIP grant to write a book on European strategic interests in Africa, a study which by its completion had become highly topical – besides being as original and brilliant in conception as it proved in execution. Since I had no institutional connection with Rouvez, I was not required to recuse myself from the deliberations, though we would soon hold ourselves to stricter standards. And in my case, I did not need to defend the proposal, since peer and internal review had given it adequate support. Rouvez was going to be dependent on this funding for at least a year.

I left for a sabbatical research trip in the Philippines after his grant had been approved but before checks had been cut; and returned a few months later to find, after having to press him hard, given his dignity and old-world manners, that his institute was having to cannibalize other budgets to pay him; the check was well, several months late. Indeed it hadn't arrived. I had visions of his returning to the evening catering which had got him through graduate school. Why hadn't he told me? Because he didn't want me to interfere on a personal basis with what was a professional issue, as he put it. But it surely looked otherwise. The institute staff, terrified of Sam, had come up with no explanations either. Alain, it seemed, was paying an exorbitant price for having a gay friend.

This was the day of the Barney Frank self-outing and minor scandal, the fall of 1989. I went in to see Sam. Of course he knew the real reason why I was there, though we had a lengthy agenda. 'I've held up this check to protect you, Scott, given the mood in Washington over the Barney Frank affair . . . ' Sam never wearied in doing me favors.

'What in God's name does that have to do with a decision by the presidentially-appointed board of directors, instructing you to pay out to this gentleman some $45,000?'

'Well, isn't it obvious? As your lover . . . he and the grant are in a position to embarrass you, and us . . . I have to protect you, and of course the institute . . . '

I was incredulous. Alain is straight. Yes I was enormously fond of him, and regard and respect him. An institute official had dined at my house in late summer and seen him there, with no date – and me with no date. Two and two became seven right up to the director.

'Don't I wish . . . what I would give for Alain to be gay! Let's get that check to Alain *today*', I said. We chuckled, laughed, and got on with it. But it wasn't funny, because even that recently such an insinuation might have cost Alain his grant. This board member was *seriously* unamused.

## Notes

1. See Arthur Schlesinger, Jr., making the point that there were more gays in Reagan's administration than in Carter's. *Wall Street Journal*, 11 May 1988, p. 20.
2. W. Scott Thompson and Kenneth M. Jensen, eds, with Richard N. Smith and Kimber M. Schraub, *Approaches to Peace: An Intellectual Map* (USIP, 1991).
3. 'Lexis-Nexis' has 64 references in the *Washington Times* to him between early summer 1989 when the campaign started up to a few months after his November 1989 death. See Michael Hedges and Jerry Seper, 'In death Spence stayed true to form', 13 November 1989.

Chapter eight

# *Friends Made, Friends Lost*

*The past is not fugitive, it stays put.*

● The Guermantes Way

CHARLES Ryder's cousin Jasper enunciates one of the ambivalent themes of *Brideshead Revisited* when he visits him in what is evidently Waugh's old Oxford college, to give some gratuitous advice: 'You'll find you spend half your second year shaking off the undesirable friends you made in your first.' That was true as I made my way into the gay world, though it took more like four years.

Of course in coming out you also shed – or lose – many of your straight friends, and more of your acquaintances: some simply because the friendship was based on shared experiences no longer shared, family outings, say. In the mid-1980s, however, most élite American men would not own up to having a gay friend, and many wouldn't recognize any but the most obvious in any case. It was hard for most of my friends to make the adjustment, but the loyal ones quickly sorted themselves out.

But I was in the unusual position that the Nitze family, until then to my delight, had co-opted a great many of my circle of friends, including some of the closest, going all the way back to Andover. I thus had to write off at the start those who had substantial financial ties with the family, like one fraternity brother in whose business the family had invested $250,000; he behaved accordingly ever after. In time there would even be inducements to be disloyal to me personally – to no less than my friend of longest standing.

As to every exposed minority, the upholders of the untested decencies insisted that my 'real' friends would stick by me, but in fact some I truly believed to be such did not. The reason was too often sadly simple. Staying with your coming-out friend is mostly a matter of elementary confidence and assurance of one's own masculinity and identity, at least enough to override one's probable distaste for the gay side of things along with enough appreciation for the friend's other qualities. Over and over one can pick out from a group those uneasy with themselves and therefore boastful on 'masculine' issues, who predictably will be those who walk away when homosexual issues come up, particularly if someone casually mentions that he is gay. Recently I had opportunity to test this proposition. A mixed group of fifty teachers from around America had a party at my house, one of whom (more or less the group leader), from San Francisco, was openly gay. I told the gay one to watch, and suggested which men would walk away from a circle standing in the garden if I made a reference to my homosexuality. I then approached the group and when one asked what I was working on, I mentioned this book. The two unmarried men, plus another married, sauntered away; four remained, including two well-read middle-aged woman, and two men who were not nervous about their identity. The first three were as predicted, one of whom I guessed to be closeted.

And so it was even with one's once close friends.

Over and over, the men with whom I had dealt at high levels of government stayed friends – if they were *hommes serieux*. Of course they invited Paul Nitze's reprobation in doing so, but because of their attachment knew he could not enforce a ban or even criticize them for fraternizing with me. Robert Ellsworth, former Congressman, Deputy Secretary of Defense and ambassador to NATO, sponsored chamber concerts with me at my house on and off for five years after I had come out – and he was a long-time friend of Paul's. The story has made amply clear that Jim Woolsey remained the most loyal and most helpful of friends.[1] I had the feeling from the start of Nina's and my crisis that Jim had figured out that I was gay, if only because his accomplished wife Sue, now the head of the National Academy of Sciences, had become a close friend of Nina's and well knew her pain. I think that Jim had also already divined his karma, knew that he was going to be a far more successful figure in Washington foreign policy circles than his mentor Paul had been (at fifty he reached the highest formal rung of the ladder to which Paul had ever got), and knew that he didn't have to kowtow to him where friendships were involved; by this time Paul needed Jim more than Jim needed Paul.

Once, at Blair House, I introduced my then lover to Colin Powell when he was National Security Adviser – specifically as my lover, and though my doctor friend manifestly did not know who Colin was, we had a delightful conversation, with Colin at no unease whatsoever;[2] indeed he brought the news that evening that my reappointment to the Peace Institute board had been announced in his shop, which was a happy surprise. Dr Wilcomb Washburn, then an assistant director of the Smithsonian and a great Redskins fan, I thought would be uneasy were I to bring my lover to his and his wife Kathy's Eastern Shore mansion for a summer weekend; it turned out he had been Gore Vidal's roommate at Exeter; our friendship was not even challenged.

At this time I was making a point of telling everyone with whom I had made a social engagement *before* coming out, for a date that happened to be after I crossed this threshold, that my life had changed, and gave them an opportunity to withdraw from the arrangements. Mitchell Reiss, who if talent matters will be President someday, had been a student at Fletcher, an Oxford D.Phil., a Columbia JD, and a White House Fellow on the NSC staff. His stunning English then-fiancée Elisabeth Anselmi was in town and they were due to spend a weekend with me at my Virginia farm in the fall of 1985. I wrote and suggested they might not wish to . . . and they called and said they'd never heard anything so stupid. Mitchell, with whom every gay man was in love when at Fletcher, was so easy about his masculinity that it never occurred to him that such would be a factor in choosing his friends, though of course we could joke about it endlessly. And good party-givers, like my old friend Edward Wilson, the art investor and sporting-goods heir, whose company I have enjoyed since Oxford, and who with his whole family stood by me during the long divorce, invited me to his parties as much after as before. It may be partly because they appreciate people, like their daughters' theater colleagues, who aren't bland. And oh yes indeed, I had become less bland – as I recovered the old saltiness and met once more the bumps that had been softened and smoothed out of me during a time among the swells.

But the coin had its obverse side. The most prominent gay man in Washington, Mrs Reagan's friend Robert Grey, turned quickly away when, at a White House party, I introduced my lover as 'my lover'. The former secretary of the Eisenhower cabinet, whom I had known fairly well, wasn't going to waste time with anyone so stupid as to be *open* about his homosexuality, because such a person would have no staying power in the federal city. How many friends whispered how glad they were that I had found happiness and how nothing would change in our friendship – except, as it happened, that we would never see each other socially again, at least at their house.

The fact is that a man coming out loses much of his world. Straight people tend to be especially uncomfortable with gay men around their same-sex children, as a rule. Even my most liberal colleague insisted I refer to my lover as my 'roommate' around her adult, but unmarried, son. But I confess I wanted to lose some of that world. For there are not only the *hommes serieux*, there are the serious issues as well, and I had and was confronting one, deep inside myself but in the world at large. As I got closer and closer to the fire's center the less some of the concerns of some of my old friends seemed worth attending to. When you are redefining yourself and working up your energy to try to bring your world with you, the sporting events, political gossip, and tales of day-to-day life on the ladder upward become tedious. I know that some of my old friends complain that it was I who bumped them aside. In other words I too had a bonfire of the vanities as I created my new world, which had less and less room for uncommitted people.

The liberal and straight proverbially complain that their gay friends 'flaunt' their sexuality by letting it intrude in discussions where they themselves would be more private; of course they are confusing sexuality with sex. Alfred Kazin is said to have lamented, 'The love that dares not speak its name . . . has become the love that *will not shut up*.' It is all a matter of assumptions and is part of the transformation to civil society. A majoritarian's (straight) sexuality – and even sex – is taken for granted and intrudes continually on the gay man. My beloved late sister thought as I came out that I dwelt on sex overly – this is a continuing theme in straight discussion of gays.[3] Aside from failing to register how really cellular was the metamorphosis transforming me, she forgot that in merely discussing daily life she was discussing her majoritarian sexuality: where she would go on vacation with her husband, what the physicians at his convention would be doing with their wives, what they found boring and what exciting in their lives. The equivalent things I wished to talk about in my new life were deemed 'intrusive' – namely aspects of my new sexuality. A gay fellow-member of Washington's not precisely demotic Metropolitan Club made clear to me that he mercilessly hid his sexuality at every level of club participation. I could understand his logic, having frequently made gay allusions at the members' table amid winces, yet such is the only way, at this stage in our evolution, to communicate some sense of who I really am. Sometimes a gay man is in fact seeking understanding and help from a straight person in revealing his gayness. But in all fairness I confess that my fortunes do not rise or fall on anything happening at that club; whereas my friend finds his membership so important that he is willing to subsume his identity to it and appear more conventional than ever at the members' table.

Moreover, liberals like my sister – and also some of my colleagues – have to be put gently and unmistakably on notice, at some point, that much as we appreciate their support in principle, we *aren't* like them, we aren't just a different version; gayness is qualitatively different from straightness. 'The only thing that's the same about gay and straight people is what they do in bed', Paul Monette quotes Harry Hay, since it is our sensibilities that are so utterly different.[4] You can't grow up obsessed with stamps, Bach or butterflies, rather than baseball or soccer, and expect there to be instinctive common ground – *that* has to be developed.

Stage by stage one comes to socializing mostly within the gay world, despite its vagaries – especially since I was out of government service and no longer had official duties and roles to consume my social life. With most of one's straight friends, with whom one gets on well in the office halls of government, academe, business, or on the street, one hears the patronizing overtones ringing through a social invitation, as if a favor of enormous size has been rendered thereby. In a sense, of course, the straight person has reality on his side; the gay man as we have already seen seldom gets invited to a straight function, and therefore the hospitable straight man expects a gratitude more existential than reciprocal. This is a pity; Camille Paglia argues powerfully that 'Gay men and straight men have much more in common than do gay men with lesbians or straight men with straight women. Every man must define his identity against his mother. If he does not, he just falls back into her and is swallowed up.' No wonder she can say that the 'fate of masculinity is intimately tied to homosexuality'.[5]

Family is different. In group support meetings one hears too many heart-rending stories of parents who still can't accept homosexuality in their children – though of course there is always more in the parental intolerance than just aversion to homosexuality. But I sense that this problem with parents is becoming the exception; my friends are out with theirs, as am I with my children as well. In my case I had to drag my mother along – but she came. In 1986, after falling in love with Jeff 'as I have never loved anybody', I told her it may be 'wrong' 'but it "*is*". As far as I am concerned the rest of the world can go to hell on this point.'

> What if the *world* were gay and *you* were the exception, in falling in love with my father: would you have stopped loving him because of the PTA's disapproval? Was your love for Dad a conventionality? or was it real? And if real, how real? Do you remember how powerful it was? Physically, emotionally, intellectually, psychologically? You have to face not Jeff as such but the reality that your son has found overwhelming happiness, from which many things will flow.[6]

The bisexual's tergiversations are particularly acute. Two men who are reasonably prominent in Washington, and who by any standards are successful and highly educated, were at different stages the closest persons in the world to me. Neither is any longer in touch with me, though in the past we shared holidays, dreams, the making of a better world.

The reason is not that I have changed as such, but that they are both married, and they are both gay or bisexual. With one, I shared all the bitter-sweet pains and the charms of boyhood in that almost Arcadian setting which a western rural campus could offer barely forty years ago, before there were threats of so many sorts to dull the excitement; and if our games in the woods were, with the wisdom of hindsight, overwhelmingly gay in symbolic meaning, one encounter we had, when we were young men, was explicitly and erotically so. With the other, probably the first person I was ever in love with, when I came out to him, so did he to me. But whereas I was coming to the end of a long marriage, he had just gone into one; we were on reverse timetables. He had the same drive to have children as had I, and he had found a compatible and lovely woman for whom he cared and wished to share his life, as I once had. I do not know to what extent the two wives know of their husbands' predispositions but their double life corrodes them more than it does me. For it is a symptom of their deep anxiety and fear they have in their lives about their gayness or bisexuality, which passes into authenticity and commitment, and the fear they have that their wives – and everyone else – will find out: and that in a real sense, they themselves will at last find themselves out too.

The point of course is that society has imposed another unnecessary cost. Either society, and, in particular, couples, could deal with the homosexuality of one, as many have, so that gay friends did not 'threaten' their marriage; or, for those who have not yet made that choice, going into a marriage might not seem so essential to getting on with life.

At my thirtieth Stanford reunion, I gave a summary presentation of this book in front of the several hundred of our class who made it back. It included my freshman dorm mate Gordy Adams, now associate director of the OMB for defense and national security issues, a congresswoman and congressman, several judges, numerous lawyers, and many of my fraternity brothers, including Jim Woolsey, who also made a presentation.

I was overwhelmed by the sentiment of those who either read my short essay in the class book, and/or saw the panel discussion; I got too many hugs from woman classmates, and even a lot of good feeling from the men, for this to be accidental. Of course they were disproportionately from California, but that tells us something about where the rest of the country can be presumed to be in ten or twenty years. Maybe one can be optimistic: looking out at the audience and seeing fraternity brothers who had dropped me the moment I came out, along with those like Woolsey who courageously stood by me even though he, in his case, had a far bigger incentive to do likewise, I nonetheless concluded that people taking this step today and tomorrow will pay a far smaller price. 'Out here, Scotty, it's a nothing question by now . . . nobody *cares* any longer what your sexuality is' – meaning they care a great deal, but in no invidious way at all. If that becomes true for New York and Chicago, millions of lives could surely be happier immediately. No one should feel the need to treat old friends shabbily any more, certainly not over their sexuality.

But in seeing all these friends, and especially these tanned, healthy and apparently healthy ones, I realized how much my friendship network had changed. My children apart, almost all the people I see for dinner or dates are products of this traumatic decade, either my new gay friends around the world, or my network of friends with gay sensibilities who call themselves straight. No doubt as my old friends' children grow up and themselves have children, with society progressing apace in this period, some will come back to break bread anew.

But in the meantime I marvel at how easily gay people develop friendships – like Londoners in the Blitz and for the same reason. There is always the sense of shared danger, of the impermanence of security, and therefore the need and ability to share deeply quickly. Of course the other side of the coin is the world of the one-night stand, the ability to give and sense real meaning which both sides derive, and to wake up and know the new day will have to bring new meanings – and new partners. Foucault explained better than anyone why gay culture in its sexual dimension is to the swift: in Christianity 'homosexuality was banished and therefore had to concentrate all its energy on the act itself'.

> Homosexuals were not allowed to elaborate a system of courtship because the cultural expression necessary for such

> an elaboration was denied them. The wink on the street, the split-second decision to get it on, the speed with which homosexual relations are consummated: all these are products of an interdiction.[7]

And, finally, the impermanence with which every gay man lives was redoubled in agonizing consciousness by AIDS. A friend who has been in the gay world a lot longer tells me that Sunday is 'funeral day'. He had buried dozens of friends. Mine are still alive – though how painfully close they can hover on the edge was brought home by one who told me his great pain at his father's death was seeing his mother's greater pain, since she in looking at him and then overviewing his father's service was dress rehearsing what she must, sooner rather than later, endure again.

The gay world is different from all other worlds: there is none in which hierarchy is so detached from traditional notions of status – ancestry, wealth, rank, title, all the appurtenances of a power culture. True, highly developed gay worlds, like San Francisco's, try their best to ape and replicate traditional society (their city, after all, is the only one left in America with a 'society' columnist and where social register standing is admitted to publicly as 'meaningful') but even there, as with the rest, a good-looking man with charm has instant status, whether or not he went to college, whatever his lineage, money, debts or office.

The connections among gay worlds is bound to matter in the future. In few worlds is international interconnectedness as obvious: German diplomats and civil servants instantly press their government for every new concession and right their Scandinavian counterparts have achieved, for example (spousal entitlements to air travel from home to assignment is one of these). And truly, European gay culture is one of the great wonders of the world – though less politically developed, it has achieved far more in its societies, which is therefore a double credit to those peoples. The sense of equity deeply permeates governmental rulings and laws affecting the gay world.

In Europe gay culture in the north was well ahead of ours; in southern Europe it manifests much less as an open culture yet in some ways more permissively; precisely because it isn't open, a wider range of men seem to partake, just so long as it is in fact kept beneath one kind of surface.

But as one goes East and South the problems develop. Central Europe suffers from the repressive hangover of the communist past, which for all its flaunted leftism (which of course did extend to women's and ethnic issues) was universally unkind to gays. A distinguished young Russian friend just coming out had nightmares of returning to the chill of Moscow and the memories of gay repression with which he grew up; he looks for a job in America. Of course, the very closed-mindedness can be a protection; a friend of mine, with whom I had an affair when he was a student in America, returned home to his still totalitarian society, where he says he gets away with almost openly gay behaviour in a very sensitive position because nobody would know what to recognize. And he is even referred to by nicknames betokening effeminacy. Times will be tougher for him when the society becomes officially more tolerant – and when it has eyes to see what it had so long repressed so ruthlessly; it didn't recognize it when it was right up front.

In Latin America, Cuba is obviously the least tolerant, Mexico is much the furthest along among Hispanic societies in the Western hemisphere, surely thanks to its proximity to the United States; as far back as 1982, 4,000 gay Mexicans demonstrated in Mexico City for gay pride. But there is still a long way to go. In much of the rest of Latin America homosexuality is deeply suppressed, far less by laws than by popular culture. There is still no notion of a gay culture whatsoever. Brazil and Argentina are quite the same, but the size of their gay communities provides some strength in number (though the former has permitted gay-bashing and killing on a substantial scale).[8]

In Thailand, there is no concept of shame regarding sex, really not a word for homosexuality; the culture's keen and genuine acceptance tolerates anything intimate, so long as it happens behind closed doors. One of the reasons why the Thai gay community developed AIDS so much earlier than that in the comparably-sized Philippines is simply because of the bad luck of the specific cultural varieties of sexual practice. And what often goes on behind closed doors is the Thai man on the bottom, which is how AIDS is spread among gay men most of the time, through the fragile rectal tissues. In dramatic contrast, Filipino men may have romantic sexual friendships with other men without cultural sanction – but only as long as the Filipino is not in the passive role. Then he isn't *baklaa*, which is a pejorative, effeminate description. The situation appears to be the same in Hispanic countries, with which of course the Philippines is connected by history.[9] Few of the numerous Americans who like me have had Filipino boyfriends or lovers can honestly claim to have been the so-called active partner in their links with these lovely people. And AIDS in the Philippines is a tiny fraction of Thailand's – though there are other reasons as well.[10]

So there is a great variety of national and cultural homosexualities. And we see that the civil society has a long way to go. Our very brief survey, which could have been much longer, makes one thing clear: looking at gay rights internationally is like looking at workers' rights in the nineteenth century, or looking at women's issues prior to the nineteenth amendment.

## Notes

1. Jim met Paul at my wedding, as has been noted in several articles about him; he never forgot the source of the bounty that flowed from Paul, which showed simply characteristic class. See Michael R. Gordon, 'Campus Activist to Insider: Journey of the CIA Nominee', *New York Times*, 11 January 1993.
2. Powell has had a bum rap from the gay world personally for his role-derived position on gays in the military. My personal belief is that he would have supported Clinton's original position to drop the ban on gays serving in the military, but felt that he had made sufficient social history in being the first black Chairman of the Joint Chiefs; he could not take on yet another social 'first'.
3. In an article about a lesbian comedian's discussion of homosexuality a New York high school class, one of the first stereotypes to come up was 'Why do homosexuals feel compelled to talk about their bedroom activities?' The response was 'I don't . . . Gayness isn't about sex. But it keeps being the thing pushed on us.' Lindsey Gruson, 'Meeting gay bias face to face in class', *New York Times*, 15 October 1993, p. B5.
4. Paul Monette, *Becoming a Man* (New York: HarperCollins, 1992), p. 81.
5. Camille Paglia, *Sexual Personae* (Yale University Press, 1990), pp. 23 and 22.

6. WST to Loretta Thompson, 23 June 1986.
7. Cited in Richard Isay, *Being Homosexual* (New York: Avon Books, 1989), p. 133.
8. See 'Brazilian is first to gain asylum [in the US] for being Gay', *Washington Blade*, 13 August 1993, p. 1. In late 1994 an Argentinian Cardinal, in proposing that his country's gay community be banished, did a double service: first, in mobilizing that community like nothing had done before; and secondly in rallying the support of many straights behind the gay community.
9. See Professor Roberto Gonzalez Echevarria's review of *Before Night Falls*, by the gay Cuban writer Reinaldo Arenas: 'to play the active role does not define one as a homosexual in Cuba', and thus Arenas wanted to 'seduce men' (*sic*) in contrast to American gay men, who 'band together'. The point is clear despite the pejorative. 'An outcast of the island', *New York Times Book Review*, 24 October 1993, p. 32.
10. Though as with many other countries, testing has not yet been widespread in the Philippines, and once it begins, it may turn out that the country is somewhat closer to the Thai case than it now appears.

Chapter nine

# *Reckoning the Price*

*. . . for every event is like a mould of a particular shape, and, whatever it may be, it imposes upon the series of incidents which it has interrupted and seems to conclude, a pattern which we believe to be the only possible one, because we do not know the other which might have been substituted for it.*

● The Fugitive

WHEN we are busiest keeping our lives together and our heads above water we may be least aware of the issues which our efforts symbolize or by which they are driven. In the four years of the Bush administration, after my second term on the Peace Institute board had come through, I was working so hard on the two books I edited or organized for it, each complete with a large conference, and was so busy commuting to Boston to teach, that only toward the end did I bother to add up the costs of being gay which I had incurred. In the twilight of Bush's tenure it happened that I was finally cleared politically by the White House even for a full-time, line, appointment, and which would have been at the same level as that in the Reagan administration. That merely reminded me how odd it was that I hadn't been hitherto, having served creatively and supportively in the first Reagan administration, with many years of hard work on the USIP board following that. But blaming and holding grudges is never a very attractive foreign policy, so I tended to think little of the damages.

But something which had happened at the start of these four Bush years suddenly grew on me. Prior to my calendar 1989 sabbatical in Washington and Manila, Roger Hansen had obtained a very part-time lectureship for me at SAIS to cover for him in a single course on the Third World (which in fact I had taught at SAIS in the summer of 1983). Ironically without consulting him the school cancelled it and told me they had cancelled it *because* he was on leave; this on the eve of a new semester when surely their need would have increased. I merely wrote the faculty dean, stating I hardly wished to be where I was not wanted, but that it was a little late for me to make alternative arrangements, so would he kindly honor the monetary obligation. I may even have sarcastically included a self-addressed and stamped envelope: but I think it was more likely the 'cc' to my lawyer than honor that brought me the check by return mail. I decided to regard the whole thing with hilarity – thousands of dollars for no work. Roger and I celebrated at the Inn at Little Washington, near my farm, which Craig Claiborne has annointed the best restaurant in America.

We were soon to learn the reason for the extraordinary cancellation: the school had seriously overestimated, perhaps by well over an order of magnitude, the amount of money Paul Nitze had available to bequeath (and all of which at this point was in any case committed to his grandchildren). They didn't wish there to be any blemish – like me – at the school at the time they propositioned him, certainly no homosexual one, as Roger was able to tell me amid our mutual toasts with a 1959 Nuits St Georges and 1961 Château Haut Brion. Then Paul, bucked from his horse just after President Bush bucked him out of his administration, in January 1989 was in an emergency room and was on the critical list. Barely consulting the faculty, the board renamed the school after Nitze, hoping to beat the old man with the scythe to the door, but the old statesman had not even sought this honor.[1] The last thing the school wanted around at this sensitive point was a reprobate ex-son-in-law of the would-be donor, a dishonorable faggot at that. Or so it was teasingly presented to me by friends, not however without truth.

By the beginning of 1993, however, I felt a new surge of defiant strength and freedom. Bill Clinton had opened a new chapter for gay people, or so it seemed, which surprised me enormously: from what I knew of him at Oxford one could not expect him to initiate change over on the fringes (though I could expect better from his wife, whom I knew slightly). But for once power ennobled. And by this time, as we have seen, explicit discrimination was already becoming legally impossible in many areas, particularly in the government, so Clinton had something solid upon which to build. And from a personal point of view, now that I had talked with all my children about my sexuality, and society's evolution on their respective campuses made my situation far less oppressive for them to bear, I was unconstrained.

When I got the phone call from Sam Lewis, then in his sixth year as president of the US Institute of Peace, that he was going back to the State Department, this time as head of policy planning, a distinguished perch that Paul Nitze and George Kennan had graced in their day, I knew immediately that I would declare for his job. I would be president of the institute.

And why not? I had been present at its creation, I knew it better than anyone could from outside, and though a board member I felt like an insider most of the time, loved the staff and they seemed to like me; indeed the two ranking members of senior staff supported me and lobbied for me actively, and numerous junior members asked what they could do to help. If a gay man could be a senate-confirmed board member, why not its president, who reported to the board? I was to miss a highly critical distinction here, in that I was forgetting that I had put myself in the position of nigger *after* I had been named to the board of directors the first time around, but I had nothing but confidence when I threw my hat in the ring.

The board members who were free to choose anyone were all apparently friendly, all had been guests in my house at least once and some many times, and there were friends dating back to Stanford days. Within hours I knew that I had three solid members of the board openly supporting me, and I could be confident that when Secretary of Defense Les Aspin's nominee got on board, Les would be friendly enough, from a long association, to instruct him to support me – and if the nominee were Walter Slocombe, no doubt the support would be enthusiastic. Which in the event it was. So I started with a third of the board openly on my side.

There was also the fact that Paul Nitze was so preoccupied and excited by his marriage to a woman the age of his younger children, on the eve of his eighty-sixth birthday, that I assumed for once he would stay out of my affairs. Lady Leezee, as she was known, had many husbands and told friends she liked older men, especially rich ones, it seemed. She wrung a very exacting bargain in a prenuptial agreement giving her literally everything, including all the money that had come from Paul's wife of fifty-five years, who had died in 1987 of emphysema, but from whom Paul's not enormous fortune certainly got its start. Paul bought her a $2.6 million mansion beyond even his means. So that, at first from a happy point of view for Paul, and then from one equally sad – since as the months went on colon cancer centered his life – he didn't seem to be a problem for me. It never would have occurred to me that precisely because of the medical treatment, and his knowledge that I knew his sacred secret, he had to be all the more diligent and urgent to knock me out of the game, and now truly forever.

I announced swiftly, if only to deter other potentially serious candidacies. But I made clear that while I would continue my work on the board I would not only recuse myself from everything touching on the presidential search, I would strictly limit my socializing with the board during the period of its search even where there was a business context. And I made clear that the onus would be on me to preserve these good relations and the happy spirit of the board, in the likely event that they would select some person other than me. But in my heart I was sure they could not turn me down, and I worked for the six-month search period to ensure that. I prepared papers charting the institute's next five years, and found about fifty friends in high places were sending letters of support – some of course at my suggestion, some others on their own.

Principally, I wanted an open and shut test of whether a gay man could be chosen to head an institution in the city of Washington, but not just to make a point; I wanted to win. My qualifications were so obvious that I could and should win – and then by example open the door to other gay men elsewhere.

In the event it didn't work; my close friend and colleague Dennis Bark and I couldn't budge a single additional vote beyond the third of the board with which we started. After six months of waiting, anxiety, conspiracy and, I hope, dignity, my son and I got the news together, which I think was more painful to him than me. I hopped back to the rest of the day's board meeting, to meet with these splendid people, because I still had a job to do; he found that incredible. Even with the last-minute addition to the board of its only Clinton appointee, Walt Slocombe, who spoke powerfully on my behalf, and who made the argument that perhaps more should be heard from the newcoming Clinton board appointees, I lost. There were three factors through which I was defeated, all delicate, all touching on larger issues that affect others in public life.

The first and clearly the determinative factor is that my beloved old father-in-law hadn't been able to resist entering the fray: he rose above his domestic and medical involvements to furnish the most detailed divorce dirt about me to the marketplace of the search committee. More importantly, he called in a most important debt. Because Max Kampelman was relatively new and because I had barely met him – albeit he was the board member whom Paul knew best – I vastly underestimated the skill which he would show in organizing my defeat. This went back to his tie with Paul, who had skillfully allied them together, pulling Max over from the left to the right where he wished to be (in the cadre of the Committee on the Present Danger), supporting him and his friends for administration positions, even shepherding him around Washington when Max was still the amateur from Minnesota, and piling up obligations which he now could call in. Paul led Max around on a leash, and at every stage of the search there was Max laden with procedures, argumentation, and legalisms with which to defeat me.

Getting even in Washington is serious business, but when it becomes a decade-long preoccupation, as this had now become for Paul, and when the motives are unworthy and prevent people accomplished in their callings from fulfilling themselves, then surely public interests are involved. The instantly famous lament of poor Vincent Foster was that 'ruining people' in Washington 'is considered sport' – 'as flies to wanton boys, are we to the gods; they kill us for their sport' – and the stage sets of Washington knew that this was one of their few great powers . . .

My crime, after all, was not that I had divorced Paul's daughter or that I had done it in any particular manner; nor is it that I knew of Paul's homosexuality. It was that I had the audacity to practice mine.

The second and least important factor in my defeat can loosely be called ethnicity. All the board members of Jewish background opposed me, and two married to Jewish people did likewise; this was a faction in this instance that was always ready to support Max's argumentation. It also went back to the Lenkowsky affair, where I was tainted, as it will be recalled, for the first time with the brush of anti-Semitism – when Lenkowsky, for manifest perjury, became the first Reagan appointee to bite the dust before the Congress and fail of confirmation; and in his fury he lashed out at me in several directions, with long-term effects among his large circle of friends and beneficiaries. And though I do not know whether those debts were called in as such, the alliance pattern and friendships were only too well known and too clear.

When my friend Ambassador Bill Kintner told Kampelman that he had never in two decades heard anything anti-Semitic from me, Kampelman came to me and utterly denied that any such sentiment was being expressed (generally in Washington an indication of precisely the opposite). And that such a tactic would be reprehensible, or character assassination, he later said in writing. I ended the conversation with reference to Proust who likened the costs of being Jewish to being gay (or vice versa), something he knew about, being both; so I said I knew what it was to be in a minority because I was in one. When Kampelman said to me that it had never been anything but an advantage to him – a man growing up in the New York in the first half of this century and who had even changed his name – I of course knew how to take his earlier denial. What we saw at work is the old saw, that anti-Catholicism is the anti-Semitism of the intelligentsia and anti-homosexuality is the anti-Semitism of (some) Jewish Americans.

The third issue was, simply, The Price of Being Gay. When I called my mother to tell her that the vote had gone as predicted, she said – and no one was a better booster of mine – 'Darling, I knew it wouldn't happen. *That* board of *that* generation just wouldn't have been able to accept *this*.' It hadn't even occurred to me. And then, lightning through the heart, I realized she was right . . . all the little warnings I had ignored, all the studied avoidances, all the *sotto voce* comments at board meetings, all of that, the principal underlying issue was that it was 'inappropriate' for a faggot (or a 'homo [*sic*]' as I was referred to at one point) to head up a national institute.

Astonishingly, six weeks after the vote, my distinguished colleague Max Kampelman wrote me noting that he had heard of my view as to his role in the election, hinting that such was character assassination on *my* part. Predictably, he denied that my 'sexual preference' could have played any part in his choice, since, he claimed, he hadn't heard what my sexual orientation was until after the vote. This shows just how easy it is for the majoritarian world to deny simple reality. For Kampelman and I had discussed my homosexuality at the Board Retreat in May 1993, two months earlier. I seriously doubt that Kampelman meant to dissimulate; he is simply too much a survivor of the cut-throat Washington world to do it brazenly in normal circumstances. Which these weren't. The gay issue is so new that old-timers forget to take it seriously, and they fail to put it on their 'principle' docket where one appears statesmanlike – and never mendacious.

But as small comfort there was the fact that it had become important to purport that sexuality *wasn't* an issue – the effort to cover it up only made obvious how great an issue it was in this case.

When does it become an advantage to be a member of a minority if ever? My Rhodes classmate Stan Sanders, once a little All-American football player and now a highly regarded political figure in Los Angeles, used to say that being black had always been an advantage to him, coming along when and how he did. He did not thereby debunk or lighten the role of those who paid a price for being black, but he acknowledged thereby that there are phases in all liberation movements. And one might note a peculiarly painful tie the black and gay movements share: just as great power finally accrued to the black political movement a decade and a half ago, violence and drugs came to plague it in a way which only now is it facing up to, so AIDS came to challenge and overwhelm the gay movement as it finally reached its first rung of recognition. And the irony goes further. Too many gay men only came out when AIDS made further life in the closet gratuitous in any event; one thinks of Jeffrey Schmalz, whose celebrated *New York Times* magazine article about the receding attention given to AIDS appeared just days before his death in 1993; he had come out when his medical condition revealed only too clearly an advanced case of AIDS.

Right now, being gay isn't even protected, except loosely in a few cities and states, and in some of those – Colorado is the most conspicuous – we are having to fight all over again to preserve those gains. Over and over I hear of men getting favorable consideration for jobs for being Hispanic, handicapped, black, for whom the consideration is legally inscribed. And of course finally women are able to litigate to obtain their rightful place in American business and industry, with a guardian angel at the Supreme Court now looking out for them. But it took literally until 1994, and the most expensive natural disaster in American history, for the federal government to include 'sexual orientation' in its list of protected species – assistance to the victims of the Los Angeles earthquake.

True, in more and more technical circles one hears of gay men assuming the leadership of bureaux, of departments, of circles; but the closer to real visibility one gets to the outside world, the less visible one must have been about his homosexuality. The entire Clinton administration despite its well-known commitment to placing gays in their ranks had only managed to do so with less than a dozen, mostly at low levels at that, and this over a year along, this despite all the pressure and guidance from gay organizations.

## *Notes*

1. The renaming was not thought to have been a smart move among the other professional foreign service schools – especially once it became apparent that there was no Brinks' truck at the end of the cortege.

Chapter ten

# *The Road from Rehoboth*

*We do not receive wisdom, we must discover it for ourselves, after a journey through the wilderness which no one else can make for us, which no one can spare us, for our wisdom is the point of view from which we come at last to regard the world . . . I can see that the picture of what we were at an earlier stage . . . cannot, certainly, be pleasing to contemplate in later life. But we must not repudiate it, for it is a proof that we have really lived, that it is in accordance with the laws of life and of the mind . . .*

● Elstir, in *Within a Budding Grove*

THERE turn out to be two roads from Rehoboth at the start, an expansive beach town of gay celebration, and also a narrow town of villagers and merchants trashing gay establishments and denying them licenses. As with Proust's celebrated 'two ways', the two roads are symbolized by the differences we can choose as we determine how to live: there was Roger's way, which started in denial and ended in self-destruction; there was no road out for him, no exit from Rehoboth. The gay movement can do the same if the mass of its members choose to stay in the closet. And there is the way that saved at least my life, which started in tentative steps to self-liberation and culminated in a third way, enthusiastic affirmation and transcendence.

In attempting to come to terms with my gayness first suppressed then open, I tried everything, and our society now has splendid offerings – normal support structures, therapies, cults – for working through problems, all the highest offering of civil society.

I tried them all: first psychotherapy, about which it is first appropriate to ask why so substantial a percentage of gay men have availed itself of this option. One of the reasons gay men – and closeted gay men – have seen so many psychiatrists so often is because of the confessional function that medical specialty has played in our secular society, a point Foucault has made on various occasions. The second time I went to see a psychiatrist, in Boston, I was horrified to find a Fletcher student coming out of my therapist's office as I went in. In my previous session I had confessed my anxieties of bisexuality and now insisted that the whole school would know about it. The therapist appeared not to understand. Finally, when I clarified my anxiety, he responded, 'Do you think homosexuality is the only thing people come to see a psychiatrist about?' I might then, as now, have spoken for men of a certain age and said, 'Yes, mainly'.

But the larger reason is that in compressing us on society's margins, forcing us in most places to hide our identity or accept a role as, in effect, an institutionalized hairdresser (like the Filipino *baklaa* or Indian *Berdache*), society has wrought havoc on our identity, our self-esteem and self-acceptance. And the psychiatric profession has many deficiencies; our goals and theirs are at odds – until they accept homosexuality as a healthy path for those endowed with it. Hitherto so many of them have induced denial of the *fact*, avoiding the problem.

I marvel that I escaped the guilt-trip that most gay friends acquired from fathers far less 'macho' than mine, always encouraging our athletic sides, discouraging our bookish inclinations, letting us know that the inner self which of course we most cherish *precisely because it is the central 'we'* isn't any good. Erikson, with primary reference to the 'great young man' but also to the cases 'of whom we should not demand that they reveal . . . the stigmata of greatness in order to justify confusion and conflict', says so tellingly that

> rods which measure consistency, inner balance, or proficiency simply do not fit the relevant dimensions. On the contrary, a case could be made for the necessity for extraordinary conflicts, at times both felt and judged to be desperate.[1]

But even without a guilt trip a gay man has plenty more to work out. Most of us have spent the first few decades of our life wondering why everyone else seems so happy, certain, or purposeful. If the reality is always a bit more complex, the fact is that the straight teenager, while perhaps adolescing with pains here and there, has the empowering discovery by stages of his wonderful sexuality: the pleasure, the self-enlargement, the bonding therefrom. He delights in sexcapades, 'going steady' and having sex on a steady diet, and acculturating into the adult world more often than not with a relative smoothness. For most of us, we not only didn't have the pleasure of the sex (and if we did have it with women, it was at best a mixed blessing), we had the frustration of not understanding why we were different, why we had to be so unhappy. And when we come out we have to acculturate in a quite technical sense – learning the rules of engagement, whether at twenty or forty, which the straight teenager picked up at sixteen when it was natural to do so and all the world reinforced the 'educational process', and of course turned a blind eye to excesses, even criminal ones, in the sexual world. Try processing in middle age what is natural only in advanced childhood!

The point is well made by the fact that Nina was compelled to add $20,000 to her divorce settlement for my psychotherapy, given the assumptions that such a divorce process as hers would cause great turmoil for me, and I came near to using up the kitty.

Three successive psychiatrists intermittently over a ten-year period induced me to deny the problem; one tried to get at what set off homosexual fantasies as if they could thence be eliminated. I was encouraged to envisage the sort of prototypical conversion of gay anxieties to heterosexual feelings. One of these, highly gifted, was reduced to yelling, at the most intense part of my divorce-related crisis, 'But you're not gay!' when surely by then every honestly established datum, starting with his triumph-of-the-will approach, yelled back the reverse.

It was only with a fourth and last, a really heroic therapist, that I got any benefit in this area. Testing the waters as the divorce warmed up, in which he might have to play a part, I asked him how he would answer if her lawyers demanded to know whether I were gay, in the event that he was asked to testify on issues of parenting and I therefore had to waive all other medical privilege. Of course I expected him to expound how he would work around it: but instead he said that while he would of course testify positively on all parenting questions, he would elicit from them some clearer definition of gayness, and if pressed would list my encounters with other men that might so indicate. Once more I felt the moon and stars falling in on me.

But now I had somebody to believe in, as a last step before fully believing in myself; someone who established a standard of honesty and integrity for himself and those he worked to help, who was in effect telling me to get serious. Which meant, come out, and stop trying to fool myself. He wasn't going to underwrite my denial. Like the best lawyers, who on crucial matters wouldn't protect a client in court, Dr Goldman wasn't either – at any rate, not my mythic self which he could see pulling me down, like an armored knight in a swamp. Thus were my options contracting; I should face the music. And he had convinced me that facing the music was right, the security that rests on truth.

In the meantime he had more than the usual challenges in helping me find space in which to grow. In early 1985 I wrote that Dr Goldman 'forebears':

> I ranted and I raved this week about the futility of analysis. And answered myself in the process. He had created a little world for me of total acceptance and I can harmlessly thrash around in there and find answers, in the process rearranging at least some of the psyche in the process if only because I am not 'punished' for venting hostilities or dreams. So I can figure out that I'm OK. And he has to sit impassively listening to my accusations, knowing that in the accusing I'm sorting out much . . .

Well, 'at the end of every road you meet yourself', S. N. Behrman writes,[2] and when leaving Dr Goldman's office for the last time I thought I had at least reached that haunted crossroads.

I tried other therapies, including hypnosis, which can be taking refuge in unreality, but also can be another tool of empowerment. In my general effort as a 'type A' personality to learn to blend in an adequate degree of 'type B', I learned from a remarkable therapist to relax and hypnotize myself in stressful times. Often in court or while entering Ruth-Arlene Howe's slow, mindless admonitions, I was in fact out on cloud-nine, in a fairly deep hynotic trance, ready to come back when I needed to respond. To this day I hypnotize myself in appropriate circumstances like faculty meetings, plane turbulence, or bad sermons; used like dreams to release the unconscious, it is a most valuable tool.

I sampled the 'Venice Beach' alternatives, including EST, in its rough early form; in late summer 1983 I attended the EST program, which was well known in its day. For several hundred dollars cash one was padded into a hotel ballroom with a 'trainer' from ten one morning until around three a.m. the next, for two successive weekends, with time out only for dinner both Saturday and Sunday nights. And seldom time out for personal hygiene.

I was too impatient to handle the program in its entirety, and my several absences occasioned by the Soviet shoot-down of the Korean flight 007 took me away from some of the most important sessions. I was only conditionally involved with EST, and at later follow-up sessions I had trouble dealing with the 'glowing' handlers, as the more cynical among us called the ever-smiling recruiters to that cause.

But EST taught one thing and that overwhelmingly: personal responsibility. When I challenged a trainer to explain how I could take responsibility for the armed assault on me and my house earlier that year, he noted that I had accumulated a room full of expensive gear, that was surely an attractive nuisance to the house-renovators, among whom were the confessed felons. And I had often stated that I hoped the house would be robbed, because I'd then get insurance to finish the renovation; I just hadn't counted on a gun at my head.

Another thing EST taught which gay men can all benefit from – to be 'interested', not just interesting. Mark Altbush always teasingly called me his 'interesting guy' because that's how I'd described myself in the ad through which we met. Now, defiantly, as if an ad can redefine the soul, I placed one that proclaimed that I was, dammit, interested. It took a time more to sand down my ego to anywhere near that point, but at least EST headed me in the right direction.

Seven years later I took a shorter and softer version, Rob Eichberg's 'The Experience', aimed essentially at gay men, though our group of thirty included several straight people whom I got to know well. Rob taught self-respect, acceptance, an expanding consciousness, and coming out, whatever be your closet.[3] I was even then a little bent out of shape by my break-up with Jeff (though I'd split up with two other men since) and was all eyes when a new friend recited his parallel emotions. Rob ran him to ground for all our sakes, noting that his lover could be expected to have left him, given his dependence, his whine, his inability to take responsibility. Rob saw relationships on a spectrum, with a significant other barely more important, and sometimes less so, than other relationships in one's life, most critically with ourselves; and he strongly opposed phrases like 'our better half' or even 'our other half', given his emphasis on the development of autonomy and wholeness in each of us joined or not.

We learned to distinguish between the powerful position of loving, and the powerless position of being in love: being in a position to give generously, to enable, to empower, as opposed to being in the vulnerable position of someone else's control. We had to write a letter coming out to someone dear, especially family members; or if, as in my case, that was history, to an Ex, to 'complete' the experience. I wrote Jeff, converting my powerlessness to truth – and of course he never answered, which proved Rob Eichberg's point: I now was the powerful one. When we read our letters to each other in our working groups there were few dry eyes. Knowing as some of us did that Rob was not only dynamically conducting this seminar, with a chorus of alumni at the back of the room reinforcing him, but was doing it despite his AIDS diagnosis and attendant high fevers, was a not modest inspiration.

Then there were and are the formal support structures. I started in one, like so many these days held in church precincts, for gay fathers. All had horrendous stories to tell of separation and pain, but no one could match mine at that point, despite its being acted out in the supposedly liberal state of Massachusetts – but never forget that Massachusetts liberalism has a taproot that goes straight back to the hangman's noose. But also in the church (as well as club-houses) are all the other twelve-step programs, which evolved out of

Alcoholics Anonymous, and which have provided enormous personal transformation and emotional growth to gay men.

The percentage of gay men with what we can call 'twelve-step programs' is staggering, viewed impressionistically: I know of few gay men who haven't either been in counseling of one sort or another or a twelve-step program, and I include down-and-outers whose ability to finance such is surely a wonderment. And their stories of their therapy, so often of uncomprehending psychiatrists or psychologists, were often powerful. So the churches and clubhouses run overtime in gay areas, for AA members, Al-Anon (for people, like me, with alcoholics in their family), Debtors Anonymous, Adult Children of Alcoholics, Narcotics Anonymous, and even a Lovers Anonymous, for those too dependent on sex. After many years, I became convinced that in those halls, where gay men come day after day to share their stories and participate in each other's emotional growth, lie the most important support structures for urban gay men.

And in those halls is Christianity itself – the undiluted version, which a disproportionate number of gay men populate in the urban ghettos. Christianity is a religion that speaks to suffering, not to power, and that, at so many levels, is where gaydom is. We have asked for compassion, we offer to share the burden. We have turned the other cheek to the taunts of the majority: sometimes worse in the form of in-house jokes among mainstream men than insults from rednecks. Christianity is a religion of transcendence, which every gay man understands, or should. Small wonder that, in urban churches, it is not surprising to find a fourth or a fifth of the congregation to be gay. My own rector, who is straight, has thrown himself into gay issues and causes, and serves the interest of the gay community consummately. It does not surprise.

And consider the redoubt of homosexual stigma, the Word itself, to which so much argument goes back (but not from which it proceeds in fact), among those for whom a stigma attached to gays is relevant. Firstly let us note that there are all of three explicit and apparent damnations of homosexuality in the Bible, but on closer examination they become far more obviously damnations of loose sexuality; of which homosexuality should legitimately bear only its usual ten per cent of the onus. Only in Leviticus do we find an explicit condemnation, but in a context, as John Boswell convincingly argues, that is not applicable to a Christian community as moral law.[4]

But more revealingly to our arrangements, we find that the evolution of Christian doctrine favors our psychohistorical interpretation of how society – and its stigmas – evolves. St Paul's stigmas attach to wanton behavior generally. The key word in the New Testament from Paul's pen is 'malakos', that is 'soft' or 'loose', taken in recent centuries to be a broadside against homosexuals and homosexuality, but which even this prep school Greek student can translate as hardly confined to us. As Boswell says, this use of the word (in Corinthians 6:9) against gays is gratuitous. 'The word is never used in Greek to designate gay people as a group or even in reference to homosexual acts generically.'[5]

Well, the problem gets funnier. 'Malakos' came to be seen as a broadside against masturbation. But as that vast peril receded as a threat to civilization in the nineteenth century, the psychohistorical ramparts had to retreat; as jerking off no longer precluded one's entry to the Kingdom of Heaven and God in His wisdom could suffer a little autonomous pleasure, Boswell goes on, 'the condemnation has simply been transferred to a group still so widely despised that their exclusion does not trouble translators or theologians'. In other words, if you can't blame Jews for the depression, blame them for currency speculation. And also in other words, the stigma moves as necessary to keep the bonds tight among the bigoted; psychohistory moves on.

Oh, but we're not finished. In the Revised Standard Version of the Bible, 1952, the damnation – from the *same* Greek word (or, as we see from the footnotes, from the combination of *two* words) – advances a step further beyond the 1885 version, so much more so than that of gay King James two and a half centuries earlier. For now 'homosexuals' are named as such, almost a revelation in this progression, along with the other 'immoral' persons, 'idolaters', and 'thieves' who will not inherit the kingdom of heaven. One wonders when last translators were to bring such heavy baggage to their task, as to weight down rather simple words of an ancient text with so much modern angst.

But gays need not be defensive when Christianity is the issue. Has there been a doctrine or religion more applicable to gay life as it is now found at its best? I think not. Jesus's whole ministry, arguably, is the ultimate articulation of my tribe's lifestyle – its gentleness, its generosity, its compassion, and its sensibilities. Attend a gay gathering and attend a straight one of men of similar persona and note the difference in concerns and anxieties; other things being equal, gay men may be more narcissistic in their demeanor but they will be less concerned with their individual masculinity and dominance one to another; more perfumed but less dishonest in their presentation of their motives; they will like each other as men more but be less antagonistic toward (and less jocular about) women.

Jesus' usual demeanor is something we can comprehend; it is a set of sensibilities we grasp and need. But note, gay men, that Jesus didn't always take it on the other cheek; he threw the moneylenders out of the temple. And some of our forward organizations, like Queer Nation, are radically proactive like Christ with the moneylenders. The time is surely coming when we will have to organize to be like this more radical Christ, for example to throw Jesse Helms out of the Senate. Christianity relates.

I came back to Christianity as a result of a close reading of the Gospel according to Saint John. I do not care whether he was gay or not, but at the level of essence I relate to every word he spoke. And his relationship to Jesus is one that might just cause Pastor Richard Neuhaus, and the lesser associates of his anti-gay crusade, to be perhaps slightly more cautious. Or at least the historical interpretation of that relationship, if those more recent authorities have divine perspective on the contemporary bonding of Jesus and St John. For, in the Middle Ages, Saint Aelred of Rievaulx had already put pen to paper, talking, in one of the gayest encomia to love one can find, of 'heavenly marriage' and the 'more intimate love' of John and Jesus, the former of whom had his highest reach 'that he should be called [in his own words] the "disciple whom Jesus loved" '.[6] Just halfway between then and now Caravaggio gave us an even more radical depiction of St John, and Christopher Marlowe left even less to the imagination: 'St John the Baptist was Christ's bedfellow, and used to rest his head on Christ's breast, and Christ used him as the sinners of Sodom do.'[7]

As for depression, I would guess that my patched-together solution came from all of these roads, programs and halls. Depression, of course, is a system of thought wherein you believe in your own worthlessness and resourcelessness; its roots may lie in the chemical structures of the body or the more elusive orders of the mind, whatever: it ends up as the same thing. The ability to discuss your worthiness is the road out of it. If you are inclined to suspect anyone offering to throw a rope to you in the depths of your despair, you have a problem. In short, the minute you are willing to be rational, you are on the way back.

Roger, for example, set on maintaining his morbid self-hating logic against all efforts to replace it with intelligent thought, knew that he could not refute my reasoning and avoided the issue by refusing to return my calls. And his self-hatred when he left for Rehoboth was great enough to fake good feeling in his last conversation, with me and, finally, our friend Andrew Short.

My problem with depression always seemed less severe than Roger's, and was less obvious than my exuberant behavior at the other end of the spectrum. I learned how little is known about depression – and how much – by the difference in prognoses, several years before 'black dog' finally became fashionable. The medical therapist with greatest knowledge of my behavior and over many years, Tom Goldman, never had me on anti-depressants; HMOs, comprehensive 'Health Maintenance Organizations', now widespread in the United States, though, are always prone to substitute pills for the far more expensive psychiatric billable hours, and after brief interviews mine in Boston prescribed several medications which I tried with indifferent results.

The most I could figure out was that the biggest variable in my mental health was neither medication nor conversation but diet and exercise, and if I ate and drank well and worked out every day, I never had anything to worry about. Of course I didn't always. But by 1992 my children had even made me a vegetarian, and by 1993 I had completely cut out alcohol, which is of course a depressant itself, one which in numerous cases is the villain in setting a person on the road to deep depression. The problems related to it will be the politically correct successor tomorrow to today's campaigns on smoking.

The larger point is that the trials of the last decade had wrung me out, and depression was one of the most obvious symptoms of distress, but by no means the only one. Recuperation, in any event, starts in pain, and one has to deal with that at some point. I think all the programs I tried gave me something, perhaps little threads of self-worth so that, however deep I would go into despair, there were little strings going out showing me the way back if I wanted. There are payoffs, as Rob Eichberg always said, for solving one's problems. On a day that otherwise brought much pain and which I thought would lead to minor depression, I received a letter from a very dear fourteen-year-old girl attending a summer camp at Wellesley College. It went as follows:

> I don't know whether you will be proud or ashamed but tonight I took the stand. We had a speak-out . . . on whether or not Homosexual couples should be allowed to get married and/or adopt children. I wasn't on the panel, but I talked about what it was like to have a parent who was gay. I said that you were (mostly) a wonderful father and that most of the time I didn't think of you as any different. One topic was how would friends of a child adopted by gay parents get along without being made fun of. I said the friends of mine who knew about you couldn't care less (except when I'm mad at you) and that [one hopes] most people would be understanding, and if they weren't that is their problem.
>
> Some of the people made me so mad. A lot brought up the Bible and all its gay-bashing . . . they were countered with the separation of church and state stuff. Others were just ignorant. One person said that homosexuals were not even human, and that they should be punished and he was applauded!
>
> One person (a lesbian) talked about how if God created love, men and women, and was all-powerful if *she* (God) didn't believe in homosexuality she would never have created it . . . That person got a standing ovation!!!
>
> I can *really* deal! I didn't have to go, and I definitely didn't

> have to speak – but people made me *so* mad!! Love Heidi . . .
> I CAN DEAL!

This of course was from my very precious youngest child Heidi, who has brought so much happiness into many lives.

There turned out to be another way – involving acceptance, surrender, and transcendence.[8] This is not one of false heroics. Marcel's model of physical grace, (straight) masculinity, and effortless good breeding in *À La Recherche*, Robert Saint-Loup-en-Bray, yields to his inner needs and goes off to Jupien's (male) brothel while on leave from the great war in Paris: and then, as if there is a necessary connection, Proust has him killed in action on the front just immediately after. The other way is an acceptance so powerful that it transcends all other realities and makes compromise on sexuality too trivial to contemplate.

The other way usually does start in pain. I remember telling one of the gaggle of psychiatrists hovering around Nina's and my divorce case that the whole process was so bad, so horrible, that the only way one could keep it from being an unmitigated tragedy was to transcend it, to learn so much from it that (in this case) I would be a better father than I could possibly have been under the old dispensation. I now found the same lesson after my first lover and I broke up, which was just as painful a break-up – one I tried to avert by getting my lover to see the possibility of our building on the lessons of what had so thunderously occurred, and thus transcending here again; when he didn't even understand what I was talking about I realized I had to just let events take their course.

I wrote a year later, just after I had to take him to court for continuing to steal from my property, that I had to forge on toward new territory; 'I resolve that the loss is so great that the compensating growth must be correspondingly greater. Period' (Diary, 5 March 1990). 'No pain no gain', our trainers tell us in the gym, and it is true in the school of hard knocks, too. Gay men by and large have suffered considerably. This other way only works when one reaches out far beyond where he had been, and dares to go down through the dark labyrinth of one's mind, until he comes to the bottom and confronts the minotaur, the dragon that has held back his emotional growth, caused him to hide, to take easy choices, to avoid dealing with the fullness of his homosexuality, which is so totally different from heterosexuality.

I was conscious throughout my adult life, before coming out, that I was stifling myself. In 1974, on arriving at Northeast Harbor with our new baby Phyllis, a nanny, and a puppy, for a pre-summer visit, I manifestly showed the irrelevance of the material grandeur in which our lives were cast, and got right to the point, as so often with thoughts of my father in the background.

> What keeps me so bottled up these days? A sense, growing, of the tragedy of life . . . not in any trite sense, but in the rather profound sense that *when we fail to transcend*, or solve problems, we find clever stratagems for preserving our dignity [and thus] I am filled with thoughts of dignity: that it is far better to go on acting as if life is fulfilled and suppress one's disappointment: and to find fulfillment through new patterns. (Diary, 20 May 1974, emphasis added)

But how much better to solve the problems, which often can only occur through transcendence, since the material road is truly blocked? One has to find a new road to travel on *and* a new and better destination. Andrew Harvey tells how the Pasolini film, *Teorema*, affected him.

> *Teorema* convinced me that you had to be honest about your sexuality, and choose Eros, otherwise you'd be radically destroyed from within. In a way, that prepared me to seek illumination later: the intensity and pain of choosing love above all else.[9]

The gay world has shown its rationality in constructing such multitudinous support structures in society, in pressing so hard and fast for societal change despite the unimaginably low starting point. The flowering of gay literature – social science and fiction – complements the huge gay role in the other arts, where we have always been conspicuous. I find indeed that Frank Browning is surely wrong in his conclusions, namely that unlike every other cultural entity which seeks to 'secure their tribal meaning through the immutability of their codes, rights, and rituals', the gay world lives for change.

> Queer culturalists recognize and realize one another through disruption and sabotage of their inherited traditions. Employing wit and the critical parody of camp, they unravel the hidden forgeries of their own inherited cultures and then self-consciously construct new cultural forgeries that they know are destined to dissolve. That is the essence of desire in the queer paradox. To persevere is to disappear. The community of identity exists only in the state of transformation. In the culture of desire, there are no safe places.[10]

That is not a formula for success in achieving a respected identity in the modern world – only a self-preoccupied one. For we *have* developed our icons and tribal rights, far beyond desire and pleasure. The quilt is our symbol, and the trouble about all our fashions, styles, and mottos is only that the straight world picks them up and adopts them so rapidly. There are safe places, or where is our power of energy-conferring identity for the youth from Idaho or Alabama? Precisely because we do *not* recruit by blood lines and tribal membership, we have to have identifiable rules if we are going to be fruitful in the future.

Robert Nozick has inadvertently helped to make the point I wish to make. He suggests that, with respect to building a philosophy of life, one might count fifty, out of a maximum hundred, points just for living, and another thirty for being human. 'Any particular choices we made would pale in significance alongside the fact that we are alive and make choices,' he says.[11]

In those first eighty points are all that one has gained through therapy, good works, that which has shaped us in the past, and which gay men have done so much of because of where they are coming from. I have this well in mind from having reread, while writing this essay, the totality of almost forty years of diaries, and knowing that at times I made enormous efforts to figure out what was wrong, what wasn't working. The discretionary points seem far less important – and therefore courage is easier – if we look at the substantial burden we carry from our common humanity and our individual therapy. The person who got married in 1968 saw the world totally differently from the gay man of 1993; layer after layer is different in my subconscious and is reflected in diaries, personal interactions and goals. Gay men have the beautiful option of coming out publicly, reinforcing those already there, saying it's only a small part of their existence – but added up with all the other peoples', it's a very big step for mankind. It's the toughest and biggest liberation acted out on these territories since the Civil War.

## *Notes*

1. Erik H. Erikson, *Young Man Luther* (New York: W. W. Norton, 1956), p. 149.
2. As cited by John Gardner, 'The road to self-renewal', *Stanford*, March 1994, p. 34.
3. The whole point of his excellent book *Coming Out – An Act of Love* (1990) is that virtually everyone on some passionately held issue is shut in as smothering a closet as the classic one. That the concept had made the main line became clear on 12 July 1994, when the *Washington Post* argued that, now, even accordion players – and accordions – would 'come out'!
4. John Boswell, *Christianity, Social Tolerance, and Homosexuality* (University of Chicago Press, 1980), p. 113.
5. *Ibid.*, pp. 106–7.
6. Cited by Boswell, p. 226.
7. Cited in Cecile Beurdeley, *L'Amour Bleu* (New York: Rizzoli, 1978), p. 103, as attributed to Thomas Kyd.
8. I owe this realization, as so much else, to Timothy Dickinson.
9. Laura Leivick, 'The merry mystic', *New York Times Magazine*, 3 October 1993, p. 36.
10. Frank Browning, *The Culture of Desire* (New York: Crown, 1993), p. 229.
11. Robert Nozick, *The Examined Life* (New York: Simon & Schuster, 1989), p. 299.

# *Part Three*
# *A Queer Manifesto*

*. . . every memoir now is a kind of a manifesto, as we piece together the tale of the tribe.*

● Paul Monette

## *Stigma*

Our stigma is of long provenance. J. M. Roberts notes how a Byzantine emperor suffered criticism only when not 'doing his Christian duty – which included the harrying of such familiar scapegoats as Jews, heretics and homosexuals'.[1] So I near the end of this political memoir inspired by what has happened to my gay peers and to myself, to make of it a statement, which we start by labeling things as they are. When a mother can't bear to admit that her son is gay because in her conservative community this will negate the standing she has carefully contrived and accumulated, and her peers will say 'she has a nicer house – but then, [with a sneer] her son is *gay*'; and when she and her family dismiss the achievements of the family's most distinguished member – the head of a major urban institution – because he 'swishes his hips'; or when a college student, brilliant and attractive, is ashamed of his well-known father because his peers discount his own accomplishments by noting that his father bears a stigma, because he is gay – and the student wears a scarlet letter; or when socially prominent folks omit to invite a friend to their house for an important dinner party, after they hear he's gay, and (amusingly) tell him they 'wanted to invite you, but we already had a Jewish couple coming' and manifestly feel they can bear only so much stigma: then we have a phenomenon of invidious, but meaningful, social ranking. And social discrimination.

What causes a stigma to evaporate? One analogy might be the early Christians, who, as we all know from Cecil B. deMille films of the 1950s, drew a fish in the sand – the acronym ICHTHYS of course – to reveal themselves to one another. Like gays, and unlike racially stigmatized groups, they could pass like anyone else. Now by and large they didn't come out individually in the early years, because to do so meant being tossed to the lions, at least in the Hollywood version. Of course there is another key difference, in that one wasn't born a Christian; one was converted, in those early years, or at most was acculturated into the religion. Homosexuality is mostly in the genes. Nevertheless, there was a dynamic at work and as more conversions took place, more and more Christians were willing to risk coming out; one could construct a mathematical ratio as to the risk, at the margin, of coming out as a function of the number already out, and find the critical mass of those needed to be out within a society for the most rapid conversion. Ultimately the Emperor Constantine himself converted and Christianity was the new received wisdom – and from there the analogy breaks down.

But in precisely the same sense – before fantasizing of a gay emperor (though Rome again provides us with models aplenty) – we could calculate the risk to each gay man of coming out and no doubt we would find that with each coming out, less courage would be needed, until it became an unnoteworthy event. It is also the case that the more role models that are provided, and the more prominent those coming out are, then the greater the effect will be on those troubled by their homosexuality, especially teenagers.

If the argument is compelling, why don't more gay men come out? For one thing, among the notables, we haven't reached anything near a critical mass. In Washington, only four or five of the hundred or so truly prominent gay men have come out. There are, more logically, the external reasons and the internal reasons. As we have seen, there is the price a gay man pays professionally and socially; now he bears a stigma. Some people look at him – yes, even worldly people in big cities – as something of a freak; in other words all other factors get subordinated to his sexuality in the view others have of him. In some professions he might be fired, though fewer and fewer and no longer including the US government or any other large-scale business. So as we have seen, there are prices, but declining ones, as the acceptability of gay sexuality rises in society and as one finds increasing rewards internally from having dealt with this issue. After the twenty-fifth anniversary celebration of Stonewall in New York, in 1994, one straight writer after another wrote that our movement had 'come of age'.

Internally, the reluctance is usually that one hasn't completed his coming to terms with parents and siblings. Everyone has a lifelong relationship with his mother and father, even after they die; our parents exercise such power on us that, if they are homophobic, we are frightened of revealing our true selves, and doubly pained if their homophobia remains after coming out. Ironically, the first thing parents often say in a confrontation with a child coming out is disassociation of one form or the other, including often a suggestion that the child had better not suggest that such an inclination had come down through *them*. As if there were someone more appropriate, out of the other five billion people on earth, through whom to trace one's homosexuality than one's parents.

People are fearful of taking on gay causes because in most of the country there's nothing in it for them, and there *is* something to lose; it's not yet Leonard Bernstein hosting the Black Panthers at his apartment in the Dakota – though by the late 1960s gay Lenny manifestly knew what his real cause should have been.

The bottom line of denial is prestige. A gay person who lies about his identity, or a confused gay person in denial who acts and speaks to sustain his existing status rather than venture onto unchartered waters, is afraid of losing the props of everyday life. These may be (as in my case) wealth and high social status; they may be livelihood for an Air Force lieutenant or promotion for an IBM executive. Everyone is scared of losing what he has and what sustains him; and in any event people change slowly. This applies to affected non-gays, like parents, who in covering up the homosexuality of their children to themselves or to their social group are also living a lie and perpetuating the stigma – quite apart from what they are doing in mangling their relations with their heirs.

The 'opportunity cost' of not coming out should never be far from our consciousness, and this book may contain the costliest example of our century – at least the costliest an 'outing' has yet revealed. Paul Nitze's unresolved 'missile crisis', coterminous with his never resolved sexual identification, cost the nation billions of dollars, arguably, in unnecessary weapons. This is not to argue that the nation should have gone unarmed, but the particular manner in which Nitze pressed the case of particular missiles far transcended evident military designation and purpose in many cases.

A bottom line is our personal goal. We can hardly be thought to have a program and purpose in life if we are living a lie on a daily basis. Who is the great man anywhere in history who didn't have his essentials sorted out? Erik Erikson said it so precisely of Jefferson, that he was 'centered'. Surely by definition a centered man is not a closeted man. The 'right to be' is first and simply a refusal to accept any other identity than our obvious essence. If we can't be Thomas Jeffersons, we can all be Rosa Parks. Of course we shed the gratuitous denial of my 'friend' who will 'protect' me by denying the homosexuality.

## *Creativity*

Socially we have been marginal and stigmatized men; but ironically in our artistic and literary contributions, we have been embarrassingly close to the center, perhaps creating the center. And society has enormously benefitted from this. Erikson writes more generally of the misfit,

> if some did not force themselves almost against their own wills to insist, at the price of isolation, on finding an original way of meeting our existential problems, societies would lose an essential avenue to rejuvenation and to that rebellious expansion of human consciousness which alone can keep pace with the technological and social change.[2]

Whether it is Caravaggio's paintings, Benjamin Britten's operas, or Shakespeare's sonnets, the themes which reveal the artist to the gay man so quickly and to most others in time, have worked to redefine our aesthetic and our definition of life. Proust, for example, though sealed in his cork-lined room, to all intents and purposes co-sponsored, with his contemporary Sigmund Freud, society's confrontation with the unconscious and then its slow, painful, inescapable literary incorporation in to our whole life.

Here is a strain of life that produced Alexander and Socrates, Michelangelo and Leonardo, Whitman and Melville, Williams and Albee, Britten and Copeland, Auden and Isherwood, Verlaine, Maugham, Cocteau, Gide, Turing, Forster, Keynes, Santayana, and Wittgenstein. With the possible exception of that from the Jews –

and that only in the last century – it surely is the most impressive list of geniuses and cosmic talents from a marginal group in history, and that includes women, who were never demographically marginal. It is not something to be ashamed of or protected from.

But – it may be objected – deny the homosexual his marginality and he will deny society his artistic eminence, he will blend in with the mainstream; there will be no more angst to come out on great canvases or in novels from gay denial and gay pain, there will be no more sonnets like Michelangelo's to Tommaso Cavalieri or symphonies like Tchaikovsky's to his nephew. The answer is, firstly, not necessarily so; how do you know? – we *don't* know. But if so, *so what?* African-Americans contributed the only new art form from the new world, with jazz, and no doubt it was a product of black marginality. But no black is going to trade his enormous gains against a potential future artistic outpouring from suffering.

Gays are no different. We are happy to have contributed so much more than our numbers would indicate to the common culture, but we are fighting for our place in the sun, with or without artistic (and other) creation. And in any case, there is enough gay suffering still around, from which much of artistic merit may still proceed for our lifetimes. Get acquainted with a consciously gay man from Russia or China to learn how constrained one still can be; *Talking to Fish* is the only too appropriate title of a forthcoming autobiographical novel by a young gay Russian.

And what is the danger to *gay* society if we *were* socially accepted? We have already argued the position of 'marginal man'. Whether or not we maintained our creative edge, would acceptance cost us our separateness and identity? It appears the opposite. The more gays have been allowed to live openly and have felt free to do so, the more our lifestyle seems to put down roots of its own, in the form of traditions, customs, and organizations. The stigma forced most of us historically to hide within straight society; get rid of the stigma and we would do the opposite as we are already doing – as all manner of gay groups did in the march on the United Nations in June 1994. After all, it's the sexuality from which our distinctiveness proceeds, and that isn't going to change with freedom; the parallel to deaf culture, which ideologists of 'deafism' feel is threatened by the notion of hearing, is inexact. We're at the least no longer going to be thrown in jail for our sexual practices and there will be more of us, and more of us seen, as constrained people come out of their closets and explore their true selves. Dr Isay for one is optimistic on this issue. When we don't have to spend all our energy 'hiding' and 'finding secret ways to express [our] love and sexuality, there will be a release of creative energy that will benefit all society'.[3]

## *From weakness to strength*

It is now prestigious, within American society as a whole, to be black, Jewish, or a woman's rights leader. Gloria Steinem and Jesse Jackson are avidly sought – for talk shows, debates, and opinion columns. That is because even if many men haven't bought the whole package, especially in the provinces, they have conceded the point, and legislation backs it up: women and African-Americans are to have the same chance as men. Woman are still paid much less, but ask any male Wasp trying to get a job in the Clinton administration, and he will tell you how perfectly women – and other minorities, not including gays – are coming on there. There may be a lot of anti-Semitism left in western society, but Jewish people are in the mainstream, and no one seeking national office would dare offend Jewish interests. Colin Powell, whose presumed presidential aspirations are everywhere taken for granted and respected, shows how far African-American interests have come; the fact that he's 'different' as a Jamaican by origin means nothing. Literally only a generation ago, blacks were utterly on the outside and largely without spokesmen; now 'everyone', at least everyone of the urban intelligentsia, has a black friend, and if there are still *de facto* segregated areas in society (like some musical events) acceptance is tacit everywhere. Even daily discourse has changed, from where a white male point of view was assumed in formal English to one that is at least gender-neutral and racially neutral – yet the assumption remains that *everyone is straight*.

But everyone isn't. In fact, gays are everywhere, but are only 'accepted' as long as we don't say so, and that is what has to change. It is more than coming out: it is saying we are out and reminding our friends and acquaintances that we are out. Coming out itself may be a rather private affair, after all; but after that we need to testify wherever we go. Bumper stickers and AIDS pins are touching but not enough; we need to say we're gay, until everyone gets used to it. In the past we could go everywhere, only as long as we didn't say we were gay, and that is precisely what was wrong with the old order; we denied our essential reality and now we must turn that upside down. Sumner Welles could be at the pinnacle of the American social and diplomatic establishment during the 1930s and 1940s, and everyone who mattered knew he was homosexual, including his employer Franklin Roosevelt, and as long as he didn't draw public attention to it and continued to live as a rich aristocrat he stayed at the top. But he did this by denying who he was.

Another way of looking at a stigmatized group is to see its members, correctly, as weak. If they weren't weak they'd have made themselves strong and ended the humiliations that attach to a stigma. How historically have weak groups become strong? Politically, some marginal or small groups have literally seized the reins of power and perfected the use of its suppressive mechanisms to stay in power – for example as the minority Tutsi did in ruling over the majority Hutu in Rwanda, with such catastrophic current results, for centuries. This option is not available to us. Even the 'black power' model isn't available, with its attendant shade of force, because it is implausible for the gay world and uncongenial as well. But there is also the point that Annette Baker Fox makes about weak states in World War II, and which would go for (North) Vietnam during the long war with America: there is a power to just staying put, taking the abuse, but insisting on one's own central position. Armies could maraud over European terrain but the marginal states refused to give up their existence, and ultimately their sovereignty had to be reaffirmed. Vietnam just took the abuse and the bombs, stuck to its political guns, and ultimately won the war. Fox writes that what is impressive is 'the variety of circumstances under which the power of a small state, when confronted with an unwelcome great-power demand, turns out to be much greater than any inventory of its internal resources would suggest'.[4] It could be true for us. Those who are prepared to hazard their existence possess an almost ineradicable identity.

True, accepting a man as a man, despite his differentness, is difficult. I attended segregated schools until Phillips Academy (which had only one black) and thus met almost no blacks; Stanford's were token. But even in the civil rights effort in which I joined I was too terrified of the differentness of blacks to get to know any – exactly the way so many straights think of us gays today. No African-American had ever referred to himself in personal terms as a black or African-American, and thus I had never felt the opening to discuss this essential differentness. But in 1964 I attended a dinner party (and was kindly invited to stay over) that David and Evangeline Bruce gave at Winfield House in Regent's Park – and I had only too much reason to see my differentness on the occasion, at least as something of a David Copperfield peering over the wall yet from inside, since my shoes had fallen apart and I had brought no seconds in my overnight bag. Needless to say I was far too intimidated by Ambassador Bruce to ask for a rescue. Ironically, it was Attorney General Robert F. Kennedy – who had arrived *in medias res* with sister-in-law Jacqueline for the next day's dedication of the Runnymede memorial to President Kennedy – who sensitively observed the problem and lent me a replacement pair for the evening.

The dinner was followed by a cast party for an American troupe made up largely of Southern African-Americans. One I befriended and he visited me at Oxford that weekend. He saw my problem from the first, so he confronted me in a pub and said, 'Look, I'm here for the weekend. We've got to deal with each other. I'm not a toy or a liberal creation. I'm a man and you have to respect me on my own terms. Until then we've nothing to say to each other, do we?' At the end of the visit he laughed in his hearty and heavily accented southern black way, 'It took you a hell of a lot of beer and booze to get over your inhibitions and to realize that in most ways I'm just another guy like you.' He didn't know how right he was.

So the stigma works, everywhere that gays can't pass and also where they can; there are only a few liberal urban ghettos that have come to terms. It works at every level of the judiciary, throughout the military, and in the commanding social heights of the country: at the prestigious clubs, where being known as gay would in almost all cases be a membership veto (if usually hidden or subsumed within other criteria at the more sophisticated institutions), and in prestigious societies and organizations. If gays already therein, closeted, come out and make it clear that there are more inside, that we are too talented to be kept out in any event, then the rest of those within will quickly declare themselves too.

The courage to be comes from taking a stand – against the received wisdom and established values, wherein we are judged insufficient, as lesser mortals, the way an *aficionado* of red wine considers white wine as simply an underdeveloped vinous product; where our masculinity is deemed inadequate because it expresses itself in a different way – in fact in often so much more humane a way, as compassion, as a developed aesthetic.

We will all take our stand from different cues. Mine came at the start of my ten-year crisis but gave me the resolve to carry through. In March 1982 I had bought two elegant over-the-shoulder male handbags of the sort popular among European men, and, to an extent, American gays, while at a conference in Italy. My shopping mates in Bellagio, a village beside Lake Como, were Ambassador Kenneth Adelman and François Heisbourg, then an aide to the French defense minister, the latter of whom also bought several. They were handy for travel, including at home.

After the long hot Washington summer trying to calm things down with Nina and after a long day at my office calming down bureaucratic crises, I came back to the Nitze residence to dine with my friend Ronald Steel, the well-known writer. The Nitzes I thought to be all in Northeast Harbor, but suddenly Paul Nitze arrived, for a meeting the next morning at the White House that I was also attending. We asked if he would care to join us at a restaurant for dinner (the cook being off). He could only reply, 'Oh, there's Scott's *purse*', signifying also that he knew the divorce was underway. I have alluded to the lack of taunting I received on the schoolgrounds of my childhood; I didn't look like a sissy. Now I was getting it in full measure, as intended. I was meant to feel like three-fourths less of a man for his comment, and my cup was to run over with his contempt. There was a dead silence as Paul and I both realized the force of his thrust. I finally replied, 'Yes, that's my purse . . . do you care to join us?' knowing of course he now wouldn't. Paul Monette, who *was* taunted as a kid for being a sissy, wrote of a similar jab inflicted at a far younger age, 'Something that still winces that I wasn't enough of a man . . . '.[5] The gay experience is universal.

I refused to be demeaned, and from that moment though my moves were largely unconscious and often unstrategic as well as tactless, they drove to a single purpose, *being* my real self, realizing my real self, whatever the cost, taking a stand. And whatever the cost it could only be lower than the alternative.

There is no doubt that gay pride days and marches on Washington expand our political power. But they do it slowly, merely reinforcing in mainstream America's eyes the notion that gays are with us – but 'out there'. What they need to know is that we are *right here*. My own preference is to make a reference, at least, in every conversation with a straight person or straight group, to 'my social group', or to 'us gays' or 'as we gays see it', just to accustom my interlocutors to my interests and to that set of values as well as to let them know that we're not going away. The incredulity – matched by studied and learned insouciance – at the members' table of the Metropolitan Club can be stunning, still more so when I greet a gay friend in the foyer with the kiss that is our custom.

I make a point at least several times in the progress of every semester-long class I teach to make reference to my vantage point as a gay man, both to emphasize the sociology of knowledge – and whence particularities of my outlook – and, secondarily, to familiarize my students with so novel a concept: a homosexual who isn't ashamed of it. The Monday after the march on Washington I made a one-minute announcement in class about the importance of what had happened, precisely as I had a generation earlier after a black march on Washington in which I had also taken part. All this could remind everyone that we may look the same as they do, but we are not the same.

The manifesto at its center is a refusal to accept marginal status, it is to insist as gay men that we too are mainstream. We live right there in the mainstream, suburbs and city, work in mainstream jobs, pay mainstream taxes and are everywhere, despite which we are deemed marginal almost everywhere. In a search for common ground with straight society, we assert that we are part of civil society, sharing common and mainstream turf with our brothers and sisters.

I have written over and over how in ignorance I had insisted in court, in legal confrontations over the children, and at the White House over an appointment, that I expected to be treated as the élite member of society that I was, at the very least as no worse than anybody else. The hits I took forced me to a stand, and made me realize we will only reach our goal if all of us do no less. After all, no one could have been more mainstream than I was, living the American dream of the highest education, achieved on scholarship, fathering three smart kids, and moving up through life to fulfill so many of the dreams a small-town youth could have. And I never ceased to be 'mainstream' in my public life – eating lunches at the Metropolitan Club, teaching at a famous school, but for the past decade declaring my homosexuality right there at the center.

So now it's time for America to grant us the respect we are due. It is veritably with an ideology that we must move. It is at the least a *Weltanschauung*, but more, namely 'the acceptance of one's one and only life cycle as something that had to be and that, by necessity, permitted of no substitutions'.[6] We are not asking for tolerance; we are in sight of that in some of the country and throughout our highest professional élites. Rather we want the same respect that we offer and willingly give. It is a revolution of aspiration, not desperation – it is *away* from the lives of quiet desperation, at best, that we all grew up in. This is a patriotic manifesto; it is unfitting that a tolerant America not come to terms with this its last great minority within.

## Allies

What keeps straights from aligning themselves politically with gays, the way many of us did with blacks from the 1960s onwards? The really critical difference is not the issue of discrimination but once again of stigma: a white liberal can stand being considered wet or wobbly, but he can't add effeminate to that. He can crusade for African-Americans or women, because he is in no danger of being confused with a black or a woman. If there were no stigma to homosexuality, then the white liberal could care less whether someone thought him gay when he stood up for gay causes; he could evaluate the costs of his support in functional, rather than affective, terms. The critical blockage for assembling coalitions lies in simple human realities: for example the closeted gay human rights volunteer, in a key position in a Washington organization, prevents his organization from taking on gay issues to the extent one might expect of them, because of his own anxieties about himself. We can't solve his personal problem for him; but to the extent that we remove the stigma we lower the cost to him of acting on his conscience. It is worth noting that not until mid-1994 did a single, straight, prominent member of Washington's political-diplomatic establishment come out in public support of gay rights – Ambassador Mort Abramowitz, president of the Carnegie Endowment for International Peace, an enlightened haven where I wrote a book.

Frank Rich, whom we have previously cited on the extraordinary extent to which gay perspectives, fashions and styles have woven themselves into American life in the past several decades, concludes with a caution that is just as relevant today as then:

> But if homosexuality as a social and biological phenomenon has entered the mainstream of American life, it's far from clear in the AIDS era to what extent heterosexuals embrace actual homosexuals – or the other way around. It's the nature of the melting pot that Americans can absorb black music or Jewish literature or gay aesthetics even as they keep their distance from the blacks, the Jews, and the gays themselves – especially if these minority groups are too poor or assertive or ill.[7]

But there is a difference, we must remind our potential straight allies; the white Protestant cannot *be* a Jewish or black person; there surely is a bit of gayness in him, or a phase, that should link him to the gay person but historically has threatened him and thus created a far larger barrier than with the Jew or black.

In any event it is not we who should change our homosexuality, except in the direction of greater not less assertiveness. It is society that must change, that must come to terms with us and respect us not just for our accomplishments and contributions, but for our painful road to self-realization. Paul Monette put it so well:

'A man ought to be free to find his reason. Not that freedom alone will serve it up: it requires the gods' own fury of luck to get two people to meet. But when it finally happens, two men in love can't rejoice out loud – joy of the very thing everyone burns for – without bracing for the rant of prophets, the schoolyard bully, and Rome's "intrinsic evil". I try to remember that we fight as a ragged people to outlast the calamity so that others can sleep as safe as my friend and I, like a raft in the tempest.'[8]

Sometimes we have to risk our happy acceptance at High Table, the altar of an Oxford college dining room, where faculty and master sup. In spring 1993, Sir Robin Renwick, the deft British ambassador to the United States, whom I had known when he was head of chancery in the early 1980s, flatteringly had me sit at his table at an embassy stag dinner, along with the ranking guest Senator Sarbanes and several other Washington luminaries. At one point when the then-current topic, the military gay ban, came up, I simply enquired, a little too loudly and cheekily for it to be ignored, as to which of my nine table-mates were working for gay rights, as for example Sarbanes and I had worked for black civil rights. I was especially pointed to the African-American on my right. I could sense Robin's calculation: not all his diplomatic skills, and few have more, could likely change the subject fast enough. Thus assessing, he grinned whimsically and leaned back, to enjoy the kill.

Dr Charles Krauthammer instantly differentiated homosexuality and black civil rights; I responded that there were also differences between women's and black civil rights; each constituency necessarily has a different constellation of concerns, but they are generically related in responding to tolerated social bigotry that restricts access to civil society. I got help from my old friend Christopher Hitchens, the *Vanity Fair* columnist, who has always enjoyed a good fight for equity. We got nowhere as such; but my guess is that for all at our table, it was the first bash on gay rights as a civil right, and all would be thinking more about it in the future.

We have to do this at every opportunity, until we of the gay world really do have allies. I have to add that, when the Rhodes Scholars were invited *en masse* to the embassy on Massachusetts Avenue during the June 1993 reunion, a few months later, I got no subtle or unsubtle reprimand from the ambassador – and I had even brought my boy-friend with me, *pour encourager les autres.*

## *Gay power*

We need courage. Consider how much of the gay leadership is filled by the smaller proportion of lesbians. And I note how personally gutsy they always seem, by comparison to gay men, for whom courage just isn't the long suit. Well, that's the popular image, isn't it? Amazon Jane and Casper Milquetoast . . . even when we think of the large percentage of gay men who are not effeminate.

But can't we do better? Let's be frank. Political change starts with and is about ideas – many of which are explored herein. But it is also about power. We have already considered the psychological sources of our potential power. The black movement had a primary leader, Dr Martin Luther King Jr, and it had a philosophy, nonviolent resistance. That gave it integrity and legitimacy, but what gave it quick success was the power of mass demonstration and the violent tendencies at the margin with the fears these elicited throughout America. The number of concessions and changes of consciousness in universities and in cities that were made under the guise of 'doing what was right' is almost infinite as was the amount of hypocrisy.

I am not suggesting violence on our part; anyway, as already noted, that isn't our style apart from groups like ACT-UP on the fringe. But precisely the comparison with African-Americans reveals to us how well organized and, yes, courageous, we will have to be if we are to obtain full equality. I mean boycotting goods and stores that refuse to adopt, or are not the product of, affirmative action policies; so too schools, businesses, institutes, factories. And if not violence, they'll get bullet voting, which is already beginning to achieve results, given the political and financial affluence of the gay community and its willingness to target gay issues in the voting booth: *that* is simply a revelation of how central gay issues are to our lives. And above all, speaking out at every dinner, at every meeting: 'By the way, I'm gay.' They'll blush, they'll be embarrassed, but they will, as a friend put it, 'get used to it'. It's the necessary step.

Gay men need to think less about their wardrobe and a little bit more about political war. The first mainstream national television advertisement using (plainly) gay men as a 'come-on' for sales was by Ikea in 1994, selling good taste in decor and furnishings. The implications of this are enormous. So too the market research coming to light at the same time showing the higher educational level and disposable income of average gay households.

So what is our leverage to accomplish this better life? Do we have in us the makings of the threat that Harriet Beecher Stowe so well foretold, only after a century bringing the black progress she would have wished to see, in her famous last paragraph of *Uncle Tom's Cabin*?

> This is an age of the world where nations are trembling and convulsed. A mighty influence is abroad, surging and heaving the world, as with an earthquake. And is America safe? Every nation that carries in its bosom great and unredressed injustice has in it the elements of this last convulsion.

No, that is not serious; there is convulsion aplenty in the world but not from us gays. But there is the unredressed injustice. And in a very powerful way the gay world indeed poses a threat to those of the received wisdom. Given the ease with which we influence mainstream culture and styles, envisage firstly a wave of comings-out later this decade, followed by a critical mass of outings, to the point where all of the Kinsey 1–2's – the third of all men – are fearful that 'someone knows' about their brief fling two – or ten – years ago. Or two weeks ago. I know that the most terror-struck year of my life was in 1983, when, though my wife's legal team had no evidence of gay activity on my part, my own internalization and projection, from my knowing just how gay I was inside, caused me to attribute to them a hundred times as much power over me as I should have; I lived in fear but at that point it came from inside me.

The source of gay power is indeed in the very ambiguity of the identity of mainstream straight men. The one-third who have had gay affairs think they must fight us because we threaten them by our mutual identification; the rest call us faggots (or whatever) precisely because we also represent a part of them, which they must of course destroy given how threatening it is. If they weren't afraid of us, why would they bother to go after us?

So that's one more, but the critical final, reason why men should come out – and bring their friends with them. It will bring us power. But the point is not to take anything away from the straight world; this is a non-zero sum game. We gain and they gain, because they cannot be sure of their masculinity until they have dealt with us and freed themselves of their fear that they are us. This is a revolution where everybody wins.

## Outing

This affects one's position on outing; a well-known straight writer said, 'Every senator outed saves at least one teenager from suicide.' If that is not empirically verifiable, it is intuitively obvious: and one suspects, given the numbers involved, it would be a vast number of teenagers saved. If so, outing becomes an imperative. Outing, many of us have concluded, *saves lives*. Gay teenagers have *nine times* the suicide rate of straight kids,[8] and there can hardly be any doubt that that rate would decline dramatically it there were prominent role models throughout society, at every level, to which young people could relate. In the Jewish Orthodox Book of Rules, one of the 613 meticulous instructions for daily living overrules all the others – that is that whatever saves life transcends any and all others. All our hesitations about outing should be put aside until this crisis has calmed, because the addition of a judge, film star, quarterback or senator to our roles may save a life, several lives, many lives. One's qualms about privacy invading in outing, or anything else, surely pales beside the consideration of *saving lives*. A stigmatized group like the gay world, already bearing the largest burden of any in our nation's history, simply cannot afford another risk to life without acting by any means available to reduce it.

What is our personal responsibility in 'outing'? This controversy has obscured other fundamental issues. My own view is philosophically radical, but moderate in application. I respect *any* person's bedroom privacy and am not even slightly concerned with or interested in what straights or gays do behind closed doors. But whether a person is or is not gay is an entirely different matter. Herewith, a critical distinction. If, using the Masters and Johnson criteria, a man happens to fantasize in gay terms but to practice heterosexuality consistently (and thus to them *is* straight) then as a practical matter the issue doesn't arise anyway; and if I become privy to his fantasies, say, I would surely keep them to myself since I could only have received them in confidence. He is entitled to his privacy.

But the minute he *practices gayness*, whereas I need to be no whistle-blower (unless he actively opposes gay causes or interests), I also recognize no obligation to lie for him, because it stigmatizes one's own identity.[9] He is drawing strength from the brave world we are constructing, getting his sexual and emotional fulfillment therefrom, and insofar as we get our moral fulfilment, in part, by coming out, we would abnegate that sacred part of ourselves by lying to hide his identity. So if he has every right in our privacy-conscious society to protect his closeted homosexuality, I have every corresponding right to expose it, if it cuts our interests and I come across it openly. Of course outing is a way of forcing people into our camp, breaking their bonds and compelling them to come in; it is equally a way of forcing society to accept a large number of closeted men, with consequences and ramifications for society. By the way, if I'm not mistaken, it's a well established straight idiom that lying is, also, wrong – and therefore to cover up somebody's identity will involve lies at every stage of the way.

In practice I know the agony of these closeted men's lives. In fact I would do some such men a great favor were I to out them, and eventually they would thank me; so many are placing deadline after absurd deadline for dealing with their sexuality, meantime postponing all the healing that can only start afterwards, and denying a critical part of their lives of emotional growth.

Gay men out in the gay world, but protective of their 'identity' at the workplace, defend their position on the grounds that their sexuality 'isn't anybody's business'. Indeed a psychiatrist once argued that position at my dinner table. But that's just cowardice. The straight person isn't hiding his or her sexual identity. And in fact what the gay person is doing is *impersonating* the majority, again discussing himself, not just 'protecting' himself. He is, in Paul

Monette's term 'chameleon and ventriloquist'. In support meeting after support meeting one hears tell of gays coming out on the job (other than the military, of course) and finding reinforcement, friendship, even professional advancement owing to the higher performance from the more open atmosphere and self-esteem gained.

To be sure, there are people whose outward persona has long since taken over any inner being, whose mask has become the soul. In that case perhaps the person isn't impersonating; his relentless dance to please has become the dancer, the very spirit. A case in point might well be one of America's most powerful and distinguished political servants, David Boren, until early 1995 senior senator from Oklahoma and its former governor. He was implicitly outed last year by gay papers and referred to, implicitly, in Signorile's book, *Queer America.* Boren and I were in the same Rhodes group, and as the law of odds would have it, he and I were put on the same staircase of the same college, sharing a scout, or manservant, as if the gods wished to concentrate the stigma; the third gay Rhodes Scholar, Michael Rice, who was already more or less out at Oxford, was nearby at Queen's College and was to become a real power in public broadcasting until he tragically died of AIDS several years ago.

Every Rhodes group has its extremes, which in the nature of things and given the range of talent usually found among Rhodes scholars can be very extreme. Walt Slocombe, now Under Secretary of Defense, was in the next staircase and presided over the only bathroom to which we had access. He was known as the brightest member of our group of thirty-two; Jim Woolsey the most purposeful; and Boren by far the most political and ambitious: just as one swatch of the cloth, he spent his first vacation sending dispatches and pictures from the 'Holy Land', showing David 'walking where Jesus walked', back to Oklahoma supporters. This amused none of us but then we didn't vote in Oklahoma. I was aware that David was gay before I was aware of my own homosexuality, and our scout confirmed it, after a parade of Balliol's cutest first-year students made their way in and out of his rooms with variable consequences. But just like the corruption which David set out to sweep away with the emblematic brooms of his first Oklahoma campaign, his homosexuality was never too far from the surface – the looks of adorable young men, the rumors of trouble with pageboys at the Oklahoma capitol, and the reasonably well-attested stories of continued gay imbroglios on Capitol Hill.

The question is, since David Boren impersonates a straight person and has done so for his lifetime, is there anything inside him that is gay, and, by the way, redeemable? Who can know? His anti-homosexual rhetoric from time to time certainly absolves the gay community from any obligations to him. But at the very least had he come clean before he left the Senate for the University of Oklahoma, he would have established a political high-water mark for homosexuality, indeed he'd have been at the high-water mark for a publicly gay figure. And I doubt at that point he would have endangered his political standing in Oklahoma, as if anything could have.

His departure from Washington, almost surely prompted by his anxieties about the growing knowledge of his sexuality and fear for a deeper degree of outing, was justified – in an Op-Ed – on the grounds that the demands on his life had become too great for him to have perspective even on political issues and that he could have more influence at the community level than through the 'power and influence' he wielded in Washington; the point had come where in one month 'it took 27 days before my wife and I could have dinner together'.[10]

Only people on the way up need to schedule themselves so heavily; David had already made it, so this classically illustrates the innate frustration of the uncentered person looking for yet another conquest with which to justify himself, to divert himself from the true search for self. People in good relationships don't have to wait twenty-seven days to see their lover. What *was* David doing in the interval? Although a university presidency is not a powerless position, it pales beside the great political power Boren had accumulated and with which he could have done much good had he had a purpose and a center, aside from escaping the searching eyes of those who knew his inner self.

Our political agenda is well laid out by those who have had it in hand these past years. There have been many gains; one of the most notable is our strength amid the press corps, for whom being 'right' on gay issues is a necessary condition for political acceptability these days – even if the working press too often displays an awesome ignorance of the specific issues of paramount interest to gays. I was never so heartened as in the summer of 1992, when Sid Blumenthal told me that Ross Perot was knocked out, at least for that year, because of his statement that he wouldn't put homosexuals in his cabinet: the press simply made the judgment that anyone that 'out of it' couldn't win, and they would proceed to make their judgment self-fulfilling. Note the reportage of 'Stonewall 25'. David Broder, than whom there is no straighter (or better) reporter, tells of attending *Perestroika* with wife, son and daughter-in-law for the Saturday performance in the middle of the weekend which virtually closed New York down, and noting that the proportions were reversed: he was part of the ten per cent this time, there at the Walter Kerr Theater. And when the audience exploded at the end,

> you knew, at that moment, how lucky you had been to be there that night, on the 25th anniversary of Stonewall – an evening when another group of Americans was claiming its place in our culture and politics.[11]

Our personal agenda however transcends and undergirds the political one. My daughter Heidi's courage is what we have to emulate. We must find straight allies, more Neil Rudenstines who associate our cause with their own sense of justice and the civil society. They are there, waiting to be prodded. In the fall of 1992 I gave a lecture to a group of executives of middle-sized corporations. In the discussion, a manifestly macho president of a family corporation with a football-playing son at Yale, said that 'we need to do something about gays'. I heartily agreed but was stunned. I came out to him and suspected that if this gentleman were ready for the cause, so were countless others in similar – and powerful – positions in America.

As I completed this book, I was in Florida lecturing on world political issues to another group of CEOs; I had done this many times before, and since I was hired to elucidate political issues rather than talk about myself, I had always thought it intrusive to say I was gay (unlike when I discuss contractual ties with anyone, negotiate with a prospective employee or employer, or the like). Now, at a lunch following my four-hour presentation to a group quite conservative as one might expect, the youngest at the table, a personable and attractive thirty-two-year-old head of a security-equipment company, said that one thing we could concede Bill Clinton had done for us was to put all the issues of 'personal baggage' behind us: 'if he could survive that many skeletons in the closet, then personal issues are no longer important to us. It doesn't matter whether a politician has committed adultery, is gay . . . ' My jaw dropped. I waited for a reaction from the older businessmen. This time I had no excuse. It was clear that the older men in the group weren't just being polite. 'I agree', I said 'but look how recent such expressions are: just over five years ago I was the first openly gay presidential appointee'. The miracle isn't that there was agreement but that nothing whatsoever was said in disagreement, as if it needed no comment precisely because everyone agreed with the young executive's sentiment. *That* is the civil society.

## *The new century*

'You can feel it', Anna Quindlen wrote, 'in a hundred little ways. . . . It is so certain and inevitable, that the next century will be a time which it is not simply safe, but commonplace, to be openly gay.'[12] The world that this book circumscribes is actually two worlds, a dying one and one waiting to be born. The old one was one of hierarchy and class, affective distinctions and suppressed realities. Although by the late twentieth century it had already changed greatly, it was still the lineal descendant of courtly and knightly society of pre-revolutionary France, and of the titled world still legally at the top of the English ladder, however unsteadily thereon. It had changed because one of its secrets of survival, borrowed, in America, from the British upper class, was its willingness to initiate into its ranks and rites the vigorous members of the middle class who could restore its vitality. My children's maternal great-grandfather, Standard Oil's first president, was himself one of those – as was I three generations later, at least for a half-generation or so, in a different context. But the new century class is based on the attributes of civil society rather than effective distinctions. It is not just 'merit'. Merit is one of many measures and its use as a sole guide tends to start us back with titles again, even if professional ones this time. The new century class assumes nationality, ethnicity, even regionalisms where pertinent, and is tolerant to all of these: but transcendent is a commitment to the middle level of loyalties, between state–society–civilization and self, namely to association, religion, sexual orientation, or whatever defines self to give one's life meaning: that is to say, all that makes civil society.

But it logically follows that; to make the new century class secure, the practice of those associations of civil society, not to mention the civil society itself, must not just be tolerated but be put on a secure basis.

There follows a number of drastic changes that must occur in the next generation as the new century class grapples with the old class – and, more pertinently, with fundamentalism (or any chiliastic and/or holistic single-variable movement) from Tehran to Dallas. The legal steps are only the foundation, as always only the lowest form of morality, the merest beginning, to the building of a civil society, one where invidious distinctions disappear and acceptance is by merit. And it is coming.

## *Civil society*

What would a civil society be like? We certainly know what it *isn't*: intrusive, unaccepting, two-dimensional, unsure of self. Certainly for the gay world, it would be an extrapolation from the way the vanguard – the media – already treat us. I note a charming *New York Times* article about ninety-year-old Sir John Gielgud, which without comment, prurience or fuss, refers to his 'companion', Martin Hesler.[14] The same week's *New Yorker* has David Plante's extraordinary portrait of Francis Bacon, which not only deals with his homosexuality but also with the incredible visions that accompany it (or accompany it as everyone but Francis Bacon saw his paintings) in a manner that every gay man would dream of finding in his boss's or his mother's understanding of his persona.

But in the civil society a *quality* of person would develop and would be enabled. That is, for a large spectrum of men the choice of partners would flow from their humanity, their charm, their loyalty, or whatever other qualities are to be valued, and these might as well be found in a man as a woman: this would include millions of men who might have accepted gayness in others but never considered it as central to themselves.

I think of my own Filipino lover, a young man who I think might well have married a woman by now – he certainly had affairs and is most attractive, and he had none of the anxieties about sex with women that most married American gay men have or had; but there was a magnetic field between the two of us that brought us together emotionally and sexually that still exists in some forms to the present day. In other words, at his end there were no cultural inhibitions to being with a man, even one twenty-five years older – 'if the heart is right', as he said. Though he comes from a large and poor uneducated family in one of the least developed outer islands of the archipelago, his sensibilities were of the young central grandee of a mannerist portrait. I recall with astonishment, on one of my visits to Manila, how he volunteered, and I hired, his older brother, a taxi driver, to be my chauffeur during my stay; my friend from the start held my hand in the back seat in clear view of his brother, as if our affection was the most natural thing in the world. Love, as we see, can come across a larger cross-section of society than was hitherto thought possible – though over and over I was to be reminded that we didn't know how big a gap, back home, there could be.

My picture of the sensibilities of a civil society would feature Leon Wieseltier, a distinguished man of letters in Washington, most assuredly straight, who never fails to hug me out of affection on seeing me, and who once swung by bashful lover Jeff upright to dance with him at a party at his flat.

A civil society is one where a woman remains a woman, an African-American remains what he is, and a gay man remains gay; but they are accepted with these distinctions along with the others they present to their peers: artistic excellence, business proficiency, courtesy, orderliness, or simply a calming attitude. I care not if someone refers to me as a gay man since I am a gay man, but I do care if that reference is made to delimit my options, close professional doors, make reference to the way I (or my friends) walk, or cut me from invitation lists. So until society has become wholly civil, I would, perhaps, prefer, on first reference, to be called simply a man. My courage must be to endure, to *be*, to be myself, in an examined life. That should be the manifesto of every gay man.

There will be resistance, not just to gay rights and all rights associated therewith. For example, the religious right will continue its attempt to save the family as it was once constituted – or constituted in its imagination and as it developed in the *second* millennium of Christianity. For what percentage of 'traditional families' do we now find to have been dysfunctional? Given the enormous percentage in which child abuse occurred; the fact that in cities like Washington almost half the families are already non-traditional; the half of all marriages that now break up; and the number where the absence of psychological health in the relationships drove away some of the members: one can only look forward to a reconstitution of social relationships to a network where the nuclear family as we once knew it is only a plurality among other kinship units. We are at the point where the lead article of a major national magazine can headline – on the cover – 'When Parents are Not in the Best Interests of the Child'.[15]

In this context the fact that most gay men do not have children becomes less and less exceptional, since fewer and fewer men in general do, as marriage occurs less often out of social artifice and pressures. And as uplifting a motive in life it is to immortalize oneself through procreation, as Plato has Diotima point out through Socrates, men are more motivated (so it is argued) by the pursuit of honor.

> They are ready to run all risks greater far than they would have run for their children . . . for the sake of leaving behind them a name which shall be eternal . . .

But the interesting trend is that more and more gay people *do* have children, naturally or through adoption. If the legal record is mixed, its general direction is overwhelmingly evident, as when a conservative Virginia court gives back a child to her natural – but lesbian – mother. So that barrier and differentiation between gay and straight is breaking down apace. And in any event the same percentage of gay men will continue to spring up; gay people after all apparently beget gay children in no larger percentage than straights.

Because traditional marriage is no longer deemed the only pairing with social and legal legitimacy, the emotional investment in it is more balanced, and such units are sustained only where such is tenable – more or less the way it was in the first millennium of Christianity, especially among Jesus and his disciples and through the example they set. For after all, the Moral Majority's 'family' could hardly ensue easily from the standard of Jesus, who never married, had no siblings, whose parents were not married, and whose mother was a virgin. The emphasis for centuries – as John Boswell has so devastatingly reminded us – was on a broader family, a marriage to the church, a brotherhood among men that transcended blood ties (through the notion of 'brother' as primarily a blood-derived one). The most dramatic change Christianity brought to the concept of the family, he convincingly argues, 'was its profound devaluation'.[16] After all, for the first millennium, the biological family had far lower priority, given 'the preferability of lifestyles other than family units – priestly celibacy, voluntary virginity . . . monastic community life'. It took until the early thirteenth century for the church to declare marriage a sacrament and to require its own ecclesiastical involvement.[17]

So the race is on for the legalization of gay marriages: and if Hawaii's Supreme Court is upset in that intent by a conservative legislature, the focus will turn elsewhere, as rapidly as the closure of one hole in a overweighed dike will turn the pressure to another vulnerable spot, which in turn will burst open, for example Scandinavia where same-sex marriage is in the cards. The right to marry, after all, derives from the right to privacy, as the editors of the Harvard Law Review have reminded us, noting that increasingly Fourteenth Amendment rights are derived in court decisions regarding marriage. 'Choice in intimate relationships is no less critical for homosexuals than for heterosexuals', they write – and note that

Justice Blackmun, in his famous dissent in the *Georgia* v. *Hardwick* case, argued that the family was protected because of its contribution to 'happiness', 'not for a preference for stereotypical households'.[18] And the Supreme Court, in *Moore* v. *City of East Cleveland*, has already broadened constitutional protection beyond nuclear families to extended families.[19] So the even bigger race is on, to the Supreme Court, for the great gay test case, and the outcome, I have no doubt, will have as powerful, and even quicker, an effect on gay rights than *Brown* v. *Board of Education* had on African-American rights forty years ago.

The issue is not mere legality. When gay families are established with equal legal rights and legitimacy in the new century, it will only be the (interrupted) development of the broader concept for the family the early church propagated, and it will be the legalization of a trend that has moved inexorably in the last generation.

Meantime, in the new social reality, as civil – and secular – society progresses in this country, it is in any case becoming professional to separate the individual from family, so that we focus on his work identity exclusively, without reference to social background, sexual preference, or personal habits – which of course has the effect of helping our cause. The reunification of course comes as the civil society emerges. It was striking, in the fall of 1993, that major newspapers had substantial profiles of political candidates without reference to the very family factor that traditionally loomed so large. One *New York Times* page-long profile of Rudolph Giuliani did not even mention the existence of a Madame or a divorce.

Looking back at the ground I had traversed since my arrival at Stanford in the twilight years of Dwight David Eisenhower, I could see myself in some ways as the representative man, who having come west to school in his modest way had triumphed, and then sought to take east that model of success to change the world. That success had fallen out of the sky, it wasn't earned, and that was part of the model – one that seemed to be reapplied in my marriage to fame and fortune. But then it turned out that the world that needed changing was inside me, not outside. I was again the reflection of an epoch, because, in a less intense way, our world was changing in that way too, as therapists, EST, and communes became the new cultural beacons.

This great parallel transformation of élites is manifestly well underway. It has occurred more at the fringes of the new civil society than at its center, however. But artists, writers, teachers, psychiatrists have given it movement. It is disproportionately gay for the very reason that Camille Paglia, Frank Rich and others have noted the disproportionate influence of gay men on our life and times. At a party at my house in late 1993, Timothy Dickinson observed to Edward Luttwak that the particular affair, entitled 'Beyond Life and Art' on the invitation, had a salient relevance for me, since it was highly representative of the new century class. 'This whole decade has been for you a beginning, not an end', he said to me. And it was symbolic of our times.

## *New beginnings*

At a Christmas party in 1990 Roger Hansen and I met for the first time in over a month. Pale but at least in good physical form, he apologized for not returning any of my phone calls. 'If you feel as bad as I have, you can't come out of the fog, you can't respond.'

'Yeah', I answered. 'Responding is in effect coming out of the depression.'

'Exactly', he said. 'I just don't know that it's worth it. I'm in constant pain, there's no one in my life, I can't work, I'm just keeping up the bare minimum of my teaching responsibilities, Oh, Scott, I just don't know how long I can go on like this.'

This was the most suicidal note from Roger in two years. I resolved to keep in close touch. We had a few conversations, but Roger always put me off about getting together. Then, at the beginning of February, I remained in Boston over the weekend for a faculty retreat, staying with a beloved colleague who knew Roger and who was himself soon to die. Roger called and asked to borrow my house in Rehoboth, given how much better he was suddenly feeling. I passed on my colleague Rob West's best wishes, and told Roger how to get a key. He could go up to a restaurant where my current boy friend was working and get it from him.

Later he called and said he couldn't get the key; he went to the restaurant and lost his nerve about going in and asking for the key! I said, 'You Roger'ed it.'

'Yes, I Roger'ed it', he echoed. I was to wonder, with great pain, if that jocular phrase we used to buck up his self-esteem, through sarcasm regarding his lack of it, was a final coffin-nail. I explained how else he could get the key.

And then the fatal question.

'You have a garage in Rehoboth, don't you Scott?'

'Yes, of course. The automatic door-opener is on the kitchen counter.'

Why didn't I figure it out? He had no garage in Georgetown, why did he need one in Rehoboth? But he was going there because of his high spirits, he had said. I should rejoice, not worry. It was, in the purest CIA sense, disinformation. Indeed a therapist whom I saw afterwards in my search for help told me I should be outraged that Roger had 'done' this to me. Since my dear friend was no longer around, it was not exactly appropriate. I had at least been able to provide a chosen and comfortable place for him in which to die. He barely got that. Roger had padded his car with pillows from my bedroom but he took so many sleeping pills in the bedroom that, on entering the garage, already manifestly filled with carbon monoxide, he pitched to the cement floor, where he was found.

I didn't go to the funeral that Roger's school organized. Roger's gayness and everything else about his search for meaning were going to be papered over. And I wouldn't be welcome. At his wake, no one could deal with the homosexuality that was the central issue in his death.

In a TV interview about Calvin Trillin's book, I said that it might just have helped if one, if only one, of his colleagues had ever had the humanity to say to this suffering man, as my close friend Arthur House, a successful business executive, had said to me at a very critical juncture, 'Look, whatever you are underneath, straight, gay, bisexual, it doesn't matter to us. We accept you unconditionally.' No one ever made the slightest gesture of acceptance, Roger often complained.

In every department, on every retail floor, in every hospital, there is someone to whom a strong person, sure of his masculinity and humanity, could say that. Both would win. And it would be a blow for civil rights, for a kinder, gentler world – where there would be a general enrichment from the acknowledgement of truth in a warm-hearted way, a non-zero-sum game, in other words.

It would be a blow against the greatest enemy of the gay world, denial. We have seen denial at every level of this essay: starting and most evidently showing my denial through over twenty years of experience. But there was the denial of those seeking to protect me, up to recent days. And the denial of Paul Nitze and those around him. Denial is the process on which I seized as I prepared to come out, in looking at America's ostrich-like attitude toward the Soviets in their dangerous period of the late 1970s and early 1980s. Denial is ever-present, but it is a foundation of sand for any program or purpose of seriousness. 'For now we see in a mirror dimly, but then face to face . . .'

I want gay men to lead examined lives, not lives of attitude with its strained identity. Lawrence Chickering, in *Beyond Left and Right*, argues persuasively that we are all ends-oriented publicly and means-oriented in our private lives, which is true, but gay men must for a transitional period be utterly goal-oriented.[20] It is precisely our obsession with perfume, stance, attitude, even style that has not only diverted us from the goal of equality but has kept us looking ridiculous in the straight world. Plato says there are three parts of the soul, the rational part, the courageous part, and the appetites – or passions.[21] Certainly the gay world has since Stonewall exhibited its appetites and passions, and is paying a huge price. By that I do not mean in the slightest to imply that AIDS is a holy vengeance for promiscuity and numerous sex partners; only that, given the presence of the AIDS virus in New York and San Francisco in the 1970s and 1980s, and given the perhaps historic amount of sexual contact within that community, the gay world is paying a huge price through the fortuitous timing of the disease – with only the smaller silver lining that the disease has alerted the larger community to the gay world's needs. But the gay world is the first community where desire itself is the cultural common denominator, as Frank Browning's already cited *The Culture of Desire* argues.

Every year I celebrate spring with an azalea party, and try to guess when my three hundred old and young shrubs will ignite into their luminous abundant haze of pink, white, and scarlet. Last year past it was the latest ever, 24 April, because we wanted to take advantage of the gay march on Washington scheduled for the 25th. Even so the flowers were not out, so cold a spring it had been.

It didn't matter; no one would have noticed them anyway. Over three hundred gay men, ablaze as any azalea ever, powered up to my English brick house high over Rock Creek Park, and celebrated. A friend from Boston, gazing out over the house, the great trees, the stream, the park, and the work I had been able to do in Washington, exclaimed that he at last understood why I had not moved back. A legion of errors, a decade of depression, pain, and disappointment, with very little seeming to go right other than in my children's lives, but the light was spreading again. If Catholicism is right in teaching that despair is the worst of all sins, then there was at least one evil and vice I had plainly avoided in a bad decade. I don't know where the wellspring of that strength was.

It had all led somewhere. There was a logic to it, it followed, in Proust's terms, the laws of life, ending in a 'struggle and a victory'. My children had come to terms with their father's sexuality; or, let us say, they had realized that my sexuality was only a part of what they had come to terms with, as does any child of consciousness in dealing with complicated parents. My rich inner life had surely been as tumultuous and ultimately as triumphant as any outer life prophesied for me in an earlier incarnation. When an old friend now in power passed me recently, in his caravan of security and comfort, as I jogged Rock Creek Park, I felt pride and comradeship at the great achievement of my peers, and thought that mine, given my unruly spirit, different, not comparable by the same benchmarks, but no less full of scope, impressive, real. The grandparent I most resembled lived ninety-nine years, so I hoped to have a half century before a tombstone: but I still would expect it to say only that I was father of Phyl, Nick, and Heidi – and the first gay presidential appointee. And for the period in which I had come out, in which I was meant to have soared politically, that I had helped found both Project Democracy and the Institute of Peace. I could add that I had found an inner serenity which I have never thought mine to call upon. For all intents and purposes depression had become the swiftest passing of a cloud across the skies. So I stood there at the high end of the gardens, taking in that multitude so unthinkable to assemble so short a time ago, exploring their new-formed, new-massed multiplicity and possibility, all of whom would march with empowerment and pride the next day, and wished only that Roger had stuck around. Things were good, and they could only get better, richer, deeper.

## *Notes*

1. J. M. Roberts, *History of the World* (New York: Viking Penguin, 1993), p. 278.
2. Erik H. Erikson, *Young Man Luther* (New York, W. W. Norton, 1956), p. 150.
3. Richard Isay, *Being Homosexual* (New York: Avon Books, 1989), p. 133.
4. Annette Baker Fox, *The Power of Small States* (University of Chicago, 1959), p. 8.
5. Paul Monette, *Becoming a Man – Half a Life Story* (New York: Harper Collins, 1992), p. 55.
6. Erik H. Erikson, *Young Man Luther* (New York: W. W. Norton, 1956), p. 260.
7. Frank Rich, 'The Gay Decades', *Esquire*, November 1987, p. 100.
8. Paul Monette, *Borrowed Time* (New York: Avon, 1990), 125.
9. Shira Maguen, 'Teen suicide: The governmental coverup and America's lost children', *Advocate* 24 September 1991, p. 47.
10. I am indebted to Professor Richard Mohr for helping me to see this distinction. See his *Gay Ideas – Outing and Other Controversies* (Boston: Beacon Press, 1992). See also Warren Johansson and William Percy, eds., *Outing – Shattering the Conspiracy of Silence* (New York: Harrington Park Press, 1994).
11. 'Why I am leaving the Senate', *New York Times*, 13 May 1994.
12. 'Gay pride off-Broadway', *Washington Post*, 29 June 1994.
13. 'Happy and Gay', *New York Times*, 6 April 1994.
14. Mel Gussow, 'His own Brideshead, his fifth "Lear" ', *New York Times*, 28 October 1993, p. C10.
15. Mary-lou Weisman, 'When parents are not in the best interests of the child', *Atlantic Monthly*, July 1994.
16. John Boswell, *Same-sex Marriages in PreModern Europe* (New York: Villard Books, 1994), p. 109, and chapter 4 in toto.
17. *Ibid.*, p. 111.
18. *Sexual Orientation and the Law*, Editors of the Harvard Law Review (Cambridge, 1989), p. 96.
19. *Ibid.*, p. 94.

20. A. Lawrence Chickering, *Beyond Left and Right – Breaking the Political Stalemate* (San Francisco: Institute for Contemporary Studies, 1993).
21. See Robert Nozick, *The Examined Life* (New York: Simon & Schuster, 1989).

# Index